HITLER'S
PHILOSOPHERS

YVONNE SHERRATT

YALE UNIVERSITY PRESS
NEW HAVEN AND LONDON

For information about this and other Yale University Press
publications, please contact:

U.S. office: sales.press@yale.edu www.yalebooks.com
Europe Office: sales@yaleup.co.uk www.yaleupco.uk

Set in Arno pro by IDSUK (DataConnection) Ltd
Printed in the United States of America

Library of Congress Cataloging-in-publication Data

Sherratt, Yvonne, 1966–
    Hitler's philosophers / Yvonne Sherratt.
      p. cm.
    ISBN 978-0-300-15193-0 (cl : alk. paper)
1. Philosophers—Germany—History—20th century. 2. Philosophy, German—20th century.
3. Hitler, Adolf, 1889-1945. I. Title.
    B3181.S54 2012
    193—dc23

                                                            2012026930

A catalogue record for this book is available from the British Library.

10 9 8 7 6 5 4 3 2 1

This book is dedicated to my grandparents

Contents

Illustrations

Acknowledgements

This book has benefited from the generosity and expertise of a number of friends and colleagues. I would like to express my greatest thanks to Keith Ansell-Pearson, Cliff Davies, Ian Drury, Helen Dunmore, Mark Griffith, Henry Hardy, John Hatcher, Roger Hausheer, John Herod, Eric Hobsbawm, Mike Inwood, Edward Kanterian, Ian Kershaw, Ben Mason, Robert Mayhew, Thomas Moffatt, Alan Montefiore, Stephen Mulhall, New College, Oxford, Brian O'Connor, Helen Opie, Michael Rosen, Gerd Simon and Nigel Simmonds. Thanks also to Robert Baldock, Rachael Lonsdale, my copy-editor Richard Mason, and the anonymous readers for Yale University Press.

Dramatis Personae

Adorno, Theodor (1903–1969) Important Jewish-German philosopher, sociologist and musicologist, member of the Frankfurt School.

Arendt, Hannah (1906–1975) Leading Jewish-German political philosopher, mistress of Martin Heidegger, married to the communist Heinrich Blücher.

Bäumler, Alfred (1887–1968) Nazi professor of philosophy, University of Berlin.

Benjamin, Walter (1892–1940) Influential Jewish-German writer and thinker, close friend of Adorno and Arendt.

Bergmann, Ernst (1881–1945) Nazi professor of philosophy, University of Leipzig.

Boehm, Max Hildebert (1891–1968) Nazi, philosopher and sociologist, University of Jena.

Cassirer, Ernst (1874–1945) Leading Jewish-German philosopher.

Chamberlain, Houston Stewart (1855–1927) British-born German author, married to Richard Wagner's daughter, Eva, adored by Hitler.

Darwin, Charles (1809–1882) Leading naturalist of his times, founding father of the theory of evolution.

Faust, August (1895–1945) Nazi professor of philosophy, University of Breslau.

Fichte, Johann Gottlieb (1762–1814) Major German Idealist philosopher.

Förster-Nietzsche, Elisabeth (1846–1935) Nietzsche's sister, administered the Nietzsche Archive in Weimar after his death.

Freisler, Roland (1893–1945) President of Hitler's People's Court 1942–45, known as 'Hitler's Hanging Judge'.

Goethe, Johann Wolfgang von (1749–1832) German writer, considered the leading figure of his age.

Grau, Wilhelm (1910–2000) Nazi historian and thinker.

Grunsky, Hans Alfred (1902–1988) Nazi professor of philosophy, University of Munich.

Günther, Hans F. K. (1891–1968) German race researcher and eugenicist.

Haeckel, Ernst (1834–1919) Founder of Social Darwinism in Germany.

Hagemeyer, Hans Johann Gerhard (1899–1993) Worked in Rosenberg's 'Offices of Philosophical Information', etc.

Hegel, Georg Wilhelm Friedrich (1770–1831) Foremost German Idealist philosopher.

Heidegger, Martin (1889–1976) Phenomenological and existentialist philosopher, Nazi collaborator, affair with Hannah Arendt, etc.

Hess, Rudolf (1894–1987) Prominent Nazi politician, imprisoned with Hitler in Landsberg.

Heyse, Hans (1891–1976) Nazi Rector of Königsberg University.

Hildebert Boehm, Max (1891–1968) Nazi philosopher, University of Jena.

Hitler, Adolf (1889–1945) Chancellor of Germany from 1933 to 1945.

Höfler, Otto (1901–1987) Nazi philosopher, University of Munich.

Horkheimer, Max (1895–1973) Important Jewish-German philosopher, founder of the Frankfurt School.

Huber, Kurt (1893–1943) Conservative German philosopher and musicologist, member of the *White Rose*, executed by the Nazis.

Husserl, Edmund (1859–1938) Jewish-German philosopher, Heidegger's mentor, later betrayed by him to the Nazis.

Jaspers, Karl (1883–1969) German psychiatrist and philosopher with Jewish wife, fired from his job by the Nazis.

Kant, Immanuel (1724–1804) Enlightenment thinker, founding father of modern European philosophy.

Krieck, Ernst (1882–1947) Nazi professor of philosophy, University of Heidelberg.

Langbehn, Julius (1851–1907) German conservative writer, nationalist and anti-Semite, read by Hitler.

Lessing, Theodor (1872–1933) Jewish-German philosopher assassinated by Nazis.

Löwith, Karl (1897–1973) Exiled Jewish-German philosopher, student of Heidegger.

Marcuse, Herbert (1898–1979) Exiled Jewish-German philosopher.

Mendelssohn, Moses (1729–1786) Jewish philosopher known as 'the Jewish Socrates'.

Nietzsche, Friedrich Wilhelm (1844–1900) German philosopher, considered to be one of the most creative minds of his time.

Rosenberg, Alfred (1893–1946) Prominent member of the Nazi Party, chief racial theorist, intellectual leader.

Rothacker, Erich (1888–1965) Nazi professor of philosophy, University of Bonn.

Schiller, Johann Christoph Friedrich von (1759–1805) Leading German poet, dramatist and philosopher, strongly influenced by Kant's transcendentalism.

Schmitt, Carl (1888–1985) Philosopher and lawyer, Hitler's lawmaker.

Scholem, Gerhard (1897–1982) Jewish philosopher born in Berlin but migrated to Palestine/Israel, where he changed his first name to Gershom.

Scholl, Sophie (1921–1943) Student philosopher, member of the White Rose.

Schopenhauer, Arthur (1788–1860) Canonical German philosopher, influenced by Kant but placing 'will' as central to reality.

Schulze-Sölde, Walter (1888–1984) Nazi professor of philosophy, University of Innsbruck.

Spengler, Oswald (1880–1936) German philosopher and historian, read by Hitler.

Spinoza, Benedict (1632–1677) Major Dutch Jewish philosopher.

Treitschke, Heinrich von (1834–1896) Right-wing historian read by Hitler.

Wagner, Richard (1813–1883) Romantic opera composer; friend and mentor to Nietzsche.

Weinreich, Max (1894–1969) Jewish scholar and linguist, raised in a German-speaking family. Spoke out against collaborating Nazi academics.

Wundt, Max (1879–1963) Nazi philosopher, University of Tübingen.

Prologue

While playing as children in our grandmother's garden in Suffolk during the 1970s, my brother and I unearthed part of a skeleton. Buried at the end of an undulating path at the rear of the pretty pink thatched cottage, it lay hidden under layers of mud. Beside the skeleton we found crumbling red-brick steps leading down to a ruined air-raid shelter. Pondering the origin of the bones, we decided that they must belong to an air-raid victim and carried them triumphantly to our grandmother, who was topping and tailing gooseberries in the kitchen.

My grandmother eyed the bones with suspicion and then a memory stirred. She told us of the Second World War, of how, with no Anderson shelter, our grandfather had dug his own. She hadn't trusted it and when the Nazi planes flew over the East coast she had instead crouched with her two young children under the kitchen table. She recalled one occasion when the aircraft seemed especially loud; she had pulled her daughter away from the back door and into the kitchen as a bomb fell nearby, just missing the local school. The blast sent debris across the yard as the planes passed overhead, etched with the stark lines of the swastika.

Searching for further clues my brother and I returned to the shelter, but all we found was a littering of rusted steel which flaked to the touch. My grandmother knew nothing about the bones, but with our childish enthusiasm for adventure we longed to bring the skeleton back to life. On family walks along the Suffolk coast we would climb into the old pillboxes, imagining soldiers hidden there for long hours in the cold mud and hard stones, fearing an invasion by Hitler.

I have clear memories, too, of my grandfather, sitting in his armchair in the corner of the room, the smoke rising from his pipe, the drawl of his voice interrupted by a horrendous choking sound as he coughed into a bucket. I would follow him outside where he meandered about the over-grown garden, tipping his iron watering can into terracotta pots dripping with purple fuchias. There in the quiet, humid greenhouse, among the rank geraniums and miniature orange trees, he spoke of the war and most vividly about Nazi atrocities.

When I later began my university career as a medical student, one of the first lectures I attended was delivered by the head of the British Medical Association. The lecturer confronted his audience with an ethical dilemma: should he teach facts about the body, facts that could save people's lives, but based upon knowledge gained through human experiments conducted upon Jews by the Third Reich?

I pondered that question for many years and in due course it changed my life. I changed from medicine to study philosophy, where ethical dilemmas were at the forefront of the curriculum. Great names and their distinguished works that addressed the great riddles of life were presented to us. The German philosophic tradition seemed particularly rich and exciting. Only later did I learn that some was the work of avid Nazis.

Like the skeleton in my grandmother's garden, the sinister past of many German philosophers has remained concealed. No one mentions that some ideas taught from the podium originated in the minds of Hitler's collaborators. As students we assumed that philosophers would have rejected Nazism; after all, philosophy is descended from the *moral* sciences. Anything connected with Nazism would surely be taught as an example of corruption, not as part of the mainstream curriculum. Remembering my grandparents and the issues raised at medical school, I realized along with my fellow students that the academy held a terrible secret: the story of how philosophy was implicated in genocide.

Introduction

For over seventy years the world has been preoccupied by the horror of Nazism: the rise of a tyrant of unparalleled brutality in Europe, the nightmare of the gas chambers and the atrocities of the Holocaust. In the decades since, many stories have been told, stories of collaboration, heroism, tragedy and betrayal. Almost no group of German people from the war years has remained untarnished by the stain of Hitler. Many civil servants, ordinary workers, doctors and schoolteachers, far from being innocent bystanders, have been disclosed as central to bolstering the power of the tyrant.[1] Artists and musicians have shamefully been amongst the collaborators. Yet, since Hitler's rise to power nearly eighty years ago, no one has yet examined the part played by one quiet and unassuming group – the philosophers.

Philosophy is iconic to German culture. It holds an eminence in the nation's heritage rather as the legal Constitution does for North Americans. Philosophers were celebrities. What philosophers did, how they behaved and what ideas they promoted exerted a powerful influence upon the German imagination. However, while most celebrities are worldly, philosophers in contrast are usually regarded as otherworldly, like monks preoccupied with the ethereal realm. Lost in abstract ideas, apparently living in an ivory tower, they are seen as transcending ordinary, selfish concerns. And certainly transcending cruelty. But were they always above sordid motivations? To answer this we tell the story of Hitler's philosophers.

'Hitler's philosophers' refers to the group of thinkers surrounding Hitler before, during and after the Holocaust. It includes unwitting influences, collaborators; and we also discuss Jewish academics, as well as Hitler's opponents. This group of thinkers belonged to a common tradition originating from deep within German culture. From Kant to Nietzsche, from Alfred Bäumler to Martin Heidegger, from Hannah Arendt to Walter Benjamin, these philosophers all debated the same ideas.[2] Many of their lives were interconnected – they were students, teachers, colleagues, friends, and even lovers.

Our story begins by setting the scene of 1930s Berlin. Then in chapter 1 we introduce Hitler himself. Hitler took for granted the status of philosophy, and his egotism about the subject spread to a fantasy that he himself was a great thinker. Indeed he came to regard himself as the 'philosopher Führer'. To this end he wrote *Mein Kampf*, in which he outlined his atrocious beliefs. Albeit in a crude way, Hitler quoted from the founding fathers of the German tradition such as Immanuel Kant and Arthur Schopenhauer. He professed adoration of Friedrich Nietzsche and was fond of German interpretations of Charles Darwin. In his later years Hitler would name-drop from Germany's formidable intellectuals to his generals. He also found strands of anti-Semitism in German philosophy and usurped ideas about race, strength and war in order to legitimize his project.

Our second chapter unearths Hitler's alleged influences, disclosing the lives and ideas of Kant, Nietzsche and Darwin's German followers. Their intellectual gifts were great, but what made them so attractive to Hitler?

Philosophers from Germany's past had no choice about Hitler usurping their legacy, but this was not the case for those living during the era of the Third Reich. In chapter 3 we expose the collaborators, ambitious men competing to provide a cloak of respectability for Nazi thugs. Christian, eugenicist and Idealist philosophers are all recounted in their dissemination of some of the worst propaganda ever to appear on

European soil. Reaping the rewards of a profitable collaboration and occupying the most prestigious posts at Germany's foremost universities, we paint the portraits of obscure thinkers such as Bäumler and Krieck and famous ones like Schmitt and Heidegger. What were their backgrounds, personal stories, and why did they turn to racism and war? In chapter 4 we tell the story of Carl Schmitt, who wrote the Nazi legal constitution and gained fame and fortune as Hitler's lawmaker. In chapter 5 we read how Martin Heidegger offered a source of justification for Hitler's brand of nationalism and never made any moves to distance his admiration for authority from the rule of the Third Reich.

In the second part of *Hitler's Philosophers* we explore the lives of Jewish victims and intellectual opponents. All lost their careers, were interned, forced into exile or killed. Walter Benjamin, whose life ended in tragedy, is the focus of chapter 6. In chapter 7 we see how Theodor Adorno was affected, spending much of his life as a refugee. How did his experience as a Jew under Hitler shape his work and generate some of the most profound insights into modern society? Hannah Arendt, Heidegger's student-mistress is a controversial figure and the subject of chapter 8. We tell her story, her escape from an internment camp and her flight across Europe. How did this Jewess square her lifelong devotion to the Jewish cause with her love for a Nazi? And in chapter 9 we look at Kurt Huber, the White Rose member and martyr, a conservative opponent who was executed by the Nazis.

The unity of the German philosophical community was destroyed by the rise of the Third Reich. What happened in the aftermath? Was justice ever wrought? Our narrative concludes with the Nuremberg trials, examining whether any philosophers were prosecuted and whether the German universities were purged of the Nazis after 1945. We then confront Hitler's philosophers today. Their impact across the world has been momentous. Like Marx and Freud, many of their ideas have been assimilated into everyday parlance. But who knows which words have emanated from executed Jews, and which from their Nazi persecutors?

Our story ends by following the lives of Hitler's philosophers into their cultural legacy.

At the outset it is worth mentioning the style of *Hitler's Philosophers*. The book is written as a docudrama, bringing to life the historical era and personal dramas of the people involved. It is a work of non-fiction, carefully researched, based upon archival material, letters, photographs, paintings, verbal reports and descriptions, which have all been meticulously referenced. However, it is written in a narrative style, which aims to transport the reader to the vivid and dangerous world of 1930s Germany.

PART I

CHAPTER I

Hitler: The 'bartender of genius'

During the early 1940s the Allied bombings wreaked revenge on the Rhineland, crushing Germany's magnificent cities, and a scene unfolded on the scale of a biblical disaster. The quiet hum of a thousand distant planes was in stark contrast to the devastation they caused – over Cologne, Berlin, Frankfurt, Munich, Freiburg and the Bavarian Alps, they hunted out and destroyed German civilization.

Two decades earlier in 1923, on a quiet street in Munich in southern Germany, one man had summoned all this. 'What does it matter if a couple of dozen of our Rhineland cities go up in flames. A hundred thousand dead would mean nothing provided Germany's future was assured'.[1] The man who desired war was quite ordinary looking, rather shabbily dressed and walking with an austere gait down a grey paved street bathed in the late summer sunshine. He was at this time a mere provincial politician, but with extremist fantasies. He loved fire. He enjoyed the power of its destruction, its vivid light, rank smoke and ability to destroy in seconds that which took centuries to form. He was an impatient man with a passion for the immediate, the dramatic. He wearied of traditional politicians with their incessant talking, vacillation and timidity.

The man with the apocalyptic vision was thirty-five years of age, tramping through the peaceful promenades of Munich discussing his ideas with his friend Ernst Hanfstaengl, a high-society and cultured

German businessman.[2] The city was tranquil, the sunshine reflecting off the white neo-Baroque Justizpalast and echoing in the flat space around the square, before dancing off the warm, ochre-coloured facades of the other Gothic and neo-Gothic monumental buildings.[3] The various city parks enticed walkers into their midst and, occasionally glimpsed along the other city streets, were hanging baskets or a window box draping their blossoms and summer foliage into the street. The droning of a distant tram, the rap of a cane from a passer-by, were all that accompanied the murmur of the two men's voices, lost deep in conversation. Having recounted his fantasy of war, 'Germany will either be a world power or there will be no Germany',[4] the politician turned to musing over a film they had recently watched together. He had enjoyed the movie and was now rapt in discussion of its main features. *Fredericus Rex* (*Frederick The Great*) had been showing at the Sendlinger Tor Platz cinema in Munich throughout the long summer. The politician dwelt upon his favourite scene where the old king threatened to have the crown prince beheaded. 'This is the best part of the film,' he declared. 'What a classic example of discipline when a father is prepared to condemn his son to death.'[5] His eyes shone with glee, the image of the Rhineland aflame was conjoined with his fantasy of punishment and brutal authority. The ability to cause massive suffering without flinching was, he believed, the ultimate proof of strength. 'Great deeds require harsh measures,' he pronounced. Hanfstaengl, however, was nervous – they were on the open street and were just walking past the Friedrich Schiller monument in democratic, law-abiding Weimar Germany.[6]

Several months later, in November 1923, the politician was arrested by the Weimar police. Frustrated with the slow ebb of regional debate, he had burst into a meeting in a beer hall outside Munich, gun in hand, demanding action. Prepared to set the place on fire and destroy the entire building and all its occupants, he had been halted in his tracks. He was now at the mercy of the law he had sought to violate.

The politician was of course Adolf Hitler. Sentenced and convicted of high treason for radical political actions in the name of National Socialism, in the spring of 1924 he found himself incarcerated inside Landsberg Fortress, a penal facility in Landsberg am Lech in the south-west of the German state of Bavaria.

From the outside, Landsberg was typically Bavarian, soft brown-brick walls were framed by curved turrets with opal-coloured domes. The three storeys visible from the exterior communicated with the world by way of windows leaded with diagonal criss-crossings. Warm red tiles topped the building connecting the domed turret with the flat sloping roof. The doorway was welcoming with a broad, high arch; altogether it was a homely design, if somewhat grand in scale.[7]

Cell no. 7 was Hitler's room.[8] His windows were tall and wide, stretching across the entirety of two walls. They were wooden framed and barred, the metal cage keeping the prisoner from the outside, reflected shadows across the walls creating symmetrical lines across the floor. One looked straight out on to a wall while the other was framed by the branches of a sparse tree. The view beyond stretched across the rising oak forests and fir-clad hills of the splendid countryside. There was a narrow white-painted metal bed in one corner with a slim mattress upon it, and a couple of feet away, leaning against the other wall, was a modest, dark-stained desk with a small chair. An ample mirror hung on the wall, the furnishings giving the appearance of a student room rather than a Spartan cell.[9]

An associate once described Hitler's appearance – not a description that would have flattered the man himself, or one that reflected his popularity while in gaol:

> Hitler is not physically attractive. Everyone knows that . . . stories were circulated in the party and among sympathisers about his deep blue eyes. They are neither deep nor blue. His look is staring or dead, and lacks the brilliance and sparkle of genuine animation. The timbre of his harsh, uncommon voice is repellent to the North German. The

tone is full, but forced as though his nose were blocked. Since then this voice, guttural and threatening . . . embodies torment . . .

There is something peculiar about the magic of a personality. I found in myself and in others that one succumbs to such magic only if one wishes to succumb to it. I have noticed that Hitler made the strongest impression on such people as were either highly suggestible or somewhat effeminate or accustomed by their education and social background to formalism and hero-worship. A receding forehead, with the lank hair falling over it; a short, unimposing stature, with limbs somehow ill-fitting and awkward; an expressionless mouth beneath the little brush of a moustache – such are the traits of the outer man. His only charm lies perhaps in his hands, which are strikingly well shaped and expressive.[10]

In gaol Hitler was forced temporarily to repress his fantasies of destruction and take stock of his new surroundings. Standing in the dark shadow behind the window, he stared out across south-west Germany, steely eyed and standing stiffly upright in the pose of a soldier. His gaze was given over not to the landscape but to himself. Then with his right arm resting upon the sill, he turned his back to the window and leant against the discoloured, roughly plastered wall.[11] He likened himself to a portrait in a Rembrandt painting, hastening to remind himself that although 'Rembrandt painted in the Jewish quarter, he was at heart a true Aryan'.[12] Then, perfecting the image of the soldier's portrait from the painting *Man in a Golden Helmet*, he caught his reflection in the mirror and mused with approval: 'There you have something unique. Look at that heroic, soldier-like expression.'[13]

The prison cell was in stark contrast to all the other inmates' cells in Landsberg. Whereas theirs were bare, this one became adorned with gifts. In fact a visitor noted that Hitler 'had not so much a cell as a . . . delicatessen store. You could have opened up a flower and fruit and a wine shop with all the stuff stacked there.' People were sending him presents from all over Germany, and Hitler had grown visibly fatter on the proceeds. Moreover, the prison guards had offered him preferential treatment, indulging him this freedom of receiving gifts in his cell, and in return he would say 'take this box of chocolates home to your wife'. 'The ascendancy he gained over the officials and guards at Landsberg was quite extraordinary. The gaolers even used to say *Heil Hitler* when they came into his cell.'[14]

How was he to spend his time in Landsberg prison? Hitler had charmed the guards, but was still seething with frustration at what he considered to be the waste of his political genius. He fumed for many a long hour, ranting politics and raging to the other inmates. How long would the imbeciles that ruled the country keep him inside? Hitler's stormy outbursts would gradually recede and become interspersed with periods of calm. Then he would recover his composure and regain belief in his own authority, occupying his time dealing with visitors and answering correspondence. Some of his letters were personal or domestic, in which he thanked his friends and sympathizers for their many gifts. For example:

Landsberg on the Lech, 1 October, 1924.

Dear Frau Deutschenbauer,
A few days ago Frau Reichart was kind enough to bring me your plum cake. It was a brief reminder of the time which I spent near you when I was a soldier and also a sign that you have not forgotten me. Please accept my cordial thanks for this attention.
With kindest regards to you and your husband,
I remain,
Yours sincerely,
Adolf Hitler.[15]

In other correspondence he meted out advice and coined slogans and mottos.

Landsberg on the Lech, 10 April, 1924.

To the Hetzendorf Group

Sincere thanks for your confidence.

Our struggle must and will end in victory!

With German Heil!

Adolf Hitler.[16]

Hitler also worked on presenting himself in an authoritative style to important associates:

Landsberg on the Lech,

20.10.24.

Patriotic Defence Alliance,

District Commander Freystadt,

Upper Austria.

Attention: W. Hollitscher, District Commander.

Dear Herr District Commander,

A few days ago I received your announcement of the presentation of colours to the Patriotic Defence Alliance, District Commander Freystadt. Would you receive my belated congratulations on that occasion, and also my sincere thanks for the pledges of loyalty you transmitted to me. For the rest I have only one desire: that the day may soon come in which my former homeland is incorporated in the glorious wreath of German states, in a united Greater Germany.

With true German greeting,

Yours sincerely,

Adolf Hitler.[17]

Completing correspondence was not, however, Hitler's only pursuit during incarceration. He was later to reflect that this time in Landsberg was, in his own words, his 'University paid for by the State'.[18] In fact, 'the long days of enforced idleness in Landsberg were ideal for reading and reflection'.[19] Hitler decided to peruse a vast wealth of literature and he also embarked upon a project that he believed would demonstrate to the world his immense mental superiority.

Although he considered himself first and foremost a man of action, he believed that he did not lack other talents, and prevented by fools from fulfilling his destiny in the outside world he would therefore turn to the inner one. His mission was to construct a masterpiece, his magnum opus. After all his great hero of the eighteenth century, the philosopher Friedrich Schiller, had done just that. Hitler took an old typewriter that had been lent to him by the guards and hunched over his desk. His hands began to tremble over the keys as he hammered out the project with venom,[20] his 'left arm and leg kept trembling [and] the movement of his forearm was restricted'.[21]

As an audience to his venture Hitler ensnared his deputy Rudolf Hess. Hess had been convicted along with Hitler of high treason. He was Hitler's favourite and accompanied him in his gaol cell every day. A restless character, he had the 'habit of fooling around with the chair he was sitting on. He would sit on it the wrong way round, pass it through his legs, sit on the back, twirl it on one leg, like an amateur acrobat trying to show off', a visitor noted.[22] Hess could not bear to see Hitler exposed to any views other than his own, for he regarded himself not merely as a disciple but also as a tutor – he had studied geopolitics, doctrines of land and power.[23] Hess spoke in catchphrases, 'we must learn to be more brutal in our methods. That is the only way to deal with our enemies,' he would chant. 'He loved the word "brutal", which in German is pronounced with a rolling "r" and equal stress on both syllables, and Hitler also seemed to take pleasure in the sound of it.'[24]

With Hess hanging on his every word, Hitler lost himself in his political fancies and perceived oratorical might. Whatever the ebb and flow of his moods, Hitler was always aware of an audience, sure of the importance of his ideas and the certainty of their impression upon an imaginary, unblinking mass of men.

The book Hitler was composing from his prison cell in the midst of the Bavarian forests, although first entitled *Four and a Half Years (of Struggle) Against Lies, Stupidity and Cowardice*, was in fact the infamous one that would later become simply *Mein Kampf* (My Struggle). In it, Hitler both set out and justified his various prejudices and outlined the beginnings of the National Socialist cause. He also discussed himself and presented an idealized image of his own life and background. With his companion he began the first volume (subtitled 'A Reckoning'), starting with the chapter 'In The House Of My Parents'.[25]

Hitler had been born in Gasthof zum Pommer, an inn in the municipality of Braunau am Inn, Austria-Hungary, on 20 April 1889. 'Today,' he spoke:

> it seems to me providential that Fate should have chosen Braunau on the Inn as my birthplace. For this little town lies on the boundary between two German states which we of the younger generation at least have made it our life work to reunite by every means at our disposal. German Austria must return to the great German mother country . . .[26]

His childhood had been an unhappy one. His father, Alois Hitler, a customs official, had introduced him to violence at an early age – frequent beatings had left an indelible mark upon him. This, however, was omitted from his account. Hitler preferred instead to dwell upon issues of his supposedly German roots: 'In this little town on the Inn, gilded by the rays of German martyrdom, Bavarian *by blood*, technically Austrian, lived my parents.'[27] He described his mother as 'giving all her being to the household' and meanwhile referred to his brutal father as simply a 'dutiful civil servant'. Rather than admit the paternal bullying he simply spoke of 'an old gentleman', and mentioned in passing, 'Little remains in my memory of this period.'[28] In his observation of others, however, Hitler had the rather intimate insight of a father who 'comes home on Sunday or even Monday night, drunk and brutal . . . [when] . . . such scenes often occur that God have mercy'.[29]

Out of brutality came strength, of this Hitler was convinced. In later years he proclaimed:

Haven't you ever seen a crowd collecting to watch a street brawl? *Brutality is respected*. Brutality and physical strength. The plain man in the street respects nothing but brutal strength. And ruthlessness – women, too, for that matter, women and children. The people need wholesome fear. They *want* to fear something. They want someone to frighten them and make them shudderingly submissive. Haven't you seen everywhere that after 'boxing matches' the beaten ones are the first ones to join the party as new members? Why babble about brutality and be indignant about tortures? The masses want that. They want something that will give them the thrill of horror.[30]

Even as a younger man Hitler believed violence was constructive. He always considered it to be a nurturing force for the development of positive character traits: 'I believe that even then my oratorical talent was being developed in the form of more or less violent arguments.'[31]

Hitler flattered himself that he had risen above his circumstances, growing strong out of austerity. Life had been tough, he gloated, so much so that a weaker man might have succumbed, but *he* had passed his first test in life. Pausing and looking around his prison cell, he was for an instant overwhelmed by memories of injustice. Bitterness rose in his throat as he recollected all those who had failed to recognize his greatness during his early years – it was one thing to overcome the test of hardship but quite another to endure being overlooked. In the Austrian and German towns of Passau, Lambach, Leonding and Linz, as a boy in elementary school things had not been too bad. At first his talents had been recognized – his school had awarded him excellent marks. It was later in his first year at high school (Realschule) in Linz that they had failed him. Being of superior insight, however, he decided, by the age of sixteen, that the 'pen pushers' who shaped education could not account for one as singular as himself, so he dropped out without a degree.

From 1905 Hitler had lived in Vienna following a bohemian life, subsisting on support from his devoted mother (widowed in 1903).[32] He was rejected twice by the Academy of Fine Arts which cited 'unfitness for painting', and was told his abilities lay instead in the field of architecture. While acknowledging the correctness of their insight in recognizing his architectural talents, he resented their philistine blindness to his visual genius.[33]

Recovering from his momentary rage, as he continued typing out his life story, Hitler turned to dwell upon a happier theme – national pride. Here he exchanged proud and knowing glances with Hess. At a time during his early teenage years, he had read a book of his father's about the Franco-Prussian War of 1870–1, which had caused him to question why his father and other German Austrians failed to fight for the Germanic peoples during this war. Always wanting to perform to an audience, however, in *Mein Kampf* Hitler omitted the fact that his father had never fought for the Germans and he went on to attribute his nationalist conversion to his father – despite the absence of any such devotion.

Hitler reinvented his father in the idealized image of the Bavarian peasant: tough, determined, hard-working, simple and proud. He wrote:

> When finally, at the age of fifty-six, he went into retirement, he could not bear to spend a single day of his leisure in idleness. . . . he bought a farm, which he worked himself, and thus, in the circuit of long and industrious life, returned to the origins of his forefathers.[34]

Although it is true that Hitler's father did buy a farm, he soon sold it again as it was too large for him to run and instead he bought a suburban house in Leonding by Linz, which simply had a large garden. Ignoring this inconvenient fact, Hitler continued to idolize his father's supposedly 'folksy' heritage. Hitler invented a proud identity: he was no longer an Austrian outsider but a fervent German nationalist with genuine folkloric roots.

More proof of Hitler's nationalism was evidenced in his account of himself during the First World War. He managed to enlist and serve not for Austria but for the 16th Bavarian Reserve Infantry Regiment. Reminiscing about these years in his cell, he bragged to Hess and rubbed his hands together in self-satisfaction.

Mein Kampf was not intended, however, to be merely autobiographical, but a vehicle to promote Hitler's political views. Once more he stood in the prison cell before the mirror and pictured his own stately allure: how he had begun and attracted followers from what he believed to be his masterful oratory. In his writings he outlined in unrelenting detail his abilities to influence people, gain mass obedience, invent military strategy for the rise of Germany and, it goes without saying, a programme of obliteration of all those he regarded as inferior. He attacked social democrats, liberals, reactionary monarchists, capitalists, communists and the Jews.

From the beginning Hitler's National Socialist politics portrayed an enemy. He would soon declare: 'The National Socialist movement has the mightiest task to fulfil. It must open its eyes to the people on the subject of foreign nations and must remind them again and again of the true enemy of our present-day world. In place of the hatred against Aryans ... with whom we are bound by common blood ... it must call eternal wrath upon the head of the foul enemy of mankind as the real originator of our sufferings.'[35] He would mean, of course, the Jews. The emotional and moral filth from Hitler's claustrophobic and violent family life would be spewed out into the world and would find an invaluable scapegoat to punish. He would feel purged.

From his prison cell Hitler described how his political career had soared from strength to strength, his nationalism and rejection of the Jews being greeted by hoards of gleeful Germans. Amidst much internal wrangling, on 29 July 1921 he had realized his first dream and become leader of the National Socialist Party. Admiring his own success, he reflected from Landsberg that it had been the first time the term 'Führer' was publicly used. With great pride, he felt enormous ambitions afoot for that title.

Lingering over how he had become an accomplished speaker, Hitler reflected that by the early 1920s he was drawing in large crowds. With especial pleasure he remembered speaking on 10 April 1923 before an audience of nearly six thousand in Munich:

> In the Bible we find the text 'That which is neither hot nor cold will I spit out of my mouth' (revelation iii. 16) . . . until the present day the . . . lukewarm have remained the curse of Germany. . . . No economic policy is possible without a sword, no industrialization without power. Today we have no longer any sword in our fist – how can we have a successful economy?[36]

Surveying the vista of the German landscape outside, he reimagined the scene. He replaced trees with men, and pictured himself once more before an enormous audience. From the bird's-eye view of his second-floor cell window, he saw in his mind's eye a mass of men saluting with their arms outstretched diagonally towards him, the mass resembling the skin of a fish, the pale flesh of men's arms reflecting the shiny scales symmetrically pointing towards the fish's eye.

In spite of his success, Hitler recollected his frustration at the slow path to power. The consequent outbursts of anger and violence had resulted in his confinement, first in Stadelheim prison, Munich, in 1922. Then a year later, on 8 November 1923, he and the *Sturmabteilung* (SA), the paramilitary wing of the Nazi Party, had stormed a public meeting headed by the Bavarian prime minister, Gustav Kahr, in the Bürgerbräukeller, a large beer hall outside of Munich. Hitler declared that he had set up a new government with the former general Erich Ludendorff, and demanded, at gunpoint, the support of Kahr and the local military establishment for the destruction of the Berlin leadership. Government forces intervened and Hitler had fled to the home of Ernst Hanfstaengl and even contemplated suicide. He was soon arrested for high treason. During his trial he was given almost unlimited time to speak and his popularity soared as he voiced nationalistic sentiments in his defence speech:

> The army which we have formed grows from day to day; from hour to hour it grows more rapidly. Even now I have the proud hope that one day the hour is coming when these untrained (*wilde*) bands will become battalions, when the battalions will become regiments and the regiments divisions, when the old cockade will be raised from the mire, when the old banners will once again wave before us: and then reconciliation will come in the eternal last Court of Judgement – the Court of God – before which we are ready to take our stand. Then from our bones, from our graves will sound the voice of that tribunal which alone has the right to sit in judgment upon us. For, gentlemen, it is not you who pronounce judgment upon us, it is the eternal Court of History which will make its pronouncement upon us the charge which is brought against us. The judgment that you will pass, that I know. But that Court will not ask of us 'Have you committed treason or not?' That Court will judge us . . . who as Germans have wished the best for their people and their Fatherland, who wished to fight and die. You may declare us guilty a thousand times, but the Goddess who presides over the Eternal Court of History will with a smile tear in pieces the charge of the Public Prosecutor and the judgment of the Court: for she declares us guiltless.[37]

After the speech, this Munich personality became a nationally known figure.

On 1 April 1924, Hitler was sentenced to five years' imprisonment. Unbeknown to him at the time, as he poured forth his memoirs, he would soon be pardoned and by December 1924 would be released as part of a general amnesty for political prisoners. Including time on remand, he would serve little more than one year of his life.

Throughout this year in prison Hitler continued to recall his life and rant politics. He penned from his desk in Landsberg gaol: 'Today I am convinced that basically and on the whole all creative ideas appear in our youth. . . . It is this youthful genius which provides the building materials and plans for the future . . .'[38] In *Mein Kampf* he believed he was setting forth that very creative flow that earmarked his own genius. And part of that genius was, he believed, not only political agitation and action but his capacity for thought. From Landsberg he wrote: 'In this period there took shape within me a world picture and a philosophy which became the granite foundation of all my later acts.'[39]

From his prison window Hitler's eyes fed upon the immense forest canopy of the southern German landscape and he dwelt upon the culture that was definitively Germanic. He reflected in particular upon the philosophers. Hitler took for granted the importance of this subject: it was regarded as the pinnacle of the nation's cultural achievement, and thinkers such as Kant, Hegel and Nietzsche were as sacred to the German people as Shakespeare and Dickens were to the British, or Thomas Jefferson and Mark Twain to the Americans. 'Respect for the great men of the past must once more be hammered into the minds of our youth: it must be their sacred heritage.'[40] Hitler's fervent desire to be the most authentic of all Germans made these iconic figures deeply alluring. He had to incorporate the subject of philosophy within his sphere and he soon adopted the fantasy that he himself was a great thinker. Indeed he would soon come to regard himself as the 'philosopher leader'.[41]

In a cloud of fantasy, Hitler dwelt on how he topped even Germany's most venerated geniuses because he respected both intellect and action. He would soon ruminate on how '*insufficiently educated* minds' were 'men, crammed full of knowledge and intellect, but bereft of any healthy instinct and devoid of all energy and boldness'.[42] He was not like these '*insufficiently educated* minds', a pure philosopher, but instead, in his words, 'a great theoretician who was also a great leader . . . for leading means being able to move the masses'. Indeed, he would go on, 'the combination of theoretician, organiser, and leader in one person is the rarest thing that can be found on this earth; this combination makes for the great man'.[43]

One of the world's most eminent historians, Ian Kershaw, encapsulated Hitler's vanity thus:

> Hitler pictured himself as a rare genius who combined the qualities of the 'programmist' and the 'politician'. The 'programmist' of a movement was the theoretician who did not concern himself with practical realities, but with 'eternal truth', as the great religious leaders had done. The 'greatness' of the 'politician' lay in the successful application of the ideas of the programmist.

'Over long periods of humanity,' wrote Hitler, 'it can once happen that the politician is wedded to the programmist'. Hitler meant himself and he looked to 'aims which only the fewest grasp'.[44]

In reality, during his later years in education Hitler had been considered of singularly little talent and had failed. He had been described as a lazy student with no interest in work. Hitler was a 'dropout' in one of the most fashionable cities in Europe. In 1905 Vienna was an ironic setting for a 'drifter'. With its shimmering gold and marble arena, this grandly opulent city of the ancient Hapsburg Empire was sumptuous and dazzling. The shabbily dressed Adolf would amble past its grand imperial architecture, shuffle through the streets lined with elegant cafés and royal palaces, idle through the beautiful tree-lined boulevards. The Danube Canal overshadowed by slender limes, ashes, elms and maples; Prater park with its refined and immaculate chestnut-fringed avenues, the glittering Schönbrunn Palace, Karlskirche Cathedral and the Ring Boulevard – this was the walkway for Hitler's early failures. Now, imprisoned for violence, he relished the reinvention of his intellectual as well as his family's past.

Hitler 'read', he said, 'everything he could get hold of': 'Nietzsche, Houston Stewart Chamberlain ... Marx ...' (although much doubt has been placed upon the proficiency of this reading).[45] He claimed to be drawing upon Germany's most significant minds from the eighteenth and nineteenth centuries. Among them, 'he also claimed to have immersed himself in the theoretical literature of Marxism', which, of course, he disparaged.[46] 'I had come to know earlier in Vienna: the Marxist doctrine and philosophy,' he bragged.[47] He would rail against Marx in many later speeches. For instance: 'The splitting up of the nation into groups with irreconcilable views, systematically brought about by the false doctrines of Marxism, means the destruction of the basis of a possible communal life.'[48]

Other traditions Hitler idolized. Unsurprisingly, his ideas were infused with racist and ideological writings. In particular he was impressed by the German biblical scholar Paul de Lagarde (1827–91).[49] In his private copy of Lagarde's *German Essays*, Hitler highlighted:

> Despite their desire to be placed on equal terms with the Germans, the Jews continually emphasize their foreignness in the most obvious manner through the style of their synagogues. What is that supposed to mean, to lay claim to the honorable German name while constructing the most sacred one has in a Moorish style in order not to forget one is a Semite, an Asian, a foreigner?[50]

Other writers of whom Hitler couldn't get enough included Houston Stewart Chamberlain (1855–1927)[51] and Julius Langbehn (1851–1907). In his *Rembrandt as an Educator*[52] Langbehn celebrated Rembrandt as the ultimate perfection of the Aryan man. Then, combining images of Germanic folklore with nationalism, Langbehn hailed the notion of 'blood and soil'.[53] The right-wing historian Heinrich von Treitschke (1834–96)[54] and Oswald Spengler (1880–1936) were also read voraciously by Hitler[55] – he had borrowed copies of Spengler from the right-wing library, the National Socialist Institute in Munich, between 1919 and 1921, even before his internment in Landsberg prison.

Hitler's inclination towards perusing texts had begun years before his incarceration. In 1908 the eighteen-year-old youth was described by his friend August Kubizec 'as constantly immersed in his studies ... books were his world'. Although Kubizec's evidence is suspect, it is worth noting his claim that 'Hitler arrived in Vienna with four cases full of books. He had been a member of three libraries in Linz, and was now a regular user of the Hof library in Vienna.'[56] Another contemporary of Hitler's also wrote, 'he has a large library. He loves books; loves fine editions and fine bindings. In his Munich residence there were walls covered with bookcases. Hess's sister, a craftswoman, bound his books by hand.'[57]

Over the course of his year in Landsberg, Hitler continued with his appetite for books. His solidly bound, richly illustrated volumes included Hans F. K. Günther's[58] *Racial Typology of the German People*,[59] and J. F. Lehmann, a racist scientist and a publisher, became a major supplier of reading material for Hitler. During this time he also borrowed from Hess's assimilated notion of geopolitical power. This derived from Sir Halford Mackinder, who had referred to a 'heartland', 'the citadel of world empire' – all that which Hitler would later covet. Biographies of men of action such as Napoleon, Frederich the Great and Ghenghiz Khan also fired Hitler's imagination. None of this reading was surprising – racist and militaristic writings – no one would baulk at those.[60]

But what was astonishing was Hitler's identification with great German philosophers. As he whiled away his long months in prison, Hitler browsed, he said, Kant, Schiller, Schopenhauer, Nietzsche and Wagner, among others. His friend Kubizec later claimed that Hitler had digested an impressive list of classics – including 'Goethe, Schiller ... Schopenhauer and Nietzsche'.[61]

At first, during the onset of his prison years, Hitler had an ambivalent relationship with Germany's great thinkers. No doubt owing to a still-simmering inferiority complex from the memory of his own academic failings, he would always be rather resentful of the 'academic type' and would always berate Germany's 'rulers' who 'were *overeducated* men'.[62] Nonetheless he claimed during his time in the penitentiary, 'I had but one pleasure: my books.'[63] 'I read and studied much.'[64]

From amongst the many titles, a fascination with one particular philosopher was noted, namely the eighteenth-century Enlightenment thinker Immanuel Kant: 'Kant's complete refutation of the teachings which were the heritage of the middle ages, and of the dogmatic philosophy of the church, is the greatest of the services which Kant has rendered to us.'[65]

This claim was followed by others. 'Perhaps we are ignorant of humanity's most precious spiritual treasures. . . . In our parts of the world, the Jews would have immediately eliminated . . . Kant.'[66]

The importance of reason was something that Hitler claimed Kant had inspired in him. In the midst of a later electoral campaign speech he would spout:

> There are many who say that *reason* is not the decisive factor, but that other imponderables must be considered. I believe that there can be nothing of value which is not in the last resort based on *reason*. I refuse to believe that in statesmanship one should not regard as right any views which are not anchored in *reason* . . .[67]

Hitler's exclamations were superficial and amateur but he alleged great expertise and felt very well qualified to pontificate. Whether or not he read Kant in any seriousness from his cell in Landsberg no one will ever be quite sure. As his associate remarked, Hitler 'has been a Bohemian all his life. He gets up late. He can spend whole days lazing and dozing. He hates to have to read with concentration. He rarely reads a book through; usually he only begins it.'[68]

Alongside Kant, the philosopher-playwright Friedrich Schiller was another great favourite that Hitler liked to quote. Even before the unification of the German states in 1871, Schiller was more popular than Goethe because his writings encouraged German unity. In fact Schiller was destined to become admired not just by Hitler but by all the Nazis because he was highly patriotic and a German nationalist. Hitler would joke affectionately, 'our Schiller found nothing better to do than glorify a Swiss bowman!'[69] – referring to Schiller's most famous work, *William Tell*, which extolled Swiss nationalism. Hitler alleged a love of Schiller's philosophy. As one of his closest friends noted, 'he prefers the dramatic revolutionary Schiller to the Olympian and contemplative Goethe.'[70] Hitler explained his preference: 'Goethe's house gives the impression of a dead thing. And one understands that in the room where he died he should have asked for light – always more light.' Whereas 'Schiller's house can still move one by the picture it gives of the penury in which the poet lived'.[71] In fact, years later Schiller would become the pet genius of the Nazi generals, who would even give themselves nicknames from his plays. For example, one of Hitler's closest friends would recall: 'Even Goering began to call me the "*Questenberg* in the camp", a phrase he had invented in 1923, which was a reference to the character in Schiller's *Wallenstein*.'[72]

'The strong man is mightiest alone': this familiar quotation from Schiller's *William Tell* (Act I, scene III) formed the title of chapter 8, volume 2, of Hitler's *Mein Kampf*, and became his motto during his later years as the Führer. During the Second World War the Schiller and Goethe monument in Weimar was so treasured that Hitler had a special encasing made over it to protect it during the Allied bombings. But beside Schiller and other high-minded works, Hitler was known to possess 'in the drawer of his bedside table . . . literature of a less reputable character'.[73]

The daily prison routine framed Hitler's typing. He and Hess were interrupted only when they took regular exercise in the prison garden or ate with other inmates, and the food was certainly better than that which Hitler was used to, the gruel from the army and the meagre portions during his bohemian years in Vienna. In the evenings he enjoyed spouting ideas to the other inmates, always with Hess by his side absorbing his every word and gesture. While the guards had lent Hitler a typewriter, supporters from outside added to this generosity by keeping him supplied with a steady flow of ink and paper. The sympathetic guards allowed him to read long into the night after lights out and to stay up late discussing with Hess, if he so chose.

Hitler laid the foundations of gleanings from other thinkers such as Hegel and Fichte while in his prison cell. One commentator noted that:

> Hitler's views articulated in *Mein Kampf* ('My Struggle'), built in many ways upon more orthodox conservative German political theorists and philosophers. Hegel (1770–1831), for instance, had stressed the importance of a strong state . . . and the existence of a . . . [destiny] in history which justified war by superior states upon inferior ones.[74]

Hegel's historical view of the formation of the state from ancient origins was, in garbled form, a favourite theme of Hitler's and would often reappear in his orations:

> *For the States of the Ancient world* were not ruined by their cities. . . . The Roman Empire did not fall on account of the city of Rome, for without the city of Rome there never would have been a Roman Empire. The most natural way for the formation of great States – the way in which most great States had arisen – was to begin with a crystal-lization point of the political and later the cultural life which then, as the capital city, often gave its name to the State.[75]

Hegel's influence on Hitler has been noted by other scholars: 'it is possible to detect Hegel's view of the State having "supreme power over the individual" in Hitler's writings and speeches'.[76] Others have pointed out how 'the half educated Hitler was a mosaic of influences . . .

(including) the messianic complex of (Johann Gottlieb) Fichte (1762–1814)'.[77] Dietrich Eckart identified Fichte, Schopenhauer and Nietzsche as the 'philosophical triumvirate of national Socialism',[78] and the film director Leni Riefenstahl gave Hitler a first edition of Fichte's collected works published in 1848, a handsome eight-volume set bound in cream-coloured vellum with gold-leaf tipping on the pages.[79]

Years earlier in the mud-soaked trenches at the Western Front, when Hitler had been serving in France and Belgium during the First World War, he boasted 'I carried Schopenhauer's works with me throughout the whole of the First World War. From him I learned a great deal.'[80] Amidst the damp paths littered with misery, the overturned carts and wooden debris; in a place where the corpses of young men were built into the banks of mud and stone as if part of the landscape, the soldiers drenched in mud and injury, Hitler supposedly stalked with his bound volumes of wisdom. While ammunition was low, food scarce, gas masks available to only one in four men, and while the shells exploded all around, the young Hitler alleged he studied. He apparently pored over the words of a scholar from a hundred years previously. In ravines dug out by naked hands, barbed wire coiled above where there had once been the branches of trees, in this place and then in prison, Hitler claimed he discovered philosophy.

Decades later, during the reign of the Third Reich, amidst the clink of wine glasses and the glitter of silver cutlery, in an opulent restaurant in Berlin on 16 May 1944, the Führer would brag to his generals: 'It is on Kant's theory of knowledge that Schopenhauer built the edifice of his philosophy, and it is Schopenhauer who annihilated the pragmatism of Hegel.'[81] During the course of his musings for *Mein Kampf*, Hitler's admiration for Schopenhauer was perhaps the most notable, for 'Schopenhauer [1788–1860] glorified Will over Reason.'[82] On the topic of the purity of the Germanic language, he referred to 'his beloved' Schopenhauer: 'Only writers of genius can have the right to modify the language. In the past generation, I can think of practically nobody but Schopenhauer who would have dared do such a thing.'[83] However, Hitler would eventually become irritated by the contemplative side of philosophers, and complaining about his 'fatherly friend' Dietrich Eckart he stated: 'Schopenhauer has done Eckart no good. He has made him a doubting Thomas, who only looks forward to a Nirvana. Where would I get if I listened to all his [Schopenhauer's] transcendental talk? A nice ultimate wisdom that: To reduce on[e]self to a minimum of desire and will. Once will is gone all is gone. This life is War.'[84] Schopenhauer was out. Another German philosopher was in. But which one?

Hitler's businessman friend Hanfstaengl heard him remark: 'Now it is the heroic *Weltanschauung* which will illuminate the ideals of Germany's future. ...' 'What was this?' Hanfstaengl questioned. 'This was not Schopenhauer, who had been Hitler's philosophical god in the old ... days. No, this was new. It was Nietzsche.'[85] Hitler had moved his allegiance elsewhere. As Hitler expressed it: 'Schopenhauer's pessimism which springs partly, I think, from his own line of philosophical thought and partly from the subjective feeling and the experiences of his own life, has been far surpassed by Nietzsche.'[86]

Hitler's oratorical displays became littered with ideas hacked from Nietzsche's works. First off was the Nietzschean love of the ancients, especially his veneration for the Greeks. Hitler aped this: 'The art of Greece is not merely a formal reproduction of the Greek mode of life, of the landscapes and inhabitants of Greece; no, it is a proclamation of the essential Greek spirit.'[87] Combining Nietzsche's love of the Greeks with Hegel's depiction of the ancient origins of the Western world became a favourite theme for Hitler. Except that he used Darwinism to claim that the ancients were *biological* ancestors of the Germans. 'A cultural ideal stands before us which even today thanks to its art and to our own origin which relates us to it by our blood, still mediates to us a compelling picture of the fairest epochs of human development, and of the most resplendent bearers of its culture.'[88]

Hitler copied Nietzsche in admiring the ancient Greek ideals of strength and beauty, and even mimicked Nietzsche's phrases such as 'affirmation of life': 'The German people of this twentieth century is the people of a newly awakened *affirmation of life*, seized with admiration for Strength and Beauty and therefore for that which is healthy and vigorous. Strength and Beauty – these are fanfares sounded by this new age.'[89]

The Nazi obsession with 'public health' was no socialist ideal, but an aspiration Hitler had usurped from Nietzsche's bewitchment with ancient Greek beauty. Hitler went all the way in his veneration of Nietzsche's ideal and claimed that the Nazis were the modern renaissance of ancient culture: 'the gigantic works of the Third Reich are a token of its cultural renascence and shall one day belong to the inalienable cultural heritage of the Western world, just as the great cultural achievements of this world in the past belong to us today.'[90]

Hermann Rauschning, a Nazi Party member during the early years, observed Hitler on several occasions in the apparently typical German Romantic mood:

He loves solitary walks. The mountain forests intoxicate him. These walks are his divine service, his prayers. He watches the passing clouds, listens to the moisture dripping from the pines. He hears voices. I have met him in this mood. He recognises nobody then: he wants be alone. There are times when he flees from human society.[91]

This image of the great man wandering alone in the mountains could have been taken from a Caspar David Friedrich painting. It was in fact appropriated directly from Nietzsche, who spent much of his life coveting solitude and whose love of lonely mountain walks was second to none. But while his hero had acute sensitivity, Hitler was deaf to the nature around him. He was aware only of his own superiority and the need to escape society – people whom he couldn't dominate, he loathed.

Many scholars have noted that Hitler's homage to Nietzsche began in Landsberg prison. 'Whilst in the Landsberg fortress, Hitler claimed he read works by Nietzsche . . .'[92] In fact, he was so inspired that immediately after leaving prison, he 'often visited the Nietzsche museum in Weimar and publicized his veneration for the philosopher by posing for photographs of himself staring in rapture at the bust of the great man.'[93]

A very vital woman in her late eighties, wearing granny glasses and a bonnet, would welcome Hitler to the Nietzsche Archives in Weimar. This old lady was none other than Friedrich Nietzsche's sister Elisabeth, who had outlived Nietzsche by some years (he died in 1900). The first visit would occur in August 1934, on what would have been Nietzsche's ninetieth birthday, a decade after Hitler was released from Landsberg, and would be remembered by a friend of Hitler's who later recalled it thus:

> I thought back only a few months earlier to a visit he had paid during one of his election campaigns, while travelling from Weimar to Berlin, to the Villa Silberblick, where Nietzsche had died and where his widowed sister, aged 86, still lived. The rest of us had waited nearly an hour and a half. Hitler had gone in carrying his whip, but, to my astonishment, came tripping out with a slim little turn of the century cane dangling from his fingers: 'What a marvellous old lady', he said to me. 'What vivacity and intelligence. A real personality. Look she has given me her brother's last walking stick as a souvenir. . .'[94]

So it was that Hitler came to own one of Nietzsche's most personal possessions.

From that day on the Nietzsche catchphrases were everywhere, *Wille zur Macht*, *Herrenvolk*, *Sklavenmoral* – the fight for the heroic life, against formal dead-weight education, against Christian ethics of compassion.[95] The term 'Lords of the Earth' coined by Nietzsche, however, was already in constant use throughout *Mein Kampf*. Nietzsche 'predicted modern society would result in the "death of God"....Overall what Hitler latched on to in Nietzsche's writings were (what he took to be) his fervent criticisms of democratic forms of government, his praise of violence and war and his prediction of the coming "master race" led by an all-powerful "superman" ... who would rule the world.'[96]

Years later, after Hitler had become the Führer, he would make a speech drawing on ideas he had gained in Landsberg prison. From the Reichstag on 11 December 1941, just days after the Japanese attack on Pearl Harbor, he would declare war on the United States. He did so quoting the mythic notion of 'blood sacrifice', which he was adamant came directly from his reading of Nietzsche. He cried: 'You, my deputies, are in the best position to gauge the extent of the blood sacrifice.' In the same speech Hitler would justify an invasion of Europe using Hegel's historical idea of 'coming into being': 'In the whole history of the coming into being,' he would proclaim, 'the German Reich ... will wage the war forced upon them by the USA.'[97] Thus it was that during a year of musing in prison Hitler would find ideas to deploy in later years to justify war upon the Western world.

One of Hitler's henchmen later reflected on the Führer's 'savage bowdlerization of Nietzsche'. He wrote 'the guillotine twist which Robespierre had given to the teachings of Jean Jacques Rousseau was repeated by Hitler and the Gestapo in their political simplification of the contradictory theories of Nietzsche'.[98] Hitler, as Ernst Hanfstaengl put it, 'was not so much a distiller as a bartender of genius. He took all the ingredients the German [tradition] offered him and mixed them through his private alchemy into a cocktail they wanted to drink.'[99]

Of course, Hitler's love of philosophy involved, as everything else in his life, a lot of bluff and posturing. As Hermann Rauschning noted:

Hitler is exacting, spoilt, avaricious, greedy. He does not know how to work steadily. Indeed he is incapable of working. He gets ideas, impulses, the realisation of which must be feverishly achieved and immediately got rid of. He does not know what it is to work continuously and unremittingly. Everything about him is 'spasm', to use a favourite word of his. Nothing about him is natural. His professed love of children and animals is a mere pose.[100]

But for a man for whom every ingredient of his life was fantasy, Hitler's admiration of philosophy was no less real or valid than anything else about him.

For now, however, Hitler paced his cell in Landsberg, self-conscious about what he considered to be his assured and upright gait, indicative, he believed, of a born leader. He outlined his hatred for Jews and his passion for the master race. Dwelling upon his own Aryan nation and its superiority, again he turned to philosophy to demonstrate German supremacy. Of the German mind, he would later boast: 'In the great hall of the Linz library are the busts of Kant, Schopenhauer and Nietzsche, the greatest of our thinkers, in comparison with whom the British, the French, the Americans have nothing to offer.'[101]

But Hitler's readings of philosophy went beyond fantasies of ancient Greece and inspirations for nationalism, or even justifications for war. Nietzsche's complex analysis of morality, and in particular the ideas of pity and weakness versus strength, were digested by Hitler and regurgitated in rank form. He declared:

Unless you are prepared to be pitiless, you will get nowhere. Our opponents are not prepared for it, not because they are humane or anything of that sort, but because they are too weak. Dominion is never founded on humanity, but, regarded from the narrow civilian angle, on crime. Terrorism is absolutely indispensable in every case of the founding of a new power[102]

A year or so before his internment in Landsberg, Hitler had met the family of his greatest hero, the nineteenth-century German composer who had created the great music festival at Bayreuth. Dressed in his traditional Bavarian outfit of lederhosen,[103] thick woollen socks, and a red and blue checked shirt, Hitler arrived at Haus Wahnfried where in the music room and library he marvelled over the former possessions of Richard Wagner. In a sacred whisper, 'as though he were viewing relics in a cathedral', he articulated his reverence.[104] Later, Hitler would attend Wagner's operas from his own private box. He hated to sit in a row, be part of a crowd. And to concoct an air of mystery, he would always vanish before the first ovation.[105]

Back in Landsberg prison he wrote: 'I was captivated. My youthful enthusiasm for the master of Bayreuth knew no bounds. Again and again I was drawn to his works, and it still seems to me especially fortunate that the most modest provincial performance left me open to an intensified experience later on.'[106] Indeed Hitler's admiration knew no bounds: 'Wagner is responsible for the fact that the art of opera is what it is today',[107] 'Whatever one says, Tristan is Wagner's masterpiece',[108] 'Wagner was a man of the renaissance',[109] 'Wagner was typically a prince',[110] and so on. He referred in public speeches to 'the genius of Richard Wagner',[111] and among the great men in history he always singled out Wagner.[112]

Beyond music, Hitler's veneration of the composer in fact became one of emulation. Wagner inspired the stage for the Third Reich: from the gold-adorned and marble-floored abundance and opulence of the European opera houses, Hitler watched *Tristan and Isolde* thirty to forty times and used the stage setting of 'theatre and pageantry' for the military displays of the Third Reich:[113]

I came to see there was a direct parallel between the construction of . . . [Wagner's operas] and that of his [Hitler's] speeches. The whole interweaving of *leitmotifs*, of embellishments, of counterpoint and musical contrasts and argument, were exactly mirrored in the pattern of speeches, which were symphonic in construction and ended in a great climax, like the blare of Wagner's trombones.[114]

In *Mein Kampf*, Hitler also wrote of Wagner as one of the intellectual precursors of National Socialism, for not only his music but his anti-Semitism struck a chord. Hitler's identification with Wagner was so profound that Hitler declared 'to understand Nazism one must first know Wagner'.[115]

In devotion to his idol, from his prison cell Hitler began signing his letters with characteristic references to his composer hero. On 10 October 1924 he wrote from Landsberg to a composer friend in Munich:

> Please do not be angry with me for taking so long over my answers; but what I would like to write I may not, and what I may write I will not. So let me just thank you for the kind words etc. you were good enough to send me. This remark applied even more to your dear wife, who as Herr . . . keeps telling me, sacrifices so much of her time on my behalf. You know how much happiness I wish you and your dear wife for the New Year. I am afraid it will be one of the bitterest years in German history.
>
> I am getting rid of my anger by writing my vindication, of which I hope at least the first part will survive the trial and myself. For the rest I dream of *Tristan* and the like.
> Best wishes to you and your wife,
> Yours sincerely, Adolf Hitler.[116]

Having assimilated racist ideas from crude thinkers such as Paul de Lagarde, Houston Stewart Chamberlain and the like, Hitler had also usurped the most authoritative German philosophers of all time. From the Enlightenment he had taken from Kant and Fichte, and from the nineteenth century, Schiller, Schopenhauer, Nietzsche and Wagner. With these potent cultural trophies to hand, Hitler lived out the rest of his sentence.

During this time, 'Half the manuscript of *Mein Kampf* had been smuggled out from Landsberg gaol and they [Hitler's cronies] were in the process of setting it up in type'.[117] *Mein Kampf*, with all its potted versions of Germany's philosophical tradition, would be disseminated across the Bavarian land. By the time he became chancellor in 1933, it had sold about 240,000 copies. Later, after his meteoric rise to power, the book gained enormous popularity and for all intents and purposes became the Nazi Bible. By the end of the war, about 10 million copies had been sold or distributed in Germany (every newly-wed couple, as well as every front-line soldier, received a free copy).[118]

It was the autumn of 1924 and the Bavarian forests were rich in their cloaks of red and brown: 'To carry a philosophy to victory, we must transform it into a fighting movement',[119] Hitler would soon write, and 'the programme of a *philosophy* is the formation of a declaration of war'.[120] His programme would eventually be enacted upon the gentle Bavarian landscape: 'In new geological ages, the whole structure of the earth is changed by gigantic avalanches, piling up new mountains and creating canyons, plains and oceans. So also will the entire European social order be uprooted in mighty eruptions and collapses.'[121]

In September 1924 the warden of Landsberg prison made a report on him to the Bavarian Ministry of Justice. It couldn't have been more favourable. Hitler had been 'at all times cooperative, modest and courteous to everyone, particularly to the officials of the institution,' the report stated. 'There is no doubt he has become a much more quiet, more mature and thoughtful individual during his imprisonment than he was before, and does not contemplate acting against existing authority.' Hitler responded, 'When I left Landsberg . . . everyone wept (the warden and the other members of the prison staff) – but not I! We'd won them all over to our cause.'[122]

So it was that they released Hitler along with the bulk of his manuscript *Mein Kampf*. He was of course jubilant. He had arrived as a man of action and left, he fancied, as the 'philosopher leader'.

When Hitler was freed from gaol on 20 December 1924, he returned to Munich where he received a grand welcome. Supporters had fed and looked after his dog, Wolf, during his absence and his rooms were piled high with food, drink, flowers and laurel wreaths. He enjoyed the gifts, drank the wine, indulged in the chocolates – friends commented that he was even putting on weight. Smiling in acknowledgement at the phrases of admiration from the numerous greeting cards, he gleefully got back to normal life. He walked his dog. Times had changed though, and politics in Weimar Germany were no longer such a desperate affair. A fanatic like Hitler was less suited to these quieter times. Nevertheless, he continued with his cause fervently unabated.

Drawing on his band of supporters, Hitler went to work. He began to pull together his political mission, resuming leadership of the party, outlining plans, organizing committees and meetings, composing speeches and addressing conferences. All this placed him firmly back in the driving seat, as the leader, the man of action – that which he most wanted to be.

Hitler didn't just plunge himself into all this political activity by putting his prison year behind him, however. Instead, he decided to make use of the material he had read, realizing its value in promoting his career. In this quieter period, he could pose as an intellectual politician and name-drop to his audience – philosophical works were such high-status acquisitions. Combing through influential ideas with the gravitas of a general stroking his moustache, he pulled out endorsements from the grand masters. Practising his image as the 'philosopher leader', for others and for himself, posing before the mirror in his Munich apartment much as he had done during his time in Landsberg prison, he rehearsed gestures and expressions to lend appropriate weight to the mighty names he quoted. In private conversations, in correspondence and in public speeches he recounted the words of the nation's forebears and made them his own.

On 27 February 1925 before a clamouring crowd of over five thousand in the Munich beer hall, precisely where he had made his previous ill-fated putsch, Hitler made his first speech after his release from Landsberg:

We are met in a Celebration (*Feierstunde*) in memory of the day on which for the first time we sought to change the fate of Germany. The result of that attempt was sixteen dead, more than a hundred severely or slightly wounded. . . . My heart overflowed with joy when I saw the first report of these trials, when I read in the *Munich Post* – which was sent to us at the time – 'The men of the Shock-Troops are just as insolent and shameless as was their lord and master'. Then I knew that Germany was not lost. That spirit would gnaw its way through anything . . .[123]

In excited memory of the putsch Hitler then recited themes from revered manuscripts to impress and sway his audience.[124] Recapitulating his own version of ideas from Kant, Hegel, Nietzsche and German Idealism, he embellished this speech. Before his massive audience he borrowed from Nietzsche and portrayed himself as a prophet. 'If you will read again my final speech in the great prosecution you will be in a position to say that as a *prophet* I foreshadowed the only possible way for progress in the future . . .'[125] Copying Hegel, Hitler preached of a force within history: 'Just think: over a period of some two thousand years we can follow the German people in history, and never in the course of history has this people possessed this single formation both in the conceptions of its thought and in its action . . .'[126] From German Idealism, Hitler stole the notion of a single idea animating world history. 'The miracle is that [there] arose this mighty unity in Germany, this victory of a Movement, of an *idea* . . .'[127]

Hitler ended his commemoration of the putsch by claiming dominion over the books he had read in gaol. But it was not enough for him to spout great learning. From the pose of the intellectual, to the glory of the author, to the almighty leader, Hitler's ambition now was to become the idea that others would emulate. He was the subject that others would read and learn from. Not merely the philosopher, Hitler vowed to change the world and thereby become living philosophy:

This is the miracle we have wrought. We are the fortunate ones, for we need not learn the story from books: we have been chosen by fate to live this miracle in our own experience. . . . Other generations – they learn of sagas of heroes, of the expeditions of heroes: *we have lived this saga.* . . . We are all bound together in one single mighty happening. That will remain.[128]

CHAPTER 2

Poisoned Chalice

Hitler had set himself up as the 'philosopher leader' – but only in his own imagination. He had yet to convince anyone else. Ideas that he spouted from the authors whose names he dropped may have simply been the half-crazed imaginings of an ambitious and manipulative mind. Could the nation's past thinkers really have said anything in preparation for Hitler's fantasy? It hardly seemed plausible. Kant, Hegel and Nietzsche had better things to think about than pave the way for the 'mighty happening' of Nazism some hundred or more years later. To determine whether Hitler's claims were anything other than sheer sensationalism, we now turn the clock back some two hundred years.

In the eighteenth century, prior to the formation of the German nation, a very different world existed in central Europe.[1] Prussia was a notable presence and its capital, Königsberg, of great significance to German philosophers.[2] A winter's day in Königsberg, now known as Kaliningrad, could appear beautifully bright and clear, but also it could be bitterly cold. From a bird's-eye view looking down from a great height, one would have seen contrasting textures, the rough red stone of the Cathedral of Saint Nicholas, the turrets of the city's gates absorbing the winter sun, the shadowy lines of the narrow, crooked streets, the glistening palace. Noted for its castles overlooking the Pregel river and its famous seven bridges, this city had always been a meeting point of Eastern Europe and Russia. A provincial capital crowned by Teutonic church spires and eastern domes, it nestled between southern Russia and the Baltic Sea.

Over the course of the centuries, Königsberg's location meant that it was a natural gateway for the many Jews, intellectuals and others fleeing from East to West. The city, however, was geographically isolated. One philosopher once wrote 'as you know I live here in a place where new foreign books and writings appear just like comets after long years'.[3] Another complained, we are 'decried as almost a learned Siberia', and when Frederick the Great visited Königsberg in 1739, he quipped that the city was better suited to 'bring up bears than to be an arena for the sciences'.[4]

However, all this was to change – the greatest volumes of modern philosophy the world would ever see would be written there. They would be conceived and written by Immanuel Kant:

> His hair blond, the colour of his face fresh, and his cheeks showed even in old age a healthy blush ... from where do I take the words to describe to you his eye! Kant's eye was as if it had been formed of heavenly ether from which the deep look of the mind, whose fiery beam was occluded by a light of cloud, visibly shone forth. It is impossible to describe the bewitching effect of his look on my feeling when I sat across from him and when he suddenly raised his lowered eyes to look at me. I always felt as if I looked through this blue-like ether into the most holy of Minerva.[5]

Kant was born one mild, sunny April in 1724. The household in which he grew up was a busy one, and he was the fifth of nine children. He was brought up a Pietist, with the stress on intense religious devotion, personal humility, and a literal reading of the Bible. His mother died when he was but thirteen years old and he was raised solely by his strict father, who died less than a decade later. In stature, Kant was unremarkable with a diminutive, even deformed, body, and as a young man his personality was weighted with gloom. But he had remarkable self-discipline and soon developed grace, wit and ready conversation.[6] He attended his native university and graduated from Königsberg six years later.

Famously, Kant was a man of habit. He was to be found sitting beneath the same tree at the same hour each day, lost in thought. Unable to obtain a university post, he worked as a private tutor and had to wait until his thirty-first birthday before being allowed to work at the university, and then only in an unsalaried role. 'He had to wear the same coat until it was worn out, and his friends offered to buy him a new one, but he refused.'[7] The simple world of the provinces was always preferable to Kant over city life and it was in his native eastern Prussian town that he continued to reside, even turning down well-paid positions amongst the urban bustle. Eventually, he was granted a professorship and was instantly regarded with such esteem that one of his students noted it was necessary to arrive at 6 a.m., an hour before his lecture was to begin, in order to secure a seat in the lecture hall.[8]

Kant's reputation as a speaker preceded his fame for any published work. A student, Reinhold Bernhard Jachmann, witnessing his lectures, wrote that Kant 'ceased to be merely a . . . philosopher and became, at the same time, a spirited orator, sweeping the heart and emotions along with him, as well as satisfying the intelligence'.[9] For many years Kant taught but wrote little, his plentiful ruminations building into what would later become his masterpieces, *Critique of Pure Reason* and *Critique of Practical Reason*.

During this time Königsberg, although relatively quiet, was not unaffected by historical events. Frederick the Great, whom Hitler was later to admire so, had waged war on Russia, and, after the Seven Years War (1756–63), when the Prussian army lost the battle of Gross Jäagersdorf, Königsberg was occupied by the Russians. The city itself saw none of the fighting and even benefited from increased luxury and consumption: 'French cuisine replaced the more traditional fare in the houses of those who were better off. Russian cavaliers changed the social intercourse, and gallantry became the order of the day. Drinking of punch was the rage. Dinners, masked balls . . . became common.'[10]

Königsberg was fast becoming a modern, cosmopolitan city. This new era was reflected in the intellectual climate – with many of its inhabitants influenced by the fashionable ideas of the Enlightenment. Past traditions were challenged, prejudice was deemed to be overcome, and its shadow replaced by the new light of reason.

The discoveries of science heralded this era of modernity. Science claimed that true knowledge required physical evidence and this replaced mere faith or superstition as the basis of all certainty about the world. God couldn't be observed, his existence couldn't be proved, so there was no basis for faith. These ideas were terrifying to the Church as they threatened to undermine Christianity. Science also challenged philosophy, for philosophy depended upon thought rather than observation. In *Critique of Pure Reason* (1781) Kant confronted these tensions head-on and developed a system that showed how science, Christianity and philosophy could all exist together in harmony. His work propelled him on to the world stage.

Kant's main concern was to establish the importance of reason. Only things that were rational were worthy of our allegiance, and if a religion wasn't rational then it wasn't a religion at all, just a primitive set of superstitions. Crucially, in the modern world, not just religion but morality too should be rational. We could not be good people by merely following the dictates of religion, or convention, or even our own hearts. It was not sufficient to do as our parents, family, friends, predecessors, Church or other community told us. We had to think for ourselves. These ideas were explained in his treatise *Critique of Practical Reason* (1788).

In another famous short tract, *Was ist Auflkärung?* (What is Enlightenment) (1784), Kant went on to portray the world that would arise from his envisioned state of moral perfection. In a society governed by reason – peace, humanity and freedom would automatically reign. Kant was heralded as the forerunner of a modern, progressive liberalism.[11] Certainly this was how he inspired his lecture audience. The student Jachmann wrote:

> Indeed, it was heavenly delight to hear his sublimely pure ethical doctrine delivered with such powerful philosophic eloquence from the lips of its creator. How often he moved us to tears, how often he stirred our hearts to their depths, how often he lifted up our minds and emotions from the shackles of self-seeking egoism to the exalted self-awareness of pure free-will, to absolute obedience to the laws of reason and to the exalted sense of our [moral] duty to others.[12]

But what did all this hold in store for the twentieth century? How could a high-minded thinker from the Enlightenment have written anything that would stretch across the centuries and appeal to a man as coarse as Hitler?

Kant was a modern thinker – 'away with the past, with superstition and prejudice'. This drive to oust prejudice, however, left Kant with a peculiar prejudice of his own. Everything that was primitive and irrational irritated him and one ancient religion became his special target – Judaism. Kant regarded this as backward, labelling Jews as a body superstitious, primitive and irrational. His denigration went further. Because religion should be founded upon reason, Kant went so far as to deny Judaism the status of a religion at all. In his tract upon religious understanding, *Religion within the Limits of Mere Reason* (1793), he wrote 'the Jewish religion is not really a religion at all, but merely a community of a mass of men of one tribe [*Stamm*]'.[13]

Judaism, he went on, not only failed to rank as a religion but also failed to be moral. Because rationality was the basis of morality, and Jews were irrational, they were also immoral. After all, was it not true that 'Every coward is a liar; Jews for example, not only in business but also in common life'?[14] Kant went on to lament the perpetual immorality of the Jews:

The Palestinians who live among us owe their not undeserved reputation for cheating (at least the majority of them) to their spirit of usury
which has possessed them ever since their exile. Certainly it seems
strange to conceive of a nation of cheats, but it is just as strange to
conceive of a nation of traders, most of whom – tied by an ancient
superstition – seek no civil honour from the state where they live, but
rather to restore their loss at the expense of those who grant them
protection as well as from one another. . . . Instead of vain plans to
make this people moral . . . I prefer to give my opinion on the origins
of this peculiar constitution of a nation of traders . . .[15]

Kant's ideas were deeply damaging, not only because he became known
historically as the greatest thinker of the Enlightenment but also because
he was famed as the greatest moralist. This philosophical grandee, the
cornerstone of authority, provided a legitimate basis deep within
European culture for the potential criminalization of the Jews.[16]

As if this were not enough, Kant claimed the Jews had no right to an
independent existence. Judaism was obsolete. He decreed in fact that
pure morality sought 'the euthanasia of Judaism'.[17] Apart from the exception of a tiny minority of 'enlightened Jews', the rest were not morally, and
therefore not politically, equal to the Germans – they should be excluded.
In short, witnessed by the locals, sitting beneath the same tree at a regular
hour each day, this apparently innocuous, timid man set down that Jews
were materialist, immoral, obsolete and politically alien. As one commentator recently put it, Kant's 'depiction of the Jews as a group is anti-
Semitic insofar as it . . . depicts them as corrupting the body politic. . . .
Thus Kant . . . anticipated political anti-Semitism'.[18]

Kant gave his last lecture in 1796 and died in 1804. Many in
Königsberg and crowds from all over Germany came to pay tribute at his
grave. Throughout the centuries after his death the reverence continued
– a neoclassical portico enshrined his remains. A bronze tablet quotes
from his ethics: 'Two things fill the heart with ever renewed and increasing

awe and reverence, the more often and the more steadily we meditate upon them: the starry firmament above and the moral law within.'[19] It is a shame that he didn't extend such noble sentiments to include the Jews.

Hitler considered Kant a gift; he wanted away with the Jews because they were irrational, immoral and unfit for civic life. What could have delighted him more than that the trophy philosopher of the Enlightenment should have provided theories to echo his cause. But if Hitler had found a rationale for Jew hatred in Kant, this might perhaps be an isolated incident, just one particular philosopher's eccentric prejudice? Unfortunately this appeared not to be the case.

In the immediate aftermath of Kant's life, Johann Gottlieb Fichte, born in Saxony in 1762, earned a brilliant reputation. Perceived by all to be a shining beacon of truth, Fichte was an Idealist philosopher, but he also embraced military values. In 1808, in his landmark *Speeches to the German Nation*, Fichte summoned Germans to rise against foreign oppression, and on the eve of a decisive battle against Napoleon he appeared before his students armed and ready.[20] 'To action! To action! To action!' he declared; 'That is why we are here.'[21] Fichte also celebrated German exceptionalism. Germans were unique, he claimed, because their language was rooted in the Teutonic tongue, not in Latin, and the purity of the Germans needed to be preserved.[22] But if these ideas were simply expressions of nationalism, Fichte also had a blatantly sinister side. He claimed: 'I see absolutely no way of giving the Jews civic rights, except perhaps if one chops off all of their heads and replaces them with new ones, in which there would not be one single Jewish idea.'[23]

Meanwhile, by the late eighteenth century, Fichte was about to be outgunned by a new philosopher. Living from 1770 to 1831, Georg Wilhelm Friedrich Hegel became professor of philosophy at the highly influential University of Jena. With masterpieces such as the *Phenomenology of Spirit* (1807) and *Philosophy of Right* (1821), Hegel claimed that history would accomplish that which Kant merely theorized about: over the course of time the Western world would develop to become more rational and more moral. Reason was not simply an ideal but was the end point of human history. Heralded as the new leading world thinker, Hegel appeared to have outshone Kant.

But the old prejudices remained. Hegel wrote: 'The temple of ... reason is loftier than Solomon's temple. . . . It has . . . been built rationally, not at all in the way the Jews . . . have built on Solomon's pattern.'[24] Again the Jews were deemed irrational. Thus in his new, grand view of history in which he prophesized the coming of a new dawn, Hegel excluded the Jews.[25] Ostracized as they were from Europe, he relegated them to an inferior status, outside of civilization: 'The Jews continued to survive long after their *raison d'être* had disappeared – indeed they no longer had a genuine history ... but merely existed as the corpse of their extinguished essence.'[26] Just as they were seen as below par, so too was their God. Hegel wrote: 'It is only the limited Jewish national god that is unable to tolerate other gods . . . this austere, national god is so jealous.'[27] And with no doubt high-minded intentions, Hegel also put forward other potentially dangerous ideas. Advocating the strong state, he also argued that historical progress relied on conflict. Conflict, therefore, could be a positive force, and as one commentator noted: 'Hegel's ideas on the morality of war and war's function as a moral baptism of fire (in his *Rechtsphilosophie*) have had an especially disastrous effect.'[28]

Time passed and the nineteenth century matured. Illuminated in their work by candles, oil lamps and the light of the fire, men toiled with ink and quill across the porous paper of their manuscripts. As the years moved on, technology progressed and the quill was eventually replaced by the metal-nibbed pen. Unfortunately, whereas technology had developed, moral sentiments had not. During the first part of the nineteenth century the philosopher Arthur Schopenhauer (1788–1860), wrote:

Ahasverus the Wandering Jew is the personification of the whole Jewish race . . . nowhere at home and nowhere strangers . . . asserting its Jewish nationality with unprecedented stubbornness, living parasitically on

other nations. . . . The best way to end the tragic-comedy is by intermar-
riage between Jew and gentile . . . Ahasverus will be buried and . . . in a
century, the chosen people will not know where their abode was. . . .
They are and remain a foreign, oriental race.[29]

Ludwig Andreas Feuerbach, a Hegelian thinker and born sixteen years
later than Schopenhauer in 1804, described Jews as irrational and primitive. He stereotyped them as egoistic and then went further, even
accusing them of ritual cannibalism.[30] But Feuerbach's anti-Semitic ideas
were overshadowed by the notorious prejudice of Karl Marx.[31] In *On the
Jewish Question* Marx wrote:

> Once society has succeeded in abolishing the *empirical* essence of
> Judaism – huckstering and its preconditions – the Jew will have
> become *impossible*, because his consciousness no longer has an object,
> because the subjective basis of Judaism, practical need, has been
> humanized, and because the conflict between man's individual-
> sensuous existence and his species-existence has been abolished.
>
> The *social* emancipation of the Jew is the *emancipation of society
> from Judaism*.[32]

Of course Marx was of no interest to Hitler (although he claimed to have
read him), but from a very different end of the political spectrum another
man was.

The great composer and philosophical essayist Richard Wagner, born
in Leipzig in 1813, was perhaps the most virulent anti-Semite of all. In
some of his operas he turned Jew hatred into an aesthetic experience. He
firmly believed that the Jews were 'exploiters and parasites' who had
taken over German cultural and commercial life. 'I see my "Germany"
perish – for ever! . . . My artistic ideal stands and falls with Germany. . . .
What will follow the downfall of the German princes is that Jewish
German mass',[33] the 'cursed Jew-scum'.[34] In 1869 Wagner published *Das*

Judenthum in der Musik, translated as Jewishness in Music.[35] In the essay he denounced his Jewish contemporaries Felix Mendelssohn and Giacomo Meyerbeer, stating that the German people found Jewish looks and activities repulsive. In his own words: 'with all our speaking and writing in favour of the Jews' emancipation, we always felt instinctively repelled by any actual, operative contact with them'.[36] Jews were alien, he claimed, to the German spirit and their music was thus rendered superficial and without meaning. Moreover, this very superficial quality meant that they could achieve popularity and sell their music for financial gain. Wagner later became a favourite with Hitler's colleague Alfred Rosenberg, who found in the composer's reference to the Jews, 'The plastic demon of the decay of humanity',[37] a favourite catchphrase.

***

The parsonage in Rocken, near Leipzig in Prussian Saxony, where Friedrich Nietzsche was born on 15 October 1844 was a modest, though not small, dwelling, its lime-rendered exterior painted in a soft mellow tone with little white windows arranged symmetrically across its walls. A curved brick lintel marked the doorway and a wooden carved door sat snuggly to one side. The exterior was overgrown, suggesting a cottage-style homeliness, and many fruit trees jostled beside ash and birch in a once much-loved garden. The roof was laid with darkened red-brown tiles, with two neat chimney stacks above. Out of it jutted three small windows, arranged as a triangle, one above and two below, forming almond-shaped holes which the roof line framed as if with a lid. The attic windowpanes appeared as dark holes in the centre uncannily like the pupil of an eye. The topmost eye was reminiscent of a Cyclops, perhaps a fitting design for the birthplace of one of the leading visionaries of the nineteenth century, and the man whom Hitler would claim as his greatest influence.[38]

What was it that attracted Hitler to Nietzsche? Perhaps Nietzsche's life provides the answer.

Raised under the strict influence of religion, Nietzsche's upbringing bore many similarities to that of Kant. In fact, his early years were more devout even than Kant's as he grew up the son of a country parson. An intense and taciturn child, he was noticed by other children for being a creature apart, and apparently resembled Jesus in the temple. Like Kant, he encountered grief early in his life, for his father died when he was but a five-year-old boy. He wrote later, 'I did have some idea of death; the thought of being separated forever from my beloved father seized me, and I wept bitterly.'[39] The next year his two-year-old brother also died in what Nietzsche described as 'the re-opening of the tomb'.[40] This tragedy produced a sombre character and while other children were muddying their knees, Nietzsche was avidly writing down every detail of his experiences. It became a lifelong obsession, thinking, recounting and interpreting the world to himself.[41]

As a young man, Nietzsche was pale with a high forehead, an already receding hairline, and brown, austerely swept-back hair which was worn neatly parted to one side. His features were enhanced by a pair of round, fine-rimmed gold glasses which detracted little from his powerful, deep-set eyes and very intense countenance. His other most notable feature was his thick moustache, characteristic of the era. Certainly his face was more remarkable than his physique for, in keeping with the common image held of many intellectuals, he was of a slight build.

At university Nietzsche's early years were spent studying religion and classical literature. After a year in Bonn he transferred to Leipzig and continued with the classics. He then undertook a short period of military service, which was to have a profound impact upon his convictions and imagination for the rest of his life. His actual service, however, was very short-lived: he was discharged with a painful and enduring wound to the chest.

After leaving the military in 1868, Nietzsche returned to Leipzig where he made an important friendship. In the house of a mutual acquaintance, he met a man with a legendary reputation, about whose operatic works Nietzsche was passionately fond. His chest pounding, Nietzsche leant forward to introduce himself. But he recoiled in astonishment, for when the man turned towards him, the face of his dead father looked back.

Richard Wagner, the man Nietzsche was meeting, was roughly the age that Nietzsche's father would have been, and he bore a great similarity to the former pastor. After recovering from the shock, Nietzsche spent the rest of that evening discussing his love of music, philosophy and most of all Schopenhauer, becoming absorbed with Wagner in all their mutual enthusiasms. Thenceforth they were intimate friends and this awesome composer became the single greatest influence on the young man's life.

Within a year of meeting Wagner, Nietzsche's career soared. He was soon appointed professor at the Swiss University of Basel in 1869 at the astonishingly early age of twenty-four, before he had even received his doctorate. However, he found the move to Switzerland stressful, as he had never left Germany before.[42] In spite of his frail physique, Nietzsche admired the warrior spirit, none more so than that of the ancient Greeks. With a fascination for war, he served in the Prussian forces during the Franco-Prussian War as a medical orderly from 1870.[43] Ill health plagued him, however, and after bouts of dysentery and diphtheria he was forced to leave the army. His admiration for the ancient warriors found its expression more constructively, in his case, in prose rather than action. And while roaming in the Swiss Alps, mimicking his heroic ancestors, Nietzsche became absorbed in contemplation. On the higher slopes, lost in the Alpine forests, he could abandon his mind to that which he adored: the warrior spirit Schopenhauer and, of course, Wagner.

Nietzsche continued in his post as professor at Basel until 1879. For most of his life he suffered from ill health and was mired in poverty and obscurity. He never married and always lacked comfort from a source of trusted intimacy, be that family or friends. He was also plagued by fear of syphilis – caught from a single ill-fated visit to a brothel or inherited.

After leaving his post at Basel, Nietzsche's life became peripatetic as he moved across Europe from Germany to Switzerland and Italy. 'In Genoa . . . he wandered around the streets, lost in admiration'; in Turin 'the city delighted him' with 'the "aristocratic calm" of the seventeenth century'. In Italy there were few 'tiresome suburbs' and 'a unity of taste even in the colours (the whole city is yellow or reddish brown)'. He lived on minestra, risotto, meat, vegetables and bread, and dined in 'the most beautiful cafes'. However, he always returned to one beloved place, and in that place in Switzerland he composed some of his most profound prose.[44]

It was a world, a retreat, a secure, private haven where Nietzsche could sit undisturbed and think, reflect and dream. This was the house at Sils-Maria where Nietzsche spent his most fruitful summers of the 1880s. His little room was clad in pale wood, with a similar floor. The room was furnished with a brass mirror, a little Victorian sofa which was dark red and patterned with a curved back and elegant wooden surround. A wash-stand with a porcelain jug of water and bowl stood to one side of the room on a little white-painted table, and a Persian rug worn with age adorned the floor. A single bed with white bedspread and a small desk, with an oil lamp resting on it and a mahogany chair beside it, completed the furnishings. For long summer months this was Nietzsche's home, where he could allow the thoughts in his mind to flow undisturbed by all but the coaxing forest wind. And the room let in the Alpine light and the clear scent of pine.[45]

During his visits to Sils-Maria, Nietzsche was intensely productive. The fertility of his mind echoed that of the landscape and was generally evident in his prolific writing in this period. To name just some of his published books: *Untimely Meditations* (1873–6), *Human, All Too Human* (1878), *The Gay Science* (1882), *Thus Spake Zarathustra* (1883–85), *Beyond Good and Evil* (1886), *On the Genealogy of Morals* (1887), *Twilight of the Idols* (1888), *The Antichrist* (1888) and *Ecce Homo* (1888).[46] All were written in his characteristic prophetic style, all became

world classics, and many were considered to be the finest ever contributions to their respective fields.

A complex and ambiguous thinker, even during his own times
Nietzsche's works were open to very varied interpretations. In his early
period he was a Romantic. Suspicious of Christianity, he aimed not to
moderate this with reason, like Kant, but to supplant it with the passions.
Nietzsche's first great classic, *The Birth of Tragedy* (1872), sent shock
waves through the world of the German intelligentsia. Influenced by
Wagner, he developed a radical interpretation of art, and, around the
Greek god Dionysus, Nietzsche seemed to advocate a cult of wine, orgy
and song. In so doing he disturbed a conservative tradition of established
readings, modest claims and meticulous scholarship, upsetting classical
scholars and art historians in equal measure. Undeterred, he continued
on his intellectual hurricane across the landscapes of history, religion and
philosophy. Throughout his early works, against the cold chill of reason,
science and technology, Nietzsche advocated spontaneity, creativity and
the forces of imagination.[47]

Nietzsche explored many ideas throughout his life including, in his
middle period, rationalism and Enlightenment philosophy. He always
wrote in a poetic, aphoristic style, never with clarity or logic. And he was
always a controversial figure, due mainly to his dislike of Christianity
which he regarded as promoting weakness over strength. With his famous
epitaph 'God is dead', Nietzsche predicted the end of the Christian era
and in its place he prophesied the beginning of an atheistic society,
guided not by religion but by science. (This of, course, was also the era of
Darwin.) Nietzsche also often targeted democracy, criticizing modern
democratic ideals for enhancing mediocrity.[48] Nietzsche's own ideal was
a culture that would encourage not equality but greatness – great character, philosophy, literature, art, music. The one who embraced all these
would become the *Übermensch* – the 'Superman'.[49]

In spite of his own fragile constitution and his love of contemplation,
throughout his life Nietzsche often spoke in praise of war. Sils-Maria with

its peace and quiet couldn't have contrasted more with the 'devastated battlefield, mournfully bespattered everywhere with human remains, and reeking pungently of corpses'.[50] This was the scene Nietzsche described during the time in which he served as a medical orderly, on the battlefield of Wörth.[51] Earlier in the summer of 1866, before his trips to Sils-Maria had begun, the Prussian Otto von Bismarck had invaded the German confederation. Nietzsche, devastated for his homeland, had urged men to fight. He wrote: 'It has become dishonourable to stay sitting at home while the fatherland is at the beginning of a life or death struggle.'[52] Nietzsche had several encounters with war throughout his life, and because he had experienced at first hand its atrocities one might have expected his enthusiasm to have been dampened. In spite of its horrors, however, in 1884 he wrote 'one must learn from war (1) to associate death with the interests for which one fights – that makes us venerable; (2) one must learn to sacrifice many and to take one's cause seriously enough not to spare human lives'.[53] Brave words, given that after his own short encounters with the battlefield, each time he had relapsed into sickness and become 'enfeebled and incapacitated ... in ... [a very] short time'.[54] Nevertheless, this praise of war made Nietzsche very alluring in later years to Hitler.

Nietzsche may have unambiguously admired the destructive passion of the battlefield, but his attitude towards the Jews was more ambivalent. On the one hand he perceived the Jews to be the enemy of Germany. In a letter on 21 June 1871 he wrote, 'not everything has been destroyed by Franco-Jewish trivialization and "elegance" ...'[55] Later, however, he showed equal displeasure towards the anti-Semites. In 1889, towards the end of his sane life, he raved, 'I will simply have all anti-Semites shot.'[56]

After a life of vigorous contemplation, roaming the Alps and cities of Europe, and the solitude of Sils-Maria which facilitated his great productivity, Nietzsche's fears eventually caught up with him. He had suffered bouts of illness all his life, but his greatest fear had been syphilis – that this would slowly encroach upon his brain and destroy his mind. Although haunted by this possibility, he had never been a man who coveted sympathy. He had written years earlier, maybe in anticipation: 'it is . . . not even desirable for you to argue in my favour'. 'Consider me as you would an alien plant.'[57] In 1889 clinical insanity was diagnosed and Nietzsche's productive life ended. The last decade of his life was spent in the hands of his sister Elisabeth, who wheeled the now semi-paralyzed philosopher around in his wheelchair for money.

A decade after the onset of dementia, Nietzsche died in 1900, and the events that ensued became almost more influential than his life itself. In death, bolstered by the public's morbid fascination with him and his work he became a figure of great notoriety and a best-seller. His infamous work *Zarathustra*, in which he had coined the idea of the 'Superman', was printed in 150,000 copies during the First World War, and handed out to German soldiers at the front.[58] A London broadcaster even went so far as to dub the war the 'Euro-Nietzschean War',[59] and the best-selling English novelist of the time, Thomas Hardy, claimed in a letter to the *Daily Mail* that there was 'no instance since history began of a country being so demoralized by one single writer'.[60]

Meanwhile, Elisabeth Nietzsche developed and maintained archives of her brother's work.[61] She did this in the Villa Silberblick in Weimar, highlighting from among Nietzsche's known works the scribbled, dusty papers which were obscure and hidden under books and other published materials. Although these were mere casual jottings, Elisabeth selected, arranged and published them herself. They were deeply incriminating. They included Nietzsche's discussion on the possibilities of selective breeding and of educating a ruling caste, 'the masters of the earth', 'tyrants who can work as artists on "man" himself'.[62] Further, there were notes about the need to 'create conditions that require stronger men, who for their part need . . . a physical-cum-spiritual discipline to strengthen them'.[63] When the old lady, Elisabeth, wearing granny glasses and a bonnet, welcomed Hitler to the archive in August 1934, perhaps this was what he was shown.

In the archive, Elisabeth also highlighted something else that Nietzsche had written about: 'the armored Knight with the stern cold gaze who can pursue his dreadful path undaunted by his ghastly companion . . .'[64] The image of 'The Knight, Death and the Devil' derived from Dürer's painting which Nietzsche had given to Wagner. It later became adopted by the Nazi newspaper *Der Völkische Beobachter* as the brand image of the folk peasant of Nazi ideology, the Norse berserker, fighting in battle till death. Elisabeth's archive subsidized and commissioned poems, plays and paintings promoting this vision. And eventually 'The Knight, Death and the Devil' became synonymous with Hitler himself.

Elisabeth's Nietzsche seemed to supply most of the needs of the Third Reich – there was a zeal for war, a dash of anti-Semitism, the 'Superman' and nationalism. However, like the German philosophers before him Nietzsche had merely displayed *elements* of militarism or anti-Semitism, dark strands fouling an otherwise great and magnificent project. But Hitler would dwell only on this dark side, making violence and prejudice the essence of the 'prophet's' voice.

Elisabeth's version of Nietzsche wasn't the only force for anti-Semitism. The French diplomat and writer, Count Arthur de Gobineau (1816–82), had already initiated the notion of the 'Nordic race', and other nineteenth-century thinkers eagerly trod in his footsteps, conjoining prejudice with nationalist sentiment. Drawing on Fichte and some of Nietzsche's more obscure ideas[65] Paul de Lagarde, with prophetic, nostalgic sentimentalism, hailing the folkloric roots of the Germanic past, wrapped an incredibly ferocious anti-Semitism in a respectable cloak of idealism: 'the Jews as Jews are a terrible misfortune for every European people,' he declared.[66]

A few decades later Julius Langbehn in his book *Rembrandt as Educator*,[67] like Lagarde, hacked ideas out of Nietzsche and Romanticism. Of the Jews, he preached that 'they are a poison for us and must be treated as such . . . .. They are democratically inclined; they have an affinity

for the mob; everywhere they sympathize with decadence.'[68] Going even
further he wrote:

> The modern Jew has no religion, no character, no home, no children.
> He is a piece of humanity that has become sour .... The aspiration
> of present-day Jews for spiritual and material domination evokes a
> simple phrase: Germany for Germans. A Jew can no more become a
> German than a plum can turn into an apple .... Now that Jews are the
> oppressors and the enemies of all German being ... fight them to
> death.[69]

Journalists publicized these ideas. Wilhelm Marr (1819–1904), a German
journalist known as the 'Patriarch of Anti-Semitism' on account of his
best-selling pamphlet, *The Victory of Jews Over the Germans*, gave force to
the political current of conjoining anti-Semitism to nationalism.[70]
Intellectuals from the social elite, such as the conservative university
historian Heinrich von Treitschke, also 'propagated anti-Semitism as an
aspect of racist nationalism.'[71] (In addition he extracted from Hegel a
crude version of militarism; as one commentator put it, Hegel's militarism 'echoes through the thundering pathos of Treitschke's lectures on
politics'.)[72] Then the British-born Houston Stuart Chamberlain wrote
Foundations of the Nineteenth Century in which he slated the Jews and
advocated Pan-Germanism.[73] Married to Richard Wagner's daughter,
Eva, his connections made his ideas hugely influential.

Decades later Hitler would relish the development of this nationalistic anti-Semitism. One of his principal philosophers, Ernst Krieck,
drooled over Lagarde and Langbehn, and Hitler's ideologue Alfred
Rosenberg labelled himself their disciple.[74] Hitler treasured copies of
their books, but as if these nineteenth-century pseudo-Romantics
weren't malevolent enough, a new brand of nationalism was about to
emerge.[75] It originated not within Germany but from across the water in
England.

****

From the pine-clad Bavarian forests, through northern France and across the English Channel to the white cliffs of Dover, across the pastoral landscape of southern England just north to the Welsh border – all this was a very long way from the world of nineteenth-century Prussia. Yet it was here in a large Georgian house in the small market town of Shrewsbury that one of Hitler's most crucial influences was born.

The river Severn meandered past an imposing, elegant classical facade of a home dating from 1800. Faded red-brick walls and a grey slate roof were enhanced by bright, white-panelled Georgian windowpanes. Judging from the sunlight, the facade faced south. The rear windows meanwhile overlooked a shallow yard and steep drop to the river. Green lawns stretched out in welcome and, with three storeys and over five windows wide, this ivy-clad home indicated a prosperous owner. Its height and the fact it was built upon a mound meant that it overlooked the town beyond.[76]

The vista was grey, green, damp, cloudy and fertile. To the east and southeast, gardens ran down to water meadows which gave off a pungent aroma. Broad-leaf trees fringed a wide river which oozed with mist, seeping over the ground. These gardens were a source of great pleasure for the child born there:

> The kitchen garden was kept locked in the evening, and was surrounded by a high wall, but by the aid of neighbouring trees I could easily get on the coping. I then fixed a long stick into the hole at the bottom of a rather large flower-pot, and by dragging this upwards pulled off peaches and plums, which fell into the pot and the prizes were thus secured. When a very little boy I remember stealing apples from the orchard . . .[77]

The little boy stealing apples from his garden in Shrewsbury was Charles Darwin, who would change the face of the natural sciences.

Darwin was born on 12 February 1809 and lived for seventy-three years. He would grow to become a naturalist famed for his concept of evolution. In 1859 his *Origin of Species* was published and in it Darwin famously broke with a religious view of the world and instead substituted a mechanistic image of nature. He argued that there was no inherent, God-given purpose to life, that we were not part of some divine plan. Instead, he proposed all life derived from common ancestors. Then, over time, various species evolved through a process he termed 'natural selection' whereby nature changed through accidental variations. Darwin's scientific ideas became accepted as the foundation of biology. Phrases like 'survival of the fittest', 'competitive struggle' and 'adaptation' became the watchwords of the day. In recognition of his pre-eminence, Darwin was buried in Westminster Abbey, close to Isaac Newton. He was one of only five nineteenth-century British non-royal personages to be honoured with a state funeral.[78]

Although Darwin himself was trained as a biologist and naturalist, in *The Descent of Man* (1871) he wrote about human beings. This work influenced social debates, and a sinister variant of evolutionary theory emerged throughout Europe known as 'Social Darwinism'. While Darwin himself insisted that social policy should not simply be guided by concepts of struggle and selection in nature,[79] and that sympathy and compassion should be extended to all races and nations,[80] others attempted to apply his evolutionary principles wholesale to politics.

Darwin has always been at the hub of debates about Nazi racism and policies of mass extermination, and a highly controversial interpretation of his ideas appeared in the German-speaking world in the nineteenth century, governed principally by one man.

The enormously influential zoologist and social philosopher Ernst Haeckel elected himself to be Darwin's voice to the German-speaking people. He became the greatest advocate of 'Social Darwinism', and in his own time his books vastly outsold Darwin's. Moreover, he, along with fellow Social Darwinists advanced ideas that were to influence National Socialism.

Haeckel was born on 16 February 1834 in Potsdam. Much of what we know about his earliest years was told by his 'venerable Aunt Bertha'.[81] 'She lived until her death in her quiet, unpretentious home in the large streets behind Tiergarten in Berlin, reaching the age of ninety-two, but never losing her freshness of mind and memory.' She recalled Haeckel from her parlour where:

> the small old furniture and the ancient, ever ticking clock . . . made one forget oneself and lose oneself in the past. . . . In the dreamy twilight hours . . . smiling with quiet pride, she recounted . . . how her nephew [Ernst] visited her when he came to Berlin; how with unassuming ways . . . he chose to sleep in the clothes drying loft.

When he was a child, she remembered 'how Haeckel invited his friends to come . . . to share a single dish of herring salad . . . and how . . . he made seats for them of boards and tubs . . . Aunt Bertha dwelt "with entire satisfaction" upon all aspects of Haeckel's life. Coaxingly, her stories of her nephew blended softly with the old and the past of nearly a century ago.'[82]

After childhood, Haeckel studied in Vienna and Berlin. Later he became an eminent professor at Jena University. Here he combined a highly credited specialization in zoology with philosophical speculation: 'the nineteenth century begins. Nature is its salvation and salvation its most practical need. It must struggle for its existence . . . but it has improved weapons for the struggle.' Having absorbed Darwin's ideas, Haeckel began to use them in philosophy: 'Nature is God,' he cried:[83]

> All the earlier ages were but poor blunderers. The lightning flashed on the naked savage, and he fell on his knees and prayed, powerless as he

was. In the eighteenth century it dawned on men's minds that this might be some force of nature. The nineteenth century sets its foot on the neck of the demon of this force, presses him into its service, plays with him. Its thoughts and words flash along the lightning current, as if along nerve tracks, that begin to circle the globe. *Man becomes lord of the earth . . .*[84]

Haeckel's literary output was extensive. During his most active years he produced forty-two works totalling nearly thirteen thousand pages, besides numerous scientific memoirs and illustrations. He also published artwork, including over one hundred detailed, multi-colour illustrations of animals and sea creatures, for example, *Kunstformen der Natur* (Artforms of Nature).

As a philosopher, Haeckel interpreted Darwin for the German-speaking world. As a biologist-cum-philosopher in 1868 he wrote *Natürliche Schöpfungsgeschichte* (The History of Creation). Its chapter headings reveal the contents: 'Theory of development according to Kant'; 'Theory of development according to . . . Darwin'. He went on to talk about 'inheritance, propagation, adaptation, division of labour, tribes and individuals . . .' In a final chapter he discussed the 'laws of the development of mankind; differentiation and perfecting'. There is only a nuance here, however, of the kinds of ideas Haeckel was in fact promoting.[85]

From 1895 to 1899 he wrote *Die Welträthsel* (The Riddle of the Universe) and in 1902 produced a cheap edition of this text which sold 180,000 copies in Germany.[86] He was becoming massively influential. He stated that humans were animals and the only thing that set them apart from other animals was not that they were moral – as many philosophers would hold – but that they were the most highly evolved. This evolutionary supremacy was gained through conflict and the survival of the fittest. Indeed, he considered the Aryan race to be the most supremely fit. Haeckel worshipped the primitive force of nature and with this pagan mysticism supported the idea of the Political State, composed not of law, but of blood – interpreted to mean race.[87]

Setting up the pan-European 'Monist League', Haeckel lectured that man should be governed by the laws of biology. His obsession with the purity of the human race grew and Haeckel proposed eugenics to protect the strength of the Aryans. If society does not follow biology, he preached, it will become weak. He argued that any use of medicine to prolong the life of the sick interfered with natural selection. The lower classes, the diseased, the handicapped, beggars, vagrants and criminals should all be denied modern medicine and the right to reproduce. Furthermore, these weak groups contaminated the species and were a threat to its survival. Thus he preached mass euthanasia; in his words: 'redemption from evil should be accomplished by some painless and rapid poison'.[88]

Praising the ancient Greek militaristic state of Sparta, Haeckel claimed that the Spartans were a chosen people. He explained why they were so successful and superior to others: by killing all but the 'perfectly healthy and strong children', the Spartans were 'continually in excellent strength and vigour'.[89] Haeckel regarded this savage practice as justified. According to him, Germany should have followed this Spartan custom too, because infanticide of the deformed and sickly children was 'a practice of advantage to both the infants destroyed and to the community'.

A recent scholar wrote of Haeckel's impact upon Hitler:

The basic outline of German social Darwinism [was] ... man was merely a part of nature with no special transcendent qualities or special humanness. On the other hand, the Germans were members of a biologically superior community ... politics was merely the straightforward application of the laws of biology. In essence, Haeckel and his fellow social Darwinists advanced the ideas that were to become the core assumptions of National Socialism. . . . The business of the corporate state was eugenics or artificial selection. . . .[90]

In the words of another scholar: 'Hitler's views on history, politics, religion, Christianity, nature, eugenics, science, art, and evolution, however eclectic, and despite the plurality of their sources, coincide for the most part with those of Haeckel and are more than occasionally expressed in very much the same language.'[91] Haeckel gave his last lectures in Berlin in 1905, entitled in the English translation, 'Last Words of Evolution'.[92] Then, bedridden with flu, he lay in his villa in what was later to be named in his commemoration, Haeckel Street, overlooking his zoological institute. His devoted biographer wrote:

> through inexorable labour, through constant sacrifice, through storms of painful obloquy, he has lived his ideals ... beyond the graceful hills that cradle it, he sees the dark waves tossing that he had worked so hard to set in motion.[93] ... what will men say of him when the lines of history draw in and the critic will have the proper perspective?[94]

One era was fading and another emerging. Haeckel had written of himself: 'I am wholly a child of the nineteenth century and with its close I would draw a line under my life.'[95] At the beginning of the twentieth century, however, no such line would be drawn.

****

Between 1914 and 1918, Europe was embroiled in conflict. Over 60 million soldiers were mobilized across the battlefields of the First World War.[96] Vast numbers of these men lost their lives in the trenches and out of this bloodshed emerged a preoccupation with survival and a desperate form of nationalism. So while the guns of the battlefields blazed, German philosophers rediscovered the prejudices of the past.[97]

Influenced by Social Darwinism, thinkers began to embellish racist ideas. Hans Friedrich Karl Günther (1891–1968) was a German race researcher and eugenicist who later became known as 'Race Günther'.[98]

After the end of the war in 1919, he embarked on his writing career. He wrote a polemical work, the title of which echoed Nietzsche's fascination with Dürer – *The Knight, Death and the Devil: The Heroic Idea*. This was a reworking of the tradition of German pagan Romanticism into a form of 'biological nationalism'. Heinrich Himmler would later be very impressed by this book.[99] But Social Darwinists did not stop there.

Alfred Ploetz (1860–1940), a German biologist and eugenicist who had zealously read Darwin and Haeckel as a student,[100] had already written *The Efficiency of our Race and the Protection of the Weak* (1895) in which he hailed a society where disabled children, the sick, the weak and children whose parents Ploetz considers too old or young were 'eliminated'. This he called a theory of 'racial hygiene'.[101] In 1904 Ploetz became one of the principal founders of the journal *Archiv für Rassen- und Gesellschaftsbiologie* (Archive for Racial and Social Biology), which printed Nazi-style eugenics. Eugen Fischer (1874–1967), a German professor, was an editor, and the journal became one of the chief organs for the Nazi Party, providing a respectable scientific framework to consolidate terrifying theories.[102]

Meanwhile, further arguments were developing to justify violence against the Jews. The German cultural historian Arthur Moeller van der Bruck (1876–1925) wrote *Das Dritte Reich*, translated as The Third Reich, a title that would become the Nazi Party slogan.[103] In this book Jews, he claimed, misunderstood the spiritual essence of man. A Jew 'was a stranger in Europe and nevertheless mingled in the affairs of the European peoples ...' 'The effect was Jewish, because it was corrosive.'[104] Moeller then 'accepted the belief of the social Darwinists that the laws of nature and of society were identical'[105] and that natural selection justified war: war would select and ennoble the superior people.[106]

Oswald Spengler (1880–1936), a German historian and philosopher, would go one step further. Dissatisfied with the old brands of anti-Semitism, he too turned to Social Darwinism. Spengler declared that life was 'a struggle for domination' and that 'each civilization [w]as subject to the laws of ageing like living organisms'.[107] He then jumped to a dangerous political conclusion: survival of the fittest meant that if civilization did not forever expand, it would contract and die. Racial domination was not simply desirable, it was perceived as an absolute necessity – conquer or die.

One further philosopher deserves mention. The German thinkers discussed so far had all incorporated their views into their various works, so that nationalism, anti-Semitism or racism were integral to an intellectual position. One branch of philosophy, however, separated ideas from life. Gottlob Frege (1848–1925) was a logician. His work would become hugely influential and his *Begriffsschrift* (Conceptual Notation) published in 1879 meant that that year 'became the most important date in the history of the subject'.[108] By 1924, Frege was in his mid-seventies. On 30 April he wrote in his diary: 'One can remember that there are the most worthy Jews and still regard it as a misfortune that there are so many Jews in Germany and that in the future they will have full political equality with the German citizens.' He went on to express sympathy with the wish that the Jews in Germany 'would get lost, or better would like to disappear from Germany'. Frege read *Deutschlands Erneuerung* (Germany's Renewal), an extreme nationalist journal edited by Houston Stewart Chamberlain, and on 5 May 1924 Frege agreed with an article praising Hitler.[109] These ideas were never formulated in his philosophy, however, as Frege kept a rigid distinction between logical thinking and moral and political views. However, with this background of strong anti-Semitism and nationalist zeal Frege would go on to become the father of Western analytic philosophy.[110] The origins of this brand of philosophy were therefore also tainted by associations with Hitler.

Hitler's readings seemed to be validated. By the end of the First World War, anti-Semitic ideas pervaded every aspect of German thought from the Enlightenment to Romanticism, from nationalism to science. Men of logic or the passions, Idealists or Social Darwinists, the highly sophisticated or the very crude, all supplied Hitler with ideas to re-enforce and enact his dream. Theories of the strong state, of war, of the Superman, of anti-Semitism, and finally of biological racism, abounded in the nation's past. Beneath Germany's noble heritage lay this hidden, dark side. Far from being high-minded and above ordinary concerns, Germany's philosophers had provided a poisoned chalice for European civilization, which Hitler would soon use to his advantage.[111]

CHAPTER 3

Collaborators

Water had accumulated in an enormous hole in the road, and this artificial lake reflected the surrounding landscape; bombed-out apartment blocks; craggy walls rising dramatically with blunt, jagged edges; rubble heaped on the streets. This looked more like a remote wilderness than the Unter den Linden boulevard in the centre of Berlin.

Pedestrians, women in light summer dresses and men in bowler hats strolled down the road pulling luggage trolleys. A horse cart sat amidst them. Damaged cars were strewn along the gutter and burnt-out vehicles and wreckage littered the street. An old man stood watching curiously as people and soldiers walked past the university.[1] Some linden trees were still standing, but most had been destroyed or were heavily damaged.[2] In 1945 the city had lost its green and was now coloured grey, as if the Allied bombings had returned civilization to stone – the stare of Medusa.

This scene of devastation was repeated throughout Germany at the end of the Second World War. In 1933, however, a different kind of destruction was about to take place.

By the early 1930s Germany had enjoyed nearly fifteen years of continuous democracy under the Weimar Republic. The principles of peace, freedom and law were the dominant values across the nation. The universities embraced them and promoted traditions from the past that emphasized independence of thought, fairness and integrity in the curriculum. Differences of opinion were tolerated, and in spite of persistent strands of anti-Semitism in certain quarters – the thread of prejudice woven through the fabric of philosophy – Jews were, in the main, deeply integrated into intellectual life. Jewish-German thinkers had contributed to the canon for generations and had worked peacefully alongside their colleagues, emphasizing the ideals of their state's academic legacy for as long as anyone could remember.

All that was about to change. Traditional university institutions were about to be blown away and old scholarly values were about to be demolished. A blitz that was just as deliberate, damaging and far-reaching as any aerial bombardment was about to begin.

***

When Hitler came to power as chancellor in 1933 he had convinced himself and his Party that he was the 'philosopher leader'. He had found ammunition from the past to bolster his fantasy, but now he needed to convert the world. Starting with Germany, with the country's philosophers, he needed to take hold of his nation's mind, control its thoughts, make men into minions. And he would begin by destroying any ideas that weren't congruent with his own.

Hitler's task needed an overarching administrator. Although he would have loved to implement his scheme personally, he was snowed under with state administration and military matters. He was forced to delegate, but whom could he trust with this most precious undertaking? The competition for such a post was fierce, but the man he chose was someone who since his childhood had been nicknamed 'the philosopher'.[3] He was Alfred Rosenberg.

Rosenberg's job was to destroy democracy and construct a new Nazi ideal.[4] The toxic fury of Hitler's emotional make-up had to be converted into a philosophical mission; all the layers of anti-Semitism from the rank underbelly of Germany's heritage had to be put to maximum use. Freedom had to be uprooted, peace and tolerance dissolved as though they had never been, and the new Nazi world order established. Rosenberg, whose mind was almost as pernicious as Hitler's, was perfect for the job. But who was this proxy, and how would he accomplish his master's aims?

Born four years after Hitler on 12 January 12 1893, Rosenberg's birthplace was the town of Reval, known today as Tallinn, in Estonia, which was then part of the Russian Empire. (Given Rosenberg's Jewish-sounding name, his origins had to be meticulously proved, and he always insisted he came from a long line of Baltic Germans.) In his immediate family his father was a wealthy merchant from Latvia while his mother came from Estonia. The non-German origins into which he was born were, of course, typical of a number of high-ranking Nazis, including Hitler himself. However, Rosenberg always seemed very self-conscious about his outsider's status and was plagued by insecurity. One commentator wrote, 'he went through life with the insecurity of a new boy at his first school'. The problem continued into later life when Rosenberg 'seldom debated anything when face to face with Hitler; his character was a weak one'.[5]

Although not sharing the pugnaciousness of Hitler, Rosenberg did, however, have one thing in common with him. Like his idol, he had a love of architecture and studied the subject at the Riga Polytechnical Institute before going on to take engineering at the Moscow Highest Technical School. After finishing his doctorate in 1917, Rosenberg left his home country for Germany. He arrived in Munich in 1918 and by January 1919 this new immigrant had become one of the first members of the German Workers' Party, which developed into the National Socialist German Workers' Party, better known, of course, as the Nazi Party. Rosenberg's zeal was such that he became a member even prior to Hitler.[6]

In 1915 Rosenberg married his youthful sweetheart Hilda Leesmann, an ethnic Estonian, and brought her to Germany with him. However, after only eight years they divorced. Barely two years later, in July 1923, one day he saw entering a Greek restaurant 'a beautiful, slim lady in a dark

of culture to all North Germans with academic pretensions', and Schopenhauer.[14] Also in common with Hitler and other crude Nazi 'professors', he provided anti-Semitic interpretations of earlier philosophical works. He set up a list of thinkers he believed constituted the Nordic-Aryan tradition and claimed that these were proto-Nazis.[15] This 'calendar of saints', allegedly in the Nazi 'tradition', included Homer and Plato as well as names beloved by Hitler such as Schopenhauer, Wagner and Nietzsche.

Of Hegel, whom Rosenberg claimed to have read, he was critical. He did not agree with Hegel's idea of a strong state. Rosenberg wrote that: 'the state today is no longer a self-sufficient object of veneration, before which we must all bow down in the dust; the state is not an end in itself, but only a means to the preservation of the people. . . . The form of the state changes and its laws decay; the Volk remains'.[16] It is unclear how influential these ideas were with other Nazis. However, there is no disputing the impact of Rosenberg's theories of race.

Along with Houston Stewart Chamberlain, Rosenberg was infatuated with the names familiar from Hitler's library, including Arthur de Gobineau and Paul de Lagarde. One of Lagarde's aphorisms read: 'Races are God's thoughts.'[17] From this, Rosenberg challenged Christianity and developed the notion of a 'race soul'. He concluded that each race had its own soul and, in Rosenberg's own words: 'Soul signifies race seen from within. And conversely race is the external form of the soul.'[18] He was also highly influenced by Wilhelm Marr's book The Victory of Jewry over Teutonism (1873), based upon Social Darwinism. The conclusion of this book was that 'if two protagonists of opposing racial characteristics could not coexist, one was destined to destroy the other'.[19] This idea eventually became for Rosenberg the authorization for genocide.

From his office, Rosenberg studied, compiled and wrote the anti-Semitic philosophy of the Third Reich. A visitor described him in the following words:

His office was not a particularly imposing one, being an ordinary converted private house, not far from Tiergarten. He kept me waiting only a very short time. . . . I found a rather podgy but tall man, handsome to look at but also very ill. I understood he had only just recovered from a long and painful illness and he showed every sign of being in a rather unhealthy state. Many people have told me that they did not find him particularly intelligent. . . . As far as I was concerned I felt I was looking at a handsome man with a clear-cut face, quite frank and neither particularly intelligent nor unintelligent. His conversation was very matter of fact, without any brilliance. . . . He spoke with a slight Baltic accent and was, I gather, rather shy, which at first gives the impression of being curt and cold; but later he becomes much franker and pleasanter . . .'[20]

Rosenberg believed in a new 'religion of the blood', based on the supposed innate promptings of the Nordic soul to defend its noble character against racial and cultural degeneration. He believed that this had been embodied in ancient European (Celtic, Germanic, Baltic, Roman) paganism. He claimed that Jesus was a member of a Nordic enclave resident in ancient Galilee that had struggled against Judaism. Faith should serve the interests of the Nordic race. Rosenberg had written: 'Today there awakes a new faith; the myth of the blood, the faith to defend with one's blood the divine essence within the human being.'[21]

Rosenberg collected his ideas together and produced a book on racial theory which he published in 1934 as *The Myth of the Twentieth Century*. This dealt with key themes in the National Socialist ideology, such as the 'Jewish question'. Rosenberg considered it to be a sequel to Houston Stewart Chamberlain's work, which he had revered as a young man. Beside denigrating the Jews, *The Myth of the Twentieth Century* raised the Germans to potential heroic status. As one commentator put it, 'everyday people now had it in black and white: each was a superman' – simply by being born German.[22]

Despite selling more than a million copies by 1945, *The Myth* was described by Hitler as 'that thing nobody can understand, written by a narrow-minded Balt, who thinks in a fearfully complicated way'.[23] Hitler was also recorded as saying, however: 'All revolutions in world history – and I have studied them in great detail – are nothing save racial struggles. If you would only read Rosenberg's new book – the most tremendous achievement of its kind even greater than Chamberlain's – then you would understand these things.'[24]

In spite of Hitler's put-downs, Rosenberg was supported as the Nazi Party's chief racial theorist and celebrated for one of his favourite ideas, the 'human racial ladder'. He put Africans as well as Jews at the very bottom of the ladder. At the very top stood the white, or 'Aryan', race. He also developed the Nordic theory whereby Nordic peoples were the 'master race', superior to all others, including other Aryans. This Nordic master race consisted mainly of the Germans, although it included the British and several other types (from his Estonian descent he always retained a soft spot for the Eastern Europeans and argued, against other Nazi leaders, that they were a kind of Aryan). With all this theorizing, Rosenberg became so popular that he was hailed as the spiritual and philosophical educator of the Party.

At government level, Rosenberg could now infiltrate and influence academic thinking, but it needed more than an ideological and administrative apparatus to destroy the old values. Detailed changes would have to be made to the nation's educational establishments, including in teaching and research. For this Rosenberg needed collaboration from academics, and here he needed to look no further than two great champions of Nazism, both of whom were in fact philosophers.

***

On the battlefield of the First World War all was destruction. With bodies littering the trenches, burnt-out vehicles blotting the horizon and puddles of water reflecting the mud surrounding them, a soldier refused to put down his weapon. The ceasefire had been called, Germany was defeated, but this solitary soldier would not give in. He stubbornly posed as a 'Norse berserker', a 'knight' charging for 'death or the devil', and on the battlefield he stood alone, agape at defeat. For over a decade he would still carry his violent mission within him.

The soldier had a shaved head (in his later years), thickset jaw and wide neck; he resembled a bullish Gestapo man. His eyes were humourless and without warmth. The only expression that emanated from them was a hard look of power – he had more of the tough macho style of the Nazi generals than the steely-eyed superiority of the Führer. This was Dr Alfred Bäumler, born on 19 November 1887 in Neustadt, then part of Austria and now part of the Czech Republic.[25]

Like Hitler, Bäumler was born outside the German nation. And also, like that other outsider, he was fanatical about the military. Drafted into the army, serving as an infantryman from 1915 to 1918, the stories of how he had refused to put down his weapon even after German defeat became legendary. During peacetime, his weapon became philosophy and he went on to study in Munich, Bonn and Berlin. Completing his first book on Kant, published in 1923 (which sank without trace),[26] his following work was on Nietzsche, which landed him in the lap of success. And so throughout the 1920s Bäumler channelled his militaristic zeal into a National Socialist interpretation of Nietzsche's main texts. Indeed he was the single person most responsible for establishing the link between Nietzsche and Hitler:

A theory of the state is not to be found in Nietzsche's work – but this work has opened all paths towards a new theory of the state. . . . His attack on the 'Empire' arises from the feeling of a world-historical task that awaits us. He wanted to hear nothing of the state as a moral organism in Hegel's sense, he also wanted to hear nothing of Bismarck's Christian Lesser Germany ('Kleindeutschland'). Before his eyes stood the task of our race: the task of being leader of Europe. . . .

What would Europe be without the Germanic North? What would Europe be without Germany? A Roman colony. ... Germany can only exist world-historically in the form of greatness. It has the choice to exist as the anti-Roman power of Europe, or not to exist. ... The German state of the future will not be a continuation of Bismarck's creation, but will be created out of the spirit of Nietzsche and the spirit of the Great War.[27]

This and other publications and leaflets were disseminated widely through the publishing house of Alfred Kröner. The Nobel Prize winner Thomas Mann described Bäumler's work as 'Hitler prophecy', while others called him a 'Nazi hack'.[28] Edmund Husserl's protégé, the up-and-coming philosopher Martin Heidegger, would later praise Bäumler's account of the Nazi-style rendition of 'Nietzsche's work', *Will to Power*.[29]

Graduating from Dresden in 1924, Bäumler worked as a lecturer at the rather low-brow Technical University there. Initially he joined the young conservatives but he then became infatuated with National Socialism. In 1930 he co-founded the Anti-Semitic Struggle Confederation of German Culture and by the early 1930s was an open and vociferous supporter of Hitler.

When Hitler was appointed chancellor in 1933, from being a meagre, unknown and crude-minded academic, Bäumler began an immediate and dramatic ascension to fame. He became Rosenberg's right-hand man, central to the Nazification of the universities. Gaining promotion as professor of philosophy at Germany's most prestigious institution, the University of Berlin, Bäumler gave his inaugural speech. On 10 May 1933 he stood at the front of an overcrowded lecture theatre in the largest hall of the university. Greeted by a sea of students in uniform, bearing swastikas, marching with flags and banners, shouting and cheering, he performed his first major speech and, with his bullish appearance, looked very much in context – the military leader of a mass of youths.

Also in 1933, Bäumler created for Hitler the Institute for Political Education at the University of Berlin. He generated for its students the ideal of the political soldier and established 'men's houses' which repudiated 'female democrats'. Then in 1934 he took over the science department in the so-called Rosenberg Office, the office for monitoring the entire mental training and education of the Nazi Party, where Bäumler acted as a principal liaison with the universities.[30] Finally, under Hitler and Rosenberg, Bäumler was 'back in the trenches', weapon in hand, fighting with his old military zeal.

Ernst Krieck, the second of the two men Rosenberg charged with transforming the Weimar universities, was of meagre stature, balding, with a round face and fine-rimmed, gold glasses. Here was a man who couldn't have contrasted more with Bäumler. In the typical mould of a German professor, however, with his severe authoritarian expression, his formal suit and tie, he presented a rather forbidding picture.

Krieck had been born a few years before Bäumler, in Vögisheim on 6 June 1882. Unlike Bäumler (and, of course, Hitler), Krieck was of German descent; in common with Hitler his origins were humble. Krieck's family had been of modest means, being small-time farmers and bricklayers. For this particular class, the opportunity to pursue a career in education would be very hard to achieve. The only route was to enter the teaching profession, which is what Krieck did. Little did he dream to what heights he would rise under Hitler.[31]

Beginning life as a teacher in Karlsruhe, the middle-upper Rhine region of Germany, Krieck began publishing articles and books about education, for instance, *The German National Idea* (1917) and *The Philosophy of Education* (1922). For a humble teacher he was rather prolific and his efforts gained him an honorary degree from the regional university, Heidelberg. After several years as a freelance writer, Krieck then began to turn his ideological convictions into political action. He joined Bäumler's Anti-Semitic Struggle Confederation of German

Culture and in 1932 became a full-blown member of the National Socialist Party, also enrolling in the National Socialist Teachers' Association. Also in 1932 he was suspended by the democratic Weimar authorities for his Nazi agitation. Krieck was therefore a major ideologue before Hitler was even elected chancellor.[32]

Hating liberal, pacifist and individualist ideas, Krieck drew up a notion of an 'organic' community built upon nationalist, ethnic lines. His ideas about education were based upon his conceptions of the importance of race and breeding. A dominant obsession was with the annihilation of Jewish influence upon Church life. He advocated the elimination of religious ideas from Asia and the purification of an authentic German religion. Krieck's works were nothing if not prosaic, but due to their numerousness and his Nazi eminence he gained ready access to all the major publishing houses in the land. His plague of publications included *Educational Science and Pedagogy in Frankfurt, Philosophical Decision, Philosophie der Erziehung* (Philosophy of Education) and *Völkisch-Politische Anthropologie* (National and Political Anthropology).[33]

Catapulted into a prestigious post as Rector of Goethe University in Frankfurt am Mein, Krieck was also made professor of philosophy and pedagogy when Hitler came to power. A year after his promotion in Frankfurt he was awarded a Chair at the highly prestigious Heidelberg University, where he remained throughout the era of the Third Reich. He spied on his colleagues, worked for the Security Services of the SS and helped Rosenberg run a number of prominent Nazi institutions.[34]

Rosenberg, Bäumler and Krieck were to become the principal architects behind the Nazi infiltration of the universities. Once in positions of power, their programme was careful and methodical. It contained many elements of manipulation, but for them everything originated with destroying the old order. To knock down the existing democratic system was their aim, and their starting point was always the Jew.

***

At the age of seventy-four, retired for over half a decade, Edmund Husserl
was beginning to look gaunt. He had always had a strong face, broad nose
and thick beard, but now his cheeks were hollow, his hair white and his
eyes drawn and tired. He was usually to be seen in a dark, crumpled but
once fine suit, a crisp white shirt and tie. The long, bony fingers on
Husserl's left hand were stained from tobacco smoke from where he held
a pipe, smoking while thinking or reading at home in his study. His eyes,
which had been piercing in his youth from behind their thin metal round-
rimmed glasses, had dimmed with age.

A Jew from Prossnitz in Moravia, now part of the Czech Republic,
Husserl had been born on 8 April 1859. He had become professor of
philosophy in Freiburg and was famed throughout Germany for founding
an entirely new kind of philosophy called phenomenology. In this he
avoided grand-scale theorizing, instead preferring to examine the world
as a series of particular experiences. Husserl's ideas were to be found
disseminated throughout abundant lecture notes, manuscripts and
working papers, accrued over his forty years of university teaching. In
spite of his epic output, however, he only ever published six books, the
earliest of grand repute being *Logical Investigations*.[35]

Husserl received a painful letter from Freiburg University on 14 April
1933 just before he was to go on holiday. In an officious tone, it notified
him of his enforced 'leave of absence'[36] from his Emeritus Chair in the
faculty of philosophy – for being a Jew. This was part of the Baden Decree
implemented in 1933 to tackle what was referred to as the 'Jewification
of the Universities'. The aim was to remove all Semitic influences and
purify the Aryan mind.

Husserl experienced this suspension as the 'supreme affront of his
life'.[37] All his children had volunteered for service during the First World
War and his daughter had worked in a field hospital. His national loyalty,
he believed, had been beyond question. The shock of dismissal made
Husserl depressed and full of self-doubt. His holiday had been a welcome
chance to get away from the university and work and become absorbed

in the calming quiet of the mountains. He returned home to find a withered bunch of flowers that greeted the family on the doorstep of Lorettostrasse 40 in Freiburg.

Then Husserl noticed that with the flowers was a note. It was in the familiar handwriting of Elfride Heidegger, the wife of Husserl's favourite protégée.[38] The note referred to the two friends' 'separate ways in philosophy'.[39] Husserl was perplexed. This was not what he had expected. He and his protégé had always had a few intellectual differences but no significant quarrel had arisen, especially not recently. The letter went on to express sympathy for Husserl's son, Gerhart, who had also been fired from his post for being a Jew.[40] Although the message had an embarrassed tone, it continued to emphasize the differences between them. After many years of trust and friendship, his once devoted student Martin Heidegger was breaking off relations with him, and making it clear there would be no further contact between the families.[41]

Husserl had supported this young man throughout all the stages of his career. They had become colleagues and close friends; indeed, the two families had become inseparable. He ruminated: Why had the friendship been broken off? He ransacked his mind for possible recent differences. Had his criticisms been too harsh? Had his wife done anything to offend? Had they been too ungenerous with gifts, or unwelcoming as hosts? He went over their last meeting, analysing it in detail for possible sources of affront, but could find none. He was forced to deduce that it was on account of his suspension. Husserl knew the younger man was ambitious and supposed that he no longer wanted to be associated with this grey-bearded Jew.[42] A few days later Husserl discovered that he had also been banned from researching or even using the university library.[43]

Husserl's case was just one example. During the first year after Hitler came to power, under Rosenberg's guidance, there were hundreds, indeed thousands, of Jewish academics across Germany who all shared the same fate. (The notion of 'Jewish' for Hitler encompassed a very broad category of Germans – those with any Jewish racial ancestry on either side of the family. The category extended well beyond those who prac- tised the religion or culture.) In fact more than 1,600 scholars were expelled from their posts.[44] The majority of these were 'racial' Jewish academics who were forced into retirement or sent into exile. Soon, those with any Jewish associations such as the philosopher and psychiatrist Karl Jaspers – who had a Jewish wife – were forced into early retirement.[45]

Expelling the Jews throughout the year of 1933 was the first act of aggression in the universities. It was soon followed by more. Semitic thought was outlawed from the curriculum. The thinker of the Enlightenment – Moses Mendelssohn – was targeted. In contrast to other eighteenth-century thinkers such as Kant, who came mainly from the Protestant tradition, Mendelssohn was of Jewish origin. Moreover, whereas Kant and many European intellectuals believed that the Enlightenment had replaced religion, Mendelssohn thought that the Enlightenment stemmed from roots deep within Judaism. His books were outlawed from all educational establishments. Similarly, his grandson, the great composer Felix Mendelssohn, had his works banned, and his grandson Albrecht Mendelssohn-Barthodly, a professor of law who lived during the Nazi era, in turn was fired from his post and forced into exile. In short, the whole Mendelssohn family line of cultural and educational achievement was to be obliterated by Hitler.[46]

The works of Benedict Spinoza, the seventeenth-century Dutch canonical philosopher of Portugese-Jewish descent, were also removed from the syllabus. Dr Hans Alfred Grunsky, professor of philosophy at Munich during the Third Reich and chief reader in philosophy at Rosenberg's offices, had this to say: 'Spinoza . . . was a trade-Jew like his co-racialists who, only camouflaged as a Teutonic mystical thinker, thought of creating a new Tora that would bring all nations under the laws of the Talmud.'[47] Spinoza was deemed a conspirator.

Then, in addition to removing Semitic thought from the curriculum, Jewish books were also outlawed. Rosenberg was instrumental in the censorship of Jewish material. He ordered the issue of blacklists for public libraries. Following the spirit of these, librarians eagerly drew up legal documents to 'cleanse' public libraries. One of these read: 'The standards for the compilation of blacklists are of a literary-political nature. The fundamental question, necessary for any political decision applies here too: Who is the real enemy? Against whom do we direct our fight?'[48] The question was answered:

Our fight is against the undermining of our inherent way of thinking and living. It is against 'Asphalt' literature which is predominantly written for the urban resident, in order to confirm and strengthen his detachment from his environment – from his Volk, from any community, and which uproots him completely. This is the literature of intellectual Nihilism. This type of literature has predominantly, although not exclusively, Jewish authors. ... As a rule it is recommended to retain a copy of even the most dangerous books in the poison cabinets of the large city and university libraries, pending the coming altercation with the 'Asphalt' literati.[49]

Other Jewish and cultural thinkers deemed 'Asphalt' included anyone connected to the traditions of Marxism, especially Karl Marx and Georg Lukacs, and any psychoanalytical thinkers, particularly Sigmund and Anna Freud. Eventually the black lists would name the Jewish philosophers Husserl, Walter Benjamin and the emerging Frankfurt School. Other opponents of the Nazis, like the religious philosopher Paul Tillich and all those who wrote socialist literature such as Friedrich Engels, were blacklisted. None of the works of these thinkers could be housed in public or commercial libraries.[50]

From censorship, Rosenberg and his cronies moved to arson. Hitler's pyromaniac fantasies were enacted through Bäumler. As a professor at

Berlin University, in May 1933 he led students in an ecstatic orgy of book burning, 'which went on for most of the night and involved breaking into private libraries'.[51] As the poet Heinrich Heine had said a century earlier, 'Das war ein Vorspiel nur, dort wo man Bücker verbrennt, verbrennt man am Ende auch Menschen – 'Wherever they burn books they will also, in the end burn human beings'.[52]

Theodor Lessing, the twentieth-century German-Jewish philosopher working in the tradition of Schopenhauer, suffered the same fate as Moses Mendelssohn – his books also went up in flames. But on 30 August 1933 in Marienbad, Czechoslovakia, as Heine had predicted, the Nazis took the elimination of Jewish ideas one step further. Emissaries of the Nazi regime murdered Lessing while he was in exile. He died in the Marie Bader hospital at the age of sixty-one. The assassins had been sent there expressly to kill him.[53]

In the space of only a few years Hitler, through Rosenberg, Bäumler and Krieck, had waged outright war upon German liberal academic culture. From expelling Jews, banning books and censoring the curriculum, Hitler had even gone on to authorize the murder of a Jewish thinker in exile. So far this assassination was an isolated incident. But the onslaught upon Jews in academia was only just beginning. A new curriculum was emerging, and Rosenberg as ever was at the helm.

To instigate the Nazi curriculum Rosenberg had to build up new institutions. On 24 January 1934 he was made 'commissioner of the Führer for the Supervision of the Total Intellectual and Philosophical Schooling and Training of the National Socialist German Workers' Party'. His task was to set up the administrative apparatus for the Nazification of the universities.[54] Structures were developed to promote the twin activities of any university, research and teaching, along party lines. Rosenberg gave generous grants to academics and philosophers to pursue Nazi research. He also awarded scholarships to students to pursue 'appropriate' topics. He censored and controlled the teaching curriculum, including deciding upon which philosophers and their writings were valid. Among the more bizarre forms of rebranding, the ancient Greek philosopher Socrates was denounced as a 'social democrat'.[55]

In addition to manipulating the curriculum through finance and censorship, Rosenberg also developed specialist research institutions. The Reich Institute for the History of New Germany promoted militant National Socialism. The Institute, developed in Berlin, had its official grand opening on 19 October 1935. The red banners of the Reich were unveiled and dripped their bright colours across the city. Nazis in brown shirts with their matching brown caps could be seen dominating the audience, and in front of them were the party dignitaries – all present in full military garb. Officials occupied the most prized seats, including Hitler's right-hand men Rudolf Hess and, of course, Alfred Rosenberg. A sea of swastika armbands raised in salute greeted the opening speeches.[56] With these and other new institutions, Rosenberg, with the help of his two leading Nazi philosophers, began to construct new fields of inquiry. The foremost of these was the 'science' of racism and the 'study' of the Jew. To this end, the Institute included a sinister special department housed in Munich: the Institute for Research on the Jewish Question.[57]

The first move of the department was to confiscate all Jewish publications, which were 'designated for an explicitly German end'.[58] This task was accomplished by the historian and philosopher Dr Wilhelm Grau, a former student of Karl Alexander von Müller, who, far from being a mere armchair scholar, had become an administrator of energy and vision. Anthropologists, biologists, medical, social and political scientists, geographers and historians, all began the new 'study of the Jew'. Jews were categorized as sub-human, biologically inferior and culturally backwards. They were measured and analysed as delinquents, or even mutants, of the human race. Evidence would be gathered by distinguished scientists and scholars across the board to vilify this 'race'.[59] Philosophers too were to play their role in this new, supposedly academic, field of inquiry.

Bäumler as ever set the tone:

For centuries, the racial-soul and folk ... peculiarities *in spite* of all
universalistic counteraction were able to produce a unity of culture.
Finally, the power abated. The international Jew, by making use of
money thinking, elevated himself to world domination and threatened
to destroy all waxing creative power ... just then the distress of the
time in the most threatened folk gave rise to the will and the cognition
which led to regeneration. Instead of the vague mixture of general
concepts and values which used to be called the spirit of humaneness
or the idea of Western culture, national socialism set up an organically
founded *Weltanschauung*. It did not content itself with the piecemeal
curing of the symptoms but *attacked the evil at its roots*.[60]

Bäumler was soon joined by others. Max Wundt, professor of philosophy
at the University of Tubingen, became the prolific author of anti-Semitic
tracts, and Dr Hans Alfred Grunsky wrote at length on the contamination of Jews as philosophers, especially on Spinoza and Jewish appropria-
tion of Hegel's philosophy.[61]

Central to the development of the new Nazi curriculum was the
establishment of the idea of German supremacy. Ernst Krieck declared:
'In the future we recognize no intelligence, no culture and no education
which does not subserve the self-fulfillment of the German people and
derive from that its significance.'[62] The Aryans, especially the Nordic
peoples, were promoted by German philosophers as the new Supermen
on racial grounds. Rosenberg's own ideas as set forth in the *Mythus* were
to be disseminated throughout the universities.

Heidelberg, with its red-brown tiled roofs and clean white-fronted
houses, surrounded by forests behind and facing the banks of the Rhine,
was a beguiling context for an international address by the Nazis. The
'old' bridge spanned the wide, calm river, the castle rose above it and
churches were interspersed with thick, dark peaceful woods, gently

undulating in all directions. There was the occasional glimpse of a fig or almond tree owing to Heidelberg's warm climate. Into the midst of this tranquillity, with much aplomb came the bustle of the 550th anniversary celebrations of the University. In front of an international audience in the grand main hall, Professor Dr Ernst Krieck spoke:

> each folk in each period must form its life according to its own law and fate and to this law of its own, scholarship, with all other spheres of life is subject. . . . The idea of humanism, with the teaching of pure human reason and absolute spirit founded upon it, is a philosophical principle of the eighteenth century caused by the conditions of that time. It is in no sense binding upon us as we live in different conditions and under a different fate.[63]

Philosophers helped Rosenberg propagate the idea of the *Volk*. The philosophy professor Dr Walter Schulze-Sölde tried to capture what he considered to be the mystical qualities of the German people: 'the German man, the Nordic man is being made a *canon* against which the validity of world views on the world is being measured'.[64]

Hitler was also elevated to a grand status. Erich Rothacker, professor of philosophy at the University of Bonn, in the last chapters of a scholarly work discussed in deadly earnest the contributions of Hitler (and Rosenberg) to the philosophy of history.[65] He quoted Hitler as saying the Germans were 'a metaphysical people who violently opposed the superficiality of western democracy'.[66]

Rosenberg's project of reconstructing the university curricula also paid great heed to the younger generation. Professors were encouraged not only to teach and undertake research in line with the new ideology but also to influence their students directly. 'Hitler spoke of how his party had infiltrated the student organisations.'[67] Bäumler and Krieck were promoted by the Nazis principally because they were considered to be essential educators. As an expert in pedagogy, Krieck demonstrated methods for Nazi re-education. Martin Heidegger was highly prized during the initial years of the Third Reich because of his potential as a popular teacher to convert the mass of students.

Krieck compiled vast amounts of literature to get the Nazi message across to the German youth. Other philosophers and educators also worked hard to try and please their master. Their most significant publication, the 'bible' of education entitled *The Nazi Primer: Official Handbook for the Schooling of the Hitler Youth,* was distributed for 'textbook use' to 7 millon young people in the Hitler Youth organization. This *Primer* had to be used by schools to instruct all children between the ages of fourteen and eighteen. Prepared in 1936, it formalized Nazi education, which was a priority for the Party. Its contents give a flavour of the crude Social Darwinist educational assumptions of the German youth. Take, for instance, Chapter IV, entitled 'Heredity and Race Fostering':

> From the teaching of genetics we learn that the individual is insepa-rably bound to his ancestors by birth and heredity. In the same manner, however, the individual is, so to say, only a connecting link in the long chain of generations. If we wish to use an analogy we can say: The individual may be compared to a wave in a great stream which flows out to the remotest past into the remotest future. The farther we trace these streams of generations back into the past, the more they converge into one main source. This analogy makes it clear that all families and branches of a people have a common origin. They all have a unified heritage which is continued into the future by means of the hereditary stream.[68]

Having defined the basis of who we are, The *Primer* explained:

> The great hereditary stream of a people can suffer many kinds of pollu-tion and injury on its journey. These can occur in two ways. In the first

place injuries can arise because diseased elements enter the blood stream of the people. ... In the second place, the blood stream of a people can be defiled by being mixed with blood that is essentially and racially foreign to it. Our fostering of race should prevent these pollutions.[69]

The education of German youth involved creating a scientific-sounding framework wherein race became the defining aspect of the human being, and pollution or contamination the greatest threat:

The German people have direct contact with only one type of foreign people: with the Jews. So for us fostering race is one and the same thing as a defensive warfare against mind and blood contamination by the Jews. The extent to which Germans and Jews cross each other's paths scarcely needs to be presented today. The Jewish hegemony in cultural and intellectual life of the last few decades has brought the disrupting and disturbing character of this people to the attention of all Germans.[70]

The *Primer* was researched and authored by a number of Nazi professors and educators. It presented material in factual textbook fashion, encompassing scientific sounding pronouncements about race, population, the nature of man, territory, culture, history and technology. As the Princeton University professor Harwood Childs, who translated the book in 1938, expressed it: 'The Nazi primer is authoritative. It is not the work of extremists or of a wing of the party. It is not an ideology of an individual, but the product of many minds, the result of a distillation process that has gone on for several years.'[71] It echoed the main themes to be found throughout schools and universities and it helped to institutionalize Nazism. Bäumler, Krieck, Heidegger and other philosophers endorsed and spread these ideas to the German Youth.

Philosophy, however, had its limits for the Nazis. Hitler's aim was to educate the masses up to a sufficient level so that Germany could rule the world. Yet they also had to retain total obedience to the Third Reich. Individuality, critical thinking, were not simply to be discouraged but to be outlawed. The concern was that a theoretical education might produce free spirits rather than obedient henchmen, and Hitler had always held a distaste for 'pure' theory. He valued what he referred to as 'experience' over theory. But how to educate through experience? Rosenberg had found the answer. For those who were 'unfortunate enough to live during times of peace', perusal of the lives of the great heroes was urged. As Rosenberg expressed it: 'A great man and his achievement seem to us a thousand times more important and instructive than an apparent clever theory, according with the law of reason. . . . For us, the battle of Leuthen is as much a training of character as is *Faust* or Beethoven's *Eroica*.'[72] Rosenberg had found what he believed to be the ultimate arena for experience – the battlefield. Having destroyed the old university values of tolerance, inclusion and democracy, peace was now under threat. In its place, permanent bloodshed was advocated. War was the perfect goal, an understanding of its value indispensable to a Nazi education.

Having preached racism, Bäumler and Krieck then responded to Rosenberg's call to war that could have been seen to be a threat to their own position – war as a superior educational tool could render theorizing obsolete. But for these devoted Nazis, ideas were weapons anyway, so to hone them for the more perfect condition of violence was an appropriate ambition.

The Oder (Odra) river was perfectly calm and still, its steel-grey colour reflecting the building before it. The rust-coloured banks gave way to sandstone paving and tree-lined walkways. The university buildings, long, perfectly symmetrical and classically designed, echoed the tranquillity of the river before them. The grey of the river, the soft sandstone of the brick and rust colour of the long elegant roofs were the only quiet, warm shades to illuminate the river scene.

At the pretty riverside University of Breslau, as the death toll during the Second World War had risen by nearly 10 million for each of the first two years, Dr August Faust, professor of philosophy, was asked in 1941 by the leaders of the Third Reich how the war was being received by German philosophers. He answered by seating himself before a desk in one of the comfortable offices of the main university and arranging himself before a large and impressive book with pen in hand.[73] He wrote out the following statement:

> all the more remarkable is the essential agreement in content which occurred quite spontaneously. The result shows the deep relationship between our *Weltanschauung* and *the philosophical root* in it and all the fields of the humanities which deal with *the problem of war*. Moreover, the essential agreement of the historical studies of the present work perhaps serves as some evidence that in German thought there were always ready powers which we National Socialists today feel to be in particular conformity with our species and timely, though they previously never could function completely because in previous history the pooling of all powers of greater Germany, which we owe to the Führer, was absent.[74]

On the issue of war, philosophers wished to show the complete unanimity of German scholarship. They all followed Rosenberg's lead.

Breslau, where August Faust signed the above statement, was the leading city of East Germany. Its Jewish community of twenty thousand prior to 1933 had played a prominent part in the life of the city. The Nazi authorities over a number of years had systematically deported this community until few remained. When Faust signed his letter of total support for war, he did so during a year in which the last surviving jews were being transported to Gruessau, Tomersdorf and other places in Silesia, and from there to Auschwitz.[75]

Although prominent Nazi names such as Faust appeared alongside Rosenberg, Bäumler and Krieck, it would be misleading to point out the role only of the Party leadership. The transition of the universities under Hitler required the wholesale collaboration of a mass of academics. Ordinary everyday lecturers had to implement every tiny detail of research and teaching, revising the curriculum along party lines and preaching it to the youth. From the outset, philosophers and other educators were included in Hitler's task of converting the nation.

Initially, when the Baden decree[76] was implemented expelling Husserl and other Jewish intellectuals from academic life, Hitler and Rosenberg encountered little opposition. No hint of outrage was apparent from those still in post, no letters, campaigns or protests. No one attempted to defend the integrity of a meritocratic ideal. Indeed, 'no significant opposition to Hitler and the party in Germany ever arose'.[77] Perhaps the lack of resistance or disapproval was due to fear? However, during the first year of Hitler's chancellorship the terror and reprisals associated with the later years of Nazi rule had not yet begun. As one commentator said of academics, 'their silence was strong'.[78]

Then, after the Jews were fired from academia in 1933 and the colours of red, black and white, the vivid lines of the swastika, started flying from university buildings, philosophers went beyond mere silence. The expulsion of so many Jews had left a considerable number of positions vacant, including prestigious professorships. New jobs and opportunities were available, and furthermore the standards required to obtain these posts were vastly reduced on account of the expulsion of highly qualified colleagues. The philosophers who remained soon spotted the potential rewards for collaboration.[79] And like vultures they moved in.

Aryan academics began to apply for promotion. Soon over fifty rapidly rose through the ranks. The list of philosophers who profited from the new regime included, for example, Dr Ernst Bergmann, who was appointed professor of philosophy at the University of Leipzig; Dr Max Hildebert Boehme became professor of philosophy and social science at the University of Jena; Dr Hans Alfred Grunsky became professor of philosophy at the University of Munich; and Professor Max Wundt from Tübingen also collaborated. Dr Otto Höfler was appointed professor of German philosophy at the University of Munich; Erich Rothacker gained a post at the University of Bonn; Dr. Walter Schulze-Sölde obtained a professorship in philosophy at the University of Innsbruck; and Dr George Steiler became associate professor of philosophy at Freiburg. These names encompass only a few of the most prominent – there were many, many more.

Once vacant posts were filled in the universities, Rosenberg staffed his various other ideological institutions. Philosophers were keen to apply. Professor Alfred Bäumler was appointed director for the Nazi Institute for Political Education at the University of Berlin. In addition to his new professorship at the University of Munich, Dr Grunsky also became chief reader in philosophy at Rosenberg's office. Gerhard Johann Hans Hagemeyer enjoyed a high position in Rosenberg's commission, in the special body for philosophers known as the Office of Philosophical Information, and Professor Dr Ernst Krieck was, as we know, honoured with the Rectorship of the University of Heidelberg. The 'Research Department for the Jewish Question'[80] in Rosenberg's Reich Institute was amongst the most sinister of the new Nazi institutions, but even this extreme project was soon populated by keen philosophers – Professor Wundt eagerly became a prominent member.

Alfred Bäumler and Ernst Krieck, proud and smiling to great applause, were appointed honorary members of The Reich Institute for the History of New Germany. The Führer also personally entrusted the Institute to Professor Dr Walter Frank[81] who, at the University of Munich and guided by Karl Alexander von Müller, had completed a doctoral dissertation on Dr Adolf Stöcker, the militant anti-Semite of the pre-war years.[82] All of Rosenberg's offices became well organized and well staffed.[83]

Through teaching, many of these philosophers also supported Rosenberg's every move. In addition to expelling Jewish colleagues and staffing academic institutions, they helped him establish the framework for Nazi 'philosophy', centred upon the vilification of Jews. Deploying the rank history of generations of anti-Semitic thought, they produced startling new bodies of racist thought, drawing on Nietzsche and Romanticism or Social Darwinism, often trying to fuse these philosophical movements.

In 1932 Hans Heyse had become professor of philosophy at the University of Königsberg and, in the same year, joined the Nazi Party.[84] Then, in recognition of his devotion to Hitler, he was promoted in October 1933 to rector at the university. He advocated the new 'leader principle', namely, obedience to the Führer: 'The new German university has only one law: from the first cause of our Germanic-German reality ... to serve the intentions and objectives of the leader of the German people.' Heyse collaborated in a Nazi-style rendition of Nietzsche's works and in 1937 was made the federal director of the Academy of Sciences. His specialities were Greek and Kantian philosophy and the history of philosophy.[85] He colluded with the Nazification of classical philosophy by declaring that 'Plato's Republic was the "Ur-form of the idea of the Reich"'.[86] According to Ernst Klee – the journalist who became famous for exposing the medical crimes of the Third Reich – during the Nazi era Heyse was nicknamed 'Comrade Plato'.

A further collaborating 'philosopher' who would become much more dominant and more notorious than Heyse was Eugene Fehrle.[87] He was a purveyor of Nazi 'folklore' and Chair of the philosophy faculty at the University of Heidelberg from 1942 to 1943. Fehrle had been an SS officer and SD informant (*Sicherheitsdienst* – Security Service of the Nazi Party, the forerunner organization of the Reichssicherheitshauptamt-RSHA, which would later be tasked with implementing the Holocaust) and was one of those most responsible for enacting the racist purges of the early 1930s under Hitler. Along with Krieck he exercised 'tyrannical rule in the philosophy faculty'.[88]

On 30 January 1939 before the Nazi Reichstag on the sixth anniversary of his coming to power, Hitler proclaimed to the German Parliament his intention to exterminate all European Jews:

> In the course of my life I have very often been a prophet, and have usually been ridiculed for it. During the time of my struggle for power it was in the first instance only the Jewish race that received my prophecies with laughter when I said that I would one day take over the leadership of the State, and with it that of the whole nation, and that I would then among other things settle the Jewish problem. Their laughter was uproarious, but I think that for some time now they have been laughing on the other side of their face. Today I will once more be a prophet: if the international Jewish financiers in and outside Europe should succeed in plunging the nations once more into a world war, then the result will not be the Bolshevizing of the earth, and thus the victory of Jewry, *but the annihilation of the Jewish race in Europe!*[89]

Twelve days earlier, on 18 January, at a conference in Germany's oldest university, Heidelberg, philosophers had been among those celebrating the anniversary of the founding of Bismarck's Reich. Before the Gothic arches and spires, the sandstone facades and slate roofs of the university's most eminent buildings, with luscious trees framing the university park, steps led into the main hallway. Past the fairy-tale library with wooden-panelled walls rising up to the ceiling and pretty brass chandeliers flickering along the walls, the corridors gave way to an imposing lecture hall. Here, Ernst Krieck gave an address that would pre-empt Hitler's own speech:

> The teutons are the nobility folk of world history. If we want to prove this in history again, *we must remove from our existence Asiatism in any shape* that has penetrated our being, *the poison and the illness of the*

European peoples. This is the racial renascence. 1938, the year greater
Germany calls to the German people to lift up our eyes that we be
adequate to the deeds of the Führer and the greatest of the German
missions.[90]

Philosophers were not in the dark about the brutal reality behind these
words. One scholar pointed out: 'the German rulers had theorists at
hand who praised their achievements in reducing the Jews and supplied
the academic formulae and the scholarly backing for each further step in
German policies, until the "extinguishment" of the "eternally hostile
forces" was accomplished . . .'[91]

From the destruction of the old values and institutions, the expulsion
of the Jews, Nazification of the curriculum and the creation of institutions to vilify Jews and deify war, many philosophers therefore played a
fundamental role in helping Hitler brand the universities as his own.
They took the anti-Semitic past raked up by Hitler and infected the new
educational establishment with it. They helped destroy democratic
values, legitimize violence and glorify war. Not only did these philosophers support Hitler's project, they took it to extremes. They latched on
to opportunities to enhance their careers, and, as the Jewish scholar Max
Weinreich commented: 'The Nazis set out with a comparatively small
number of outsiders but soon were joined by mounting numbers of
people of regular academic standing. . . . As time progressed, the bulk of
university scholars ... were entirely Nazified.'[92] From Rosenberg,
Bäumler, Krieck and Faust, the list of names who helped bulldoze the
intellectual past and establish a Nazi future was long. The list, as they
themselves expressed it, represented a community.[93]

The collaboration of philosophers was no mere academic exercise. It
is sobering to note that by the time they had launched their intellectual
attack upon the Jews, the real attacks had already begun. Naked bodies,
victims from the first concentration camps, were dumped in mass graves
like fish from a trawler, pale, iridescent skin taut over ribs and skulls.

Three years after the use of hydrogen cyanide was tested on 250 children from Buchenwald camp, and two years after the first experiment with the gas at Auschwitz, Bäumler published his study of the Jews. In 1943 he eulogized Rosenberg saying that he 'attacks the demon who has become visible and who is the mortal enemy of Germandon. He creates the feeling in his readers: *this is a matter of life and death; it can only be you or we.*'[94]

While the number of Jews in the concentration camps rose, philosophers continued producing anti-Semitic research. For example, Dr Wilhelm Grau, Acting Director of the Reichsinstitut (like Professor Walter Frank, a former student of the racist Karl Alexander von Müller), produced a huge study on anti-Semitism which was supported by a very large grant from the philosophy faculty at Munich University.[95] While images of human suffering – too horrific for the human eye – mounted, twentieth-century philosophers competed for prestige and mused over the correctness of their anti-Semitic concepts.

CHAPTER 4

Hitler's Lawmaker: Carl Schmitt

Hitler's dream was coming true, for the conquest of the universities was well underway. He had provided the desecrating vision and the furious will, while his proxy Rosenberg, through Bäumler, Krieck and a myriad of other philosophers, had bulldozed democracy, ousted the Jews from academia and provided the ideologies of race and war. But it was not enough for Hitler just to convert the German mind; this was a political vision. Democracy was buried and a new world order was rising from its grave: tyranny. Hitler needed to enshrine this with the ultimate authority – law. To do this he needed a compelling legal philosopher.

The town of Plettenberg, Westphalia, was imbued with shades of green and a cloudy atmosphere. It crouched in a valley between forested mountains. When the fog swept down into the town, the foliage of the trees and bushes lining the streets and embellishing the gardens merged with the outline of the surrounding hills so that the town was at one with nature, swallowed up into the landscape. It was in this mysterious Alpine landscape that Carl Schmitt was born on 11 July 1888, a year before Hitler.

The dramatic Alpine scenery of Plettenberg contrasted with the picturesque valleys of the Schmitt family's former residence. Both of Carl's parents had migrated from the Moselle region in France with its soft pastoral scenery and fields of grapes. There would always be a French atmosphere about Schmitt's home, which he loved, with Moselle wine a firm favourite.

The Schmitt family was a staunchly Catholic household enclosed within the Protestant area of Westphalia. This was a pocket within the largely Catholic Rhineland, which in turn was surrounded by the dominant Protestant culture of Prussia. The battles of the 1870s between Bismarck and the Catholic Church – which had been witnessed so vividly by Nietzsche – were barely suppressed in the multiple layerings of Catholic and Protestant in western Germany. Schmitt grew up in his provincial Catholic world stubbornly defensive against a hostile Protestant environment.

A small businessman of modest means, Schmitt's father educated his son in a manner befitting the lower middle classes and sent Carl to a Catholic grammar school, then to a Gymnasium in Attendorn, where his son was probably rather shocked by the liberal ideas he encountered. Darwin, science and democratic ideas were the flavour of the day in opposition to his own staunch religious views. After leaving school, Carl was urged by his father to pursue an applied training, but his mother was more socially ambitious and defended her son's aspirations to attend university. Only a degree could enable social mobility, so in 1907 Carl Schmitt went to Berlin. He enrolled at Friedrich Wilhelm University to study law, although he was equally talented in philosophy, literature and the arts. He wrote of this time:

> I was an obscure young man of modest origins . . . part neither of the governing elite nor of the opposition movement . . . that meant that, standing wholly in the dark, I looked from the darkness into a brightly lit room . . . the strong repulsion which I experienced left me no comfort with my role. The feeling of sadness which filled me, increased my distance and evoked my distrust and alienation in others. A governing elite senses anyone to be a heterogeneous element who does not find happiness in coming into contact with it, but shows himself

saddened instead. ... It leaves him the choice to adapt or remove himself. ... So I stayed outside.[1]

After spending only two semesters in Berlin, Schmitt moved to Munich and then to Strasbourg – which at the time was part of Germany – preferring the southwest, close to home. Strasbourg (like Freiburg) resisted the encroachment of Darwinism against Catholic spirituality. At the university, in the humanities and philosophy departments, Kant and Christian interpretations of his works were hugely influential. Schmitt studied widely then gained his law degree in 1910 and entered the civil service. Against the background of an administrative post his enormous talents and energy manifested themselves. He plunged himself into the philosophy of law, writing three books in just five years.[2]

Schmitt must have been a highly eligible man, for besides a promising career ahead of him, he was charming and handsome. His thick dark hair was parted neatly down the centre, his brow was straight and he had even features, which lent themselves to a slightly boyish demeanour in his youth. In later years he would look dashing, his evenly shaped face flecked with character. His natural good looks were complemented by an elegant sense of dress; he was often to be seen wearing a crisp white-collared shirt and beautifully cut dark jacket. His manners were polished and he had an air of confidence about him. Notwithstanding his articulacy, he was also proud and somewhat vain, characteristics that if matched with warmth rather than coldness might have been very attractive to women.

The state has 'the right to demand from its own members the readiness to die and unhesitatingly kill enemies'.[3] Schmitt wrote these words emphatically and in 1914 at the age of twenty-seven, as the First World War erupted and his colleagues joined up to fight. The nationalistic spirit animated Schmitt to advise others to sacrifice themselves. Meanwhile, he himself delayed joining the military for as long as possible in order to further his career.[4] After taking his exams and finishing his third book, he finally volunteered. However, almost immediately he injured himself, apparently from a fall from a horse during training (though this account has not been verified). Schmitt was then given a safe desk job far from the fighting with the army's legal division in Munich.

While (in his words) 'the European world tore itself apart' and was laid waste by 'the material and metaphysical ravages of war', Schmitt, like Hitler, dabbled in the bohemian world of Schwabing in Munich. He met avant-garde authors, expressionist painters and dada artists, including the Serbian-German poet Theodor Däubler. Schmitt wrote about Däubler's cryptic verse, which eulogized poetic battles between knights and dragons, sun and moon, forces of light and darkness. 'Referring to the ancient Persian myths in Däubler's saga, Schmitt wrote words that could have applied to Germany in 1916. Instead of striving for unity, "the Volk pushes itself on, instinctively wanting to submit and letting itself be whipped".[5] Däubler's poetry and plays were influenced by, among others, the same figures who had inspired Hitler, namely, Goethe, Nietzsche and also Wagner.

Like Nietzsche before him and in common with his contemporary Heidegger, Schmitt had a 'loathing for modernity. Never, he resolved, would he settle into bourgeois life – a hollow world of "traffic, technology, organization . . . [in which] people are interested in everything, but enthusiastic about nothing. In place of the distinction between good and evil there appeared a sublime contrast between utility and destruction.'[6] He resolved instead to cling to his faith.

During his time in Munich, in 1916 Schmitt married Pawla Dorotić, a Viennese woman who claimed Serbian aristocratic lineage. She was very emancipated and even managed to shock the propriety of the bohemians. Schmitt, proud of her exoticism, added her surname to his own and went so far as to publish under the name Carl Schmitt-Dorotić.[7] During this time Schmitt's ideas embraced Kantian concerns with the notion of higher law and an interest in questions of abstract right. After his own brief flirtation with Romanticism, he became critical of its nationalist style of politics and dissociated himself from it entirely, returning to staunch Catholicism. His politics became deeply conservative, overwhelmingly preoccupied with the issue of security. Among his many publications was *Die Diktatur* (The Dictator), a study stretching from ancient Rome to Lenin. He railed against Bolshevism and went on to write *Politische Theologie* (Political Theology), wherein he argued that society, not abstract theory, was the proper grounding for politics. Life as lived by particular people at a particular time should always form the undercurrent of government.

Schmitt's success had earned him a full professorship at Greifswald University which, being situated in the northern Baltic area, was far from home. Soon after, in 1922, he moved to Bonn University, perched near the wide and serene Rhine, which wound its way through picturesque valleys and romantic mountain scenery and was closer to the Moselle valley where his ancestors had lived.

Schmitt's first wife turned out to be a chalatan, her supposed aristocratic lineage a lie. The marriage lasted less than a decade – in 1924 he was divorced. This rift created a further rupture, namely, between Schmitt and the Catholic Church; he was excommunicated. Although his faith was sorely tried, he found happiness again and soon married his second wife, Duška Todorović, also Serbian. They had one daughter, called Anima. These were happier years and Schmitt became highly esteemed. His academic style was terse and logical, and the clarity of his writing and teaching at Bonn pleased many. His earlier Bohemian image was buried. In its place emerged a slick, well-dressed, stiff but cordial German professor.[8] With his immaculate hair and even features, he was always 'a man much concerned with status and his public image'.[9]

Basking in the glow of his success and fully appreciative of his own talents, Schmitt indulged in self-appreciation. Typically he once declared 'I desire to find an oasis of practical discussion in the desert of barbarous stupidity in which we live.' On another occasion he asked a colleague, 'who in Germany could write the foreword to the second edition of my

Politische Romantic (Romantic Politics)? You cannot because you are too lazy, and all the others are too stupid.'[10]

In 1928 Schmitt left Bonn for the Hugo Preuss Chair of Law at the Berlin Graduate School of Business Administration. Berlin was a much more significant city and this move excited Schmitt. Meanwhile, the Weimar Republic was in increasing crisis, with the far left and far right making political gains. Schmitt feared the civil discord of radical politics and supported the idea of a strong and independent state. For this reason he has been seen as a follower of Hegel, who regarded the state as pivotal in modern society.

As the Nazis gained more power, Schmitt's initial feelings were of abhorrence. He regarded them as extremist, a threat to the security of the state. So instead, for reasons of stability, he supported a presidential system against the loose constitution of Weimar (although this can be seen as a leaning towards authoritarianism). By 1932 Schmitt feared both civil war and extremist politics, whether communist or National Socialist.[11]

His suspicion about the Nazis at no point appeared to be on grounds of principle. Schmitt's diaries reveal that by this time he already harboured a caustic underlying anti-Semitism. He noticed, for example, 'repulsive, chatty Jewish women'.[12] And 'in the café, a repulsive little Jew who admired everything and laughed without stopping, but also had a pretty goat with him'[13] – presumably 'goat' is his term for a Jewess. Other, later jibes include referring to the Jews as 'lovely little apes'.[14]

One chill, bright winter morning Schmitt sat in the high-ceilinged Café Kutschera. Although it was early morning, the place was not empty. Well-dressed middle-aged men were absorbed in large newspapers that draped over the small tables like the white tablecloths beneath them. The café echoed with the sound of waiters busying about, and the chatter on the radio. The scent of fresh-roasted coffee and sweet pastries infused the interior. It was the morning of 30 January 1933 and Schmitt sat on a straight-backed mahogany chair, musing, in this Berlin café, coffee in hand. Then he heard the newsreader's clear tones announce Hitler's appointment as Chancellor of Germany. Schmitt jolted with a start from his musings.[15] First appalled and then depressed, exhausted after three years of advocating a presidential system, he confessed later in his diary of a dark night contemplating suicide. He described how Hitler's sovereign dictatorship was installed against law, and his mood was black. That evening, drinking too much wine, he wrote 'alone and depressed I leave. ... [my wife] is sick in bed. ... Hitler will succeed. ... The old man has gone crazy. It is a terribly cold night.'[16]

At home with his family, Schmitt retreated while Hitler celebrated. Schmitt was silent and grave as a victorious torchlight parade was staged by the National Socialists through Brandenburg Gate. Cautiously he observed them accumulate power and purge the German universities. He watched as those critical towards Nazism were plagued by boycott, coercion and disruption, and he witnessed the many academics including the host of philosophers led by Bäumler and Krieck pledge public support for National Socialism. Reinforcing this trend was the pro-Nazi support of Martin Heidegger. He wrote to Schmitt on 22 April 1933, urging him to join the Party.[17]

Then, out of the blue, Schmitt's mood changed drastically. On 1 May 1933 he stood in line and joined the National Socialist Party – his membership number was 2,098,860.[18] It was shortly after this, on the night of 10 May, that Nazi students at the German universities burned books by Jewish authors. As the flames tore through paper, Schmitt cheered them on and penned an article for a regional National Socialist newspaper. He rejoiced that the 'un-German spirit' and 'anti-German filth' of a decadent age had been burned out and urged the government to annul the citizenship of German exiles (whose books were burned) because they aided the 'enemy'. 'Writing in German does not make Jewish authors German any more than counterfeit German money makes the forger German,' he declared. He then mocked as unmanly anyone who appreciated Jewish authors. 'Our educated grandmothers and aunts would read, with tears in their bourgeois eyes, verses by Heinrich Heine that they mistook for German.' Schmitt had only one criticism of the book burners: they had consigned too few authors to the flames. Instead of burning only 'un-German' writers' books, they should have included writings by non-Jewish authors who had been influenced by Jewish ideas in the sciences and professions (in which, he alleged, Jewish influence was both strong and pernicious). This distinguished professor's endorsement of book burning was a major coup for Hitler's bid for respectability.[19]

A Faustian pact with the Nazis seemed to have been made. But what was the motive? Was it fear? In exchange for protection, Schmitt would offer total allegiance. He quickly proclaimed the one-party state to be the state of the twentieth century and a step towards achieving unity for the German people.[20] In return for his support, Schmitt was recognized by the Nazis as 'the most renowned national constitutionalist in Germany'.[21] Almost immediately he began to reap the fruits of collaboration in the form of honours and official appointments. Hermann Goering, SA-Gruppenführer, a favourite of Hitler's who always enjoyed patronizing artists and intellectuals, appointed Schmitt as Prussian State Councillor. Goering often ranted against Christian morality and Enlightenment humanism as 'those stupid, false, unhealthy ideals of humanity'[22] – this didn't trouble the legal philosopher in the slightest. With Goering's blessing Schmitt served on the committees of many Nazi legal institutions, including the Academy of German Law, and lectured at all their major conferences. He was appointed director of the University Teachers' Group on the National Socialist League of German Jurists and made president of the National Socialist German Jurists.

Offered important chairs in Germany's most acclaimed universities, including Munich and Cologne, Schmitt turned these down in favour of the most prestigious appointment in the land. He became Chair of the University of Berlin, a position he held until the end of the Nazi era in 1945. Whatever Schmitt's initial distaste, he had quickly acknowledged that 'Hitler was now *de facto* and *de jure* the political Führer of the German nation'.[23] He reworked many of his past articles to enhance National Socialism and began to include anti-Semitic remarks in his further publications, trying to show himself to be in tune with all aspects of Nazi ideology. Indeed he couldn't go far enough and drew up an ideal of a legal system which provided the foundations for a total authoritarian regime.

Hitler's dream was becoming enshrined in law. Schmitt's legal ana-lysis of commissarial and sovereign dictatorship, based on Article 48 of the Weimar Constitution, first formulated in 1922, provided the legal basis for Hitler's assumption of power through the declaration of emer-gency and suspension of rights of 28 February 1933. Schmitt then wrote the authoritative article justifying the enabling laws of 24 March 1933, which transformed Germany, legally, in Schmitt's analysis, from a commissarial to a sovereign dictatorship. Schmitt developed for Hitler the legal-philosophical outlines for the constitution of the Third Reich and wrote that the pivot was Hitler's status as both head of state and party leader under the 'law for securing of the unity of party and state' of 1 December 1933.[24]

Half a year later, in June 1934, Schmitt became editor-in-chief of the Nazi *Deutsche Juristen Zeitung*, the German Jurists' newspaper. Then came the Night of the Long Knives, on 30 June 1934, the Nazi purging of any opposition by multiple executions without trial. At least eighty-five members of their own party were murdered and there may have been hundreds more. Schmitt was quick to support the legitimacy and legality of the purge. He justified the political murders as the 'highest form of administrative law'. Later, Goering told jurists of the Reich of their obli-gation to defend the Führer against worldwide disapproval. Schmitt obliged. He published the influential article, '*Der Fuehrer Schutz das Recht*' ('The Führer Protects the Law').[25] Even in the words of his extremely tolerant biographer Joseph Bendersky, Schmitt, 'had become an apologist for a murderous party dictatorship'.[26]

When Carl Schmitt became a member of the Akademie für Deutches Recht, he declared in his introductory address: 'the great speeches of the Führer and his fellow combatants at the party convention under the sign of honour in Nuremberg have shown us with stirring clarity the present battle in the ideological contest with Jewry', and further, 'we must free the German spirit from Jewish falsification . . .'[27]

Schmitt's career continued to grow and he became Hitler's chief legal advisor. His expertise as a legal philosopher allowed him to embody further dictatorial measures in law and his Nazi philosophy included the removal of 'man' from the German civil code. Schmitt explained: 'For the first time, our conception of constitutional principals is again German. German blood and German honor have become the basic principles of German law, while the state has become an expression of racial strength and unity.'[28]

Moreover, as the chairman of a law teachers' conference in Berlin in October 1936, he declared: 'The Jew's relationship to our intellectual work is parasitical, tactical, and commercial. . . . Being shrewd and quick he knows how to say the right thing at the right time. That is his instinct as a parasite and a born trader.' Praising Nazi leaders' call for 'healthy exorcism', Schmitt welcomed 'the genuine battle of principles' between Jews' 'cruelty and impudence' and Germans' 'ethnic honor'. 'The Jew is sterile and unproductive. . . . He is dangerous.' Schmitt condemned mere 'emotional anti-Semitism that does not accomplish the task of driving out Jewish influence'. He closed the conference by quoting *Mein Kampf*, 'In defending myself against the Jew. . . . I am doing the work of the Lord.'[29]

Certain émigrés, appalled at Schmitt's collaboration, suggested to the Nazis that he might be a mere careerist and opportunist, not a true Nazi.[30] In December 1936 the SS publication *Das Schwarze Korps* accused Schmitt of being a Hegelian state thinker and basically a Catholic, and called his anti-Semitism a mere pretence, citing earlier statements in which he criticized the Nazis' racial theories. In response, Schmitt deepened his allegiance to Hitler. In lectures and writings he cried, 'the Führer is not an agent of the nation, but the highest judge of the nation and the highest lawgiver'.[31] Schmitt intensely increased his anti-Semitism. A conference on 'Judaism in Jurisprudence' opened in Berlin on 3 October 1936 and Schmitt concluded with a speech on 'German philosophy of law in the struggle against the Jewish intellect', identifying the problem of the pervasiveness of Jewish ideas in jurisprudence and discussing how these could be purged. He focused on the practical problems of how to identity Jewish authors, separate Semitic ideas from the mainstream, and make sure legal thought was purged. He ended his speech with, 'I repeat again and again the urgent request that you read every phrase in Adolf Hitler's *Mein Kampf* concerning the Jewish question, especially his statements about Jewish dialectics.'[32]

In 1939 Schmitt propelled himself on to the world stage when, during a Nazi conference, he read aloud from his paper. Standing on the podium at the University of Kiel on 1 April 1939, he announced that the German state (*Reich*), was the carrier of a new international world order. The Reich, Schmitt proclaimed, 'sets its own law heedless of the interference of other states'.[33] He elaborated his ideas in writing, explaining how the world was being divided into large empires, *Grossraum*; for example, he cited the United States, the new Japan, the Soviet Union, each had their empire. Schmitt regarded violence through war as a just means to secure these. Europe, Schmitt argued, would be Germany's empire – and although he now curried less favour with the Nazis, he fully endorsed bloodshed as a means for Germany to acquire Europe as its territory. Two British papers, *The Times* and the *Daily Mail* picked up on Schmitt's writings. On 5 April the *Daily Mail* reported that 'Herr Hitler and Professor Schmitt will now, it is believed, devote themselves to completing the framework of this conception, and the Führer will soon give it to the world as his justification for Germany's relentless expansion.'[34] That same day *The Times* stated, 'hitherto no German statesman has given a precise definition of his aims in eastern Europe, but perhaps a recent statement by professor Carl Schmitt, a Nazi expert on constitutional law, may be taken as a trustworthy guide'. The *Daily Mail* said that, 'Herr Hitler's key man in this policy is professor Carl Schmitt, middle-aged and handsome, who is the leading international lawyer in Germany.'[35] Repugnance towards Schmitt, especially his endorsement of violence, certainly spread across the Channel. In one of his speeches Winston Churchill denounced him, and even Vera Lynn targeted him as the enemy.

Professor Schmitt toiled as the principal Nazi legal philosopher at the University of Berlin until 1945. He enshrined Hitler's tyranny in law. He relegated democracy to a burnt memory, and, like a dark phoenix from its ashes, he allowed tyranny to rise: authoritative, powerful and legitimate.

CHAPTER 5

Hitler's Superman: Martin Heidegger

Hitler's dream seemed to be accomplished. Racism, tyranny and war were the new intellectual landscape, and philosophers had provided razor-sharp ammunition for the entire project. What more was left to achieve? In fact, there was one element still missing from the universities, and until this was in place the fantasy was incomplete.

Rosenberg, Bäumler and Krieck, along with the other philosophers of the Reich, were dominant within Germany, but beyond its borders they had no reputation. Across Europe and the rest of the world they were either shrouded in obscurity or dismissed as mere Nazi hacks. The Führer was piqued. 'In the great hall of the Linz library are the busts of Kant, Schopenhauer and Nietzsche, the greatest of our thinkers, in comparison with whom the British, the French, the Americans have nothing to offer', he bragged.[1] But these were the geniuses of the past. The Nazis needed a genius for their own times, a glorious mind that would crown their project with intellectual grandeur. Who could achieve this? Carl Schmitt was world-renowned but he was a *legal* philosopher and that would not do. What was needed was a truly Germanic mind; one who carried the legacy of German Romanticism, Nietzsche and the *Völk* into the present, and indeed into the future. That would be the icing on the cake. But where could such a man be found?

In fact someone did exist, a prophet who could sow the seeds for future generations, whose overflowing intellectual energy was venerated by a generation of students. But would a genius, a 'superman' so revered for grasping some of the most profound and complex ideas the human mind was capable of generating, be bought by someone as pernicious as Hitler?

On 10 May 1933 in Berlin, an atmosphere of expectation was building. The chill night air gave the impression of stillness, but then shapes formed, dissolved, and silver lights flickered across the city. A regular beating sound emerged as if from the ground and a faint amber glow weaved its way through the civic squares and tenement blocks. Then the rhythm altered and what appeared to be a flaming serpent arose through the darkness with a myriad of ritualistic attendants, zigzagging through the grid-like pattern of streets.

Hegel Square, Berlin – named after the iconic thinker of the nineteenth century – witnessed this long procession of students marching in order, carrying lit torches. Moving to 'Opernplatz', Opera House Square, opposite Humboldt University, they excitedly dispersed to ignite an enormous bonfire.[2] Golden flames ripped through the black sky, quickly followed by plumes of grey smoke and charcoal fumes. Then through the darkness, crowds of zealous young men in their light-coloured flat caps and military garb became visible. Uniformed gangs began to assemble with a feverish sense of importance, playing songs, making 'fire oaths' and chanting incantations, accompanied by flags billowing beside them. All inhaled the thick vapour filling the air, the odour of wood smoke. Soon charred remains would litter the ground like waste on a rubbish tip. But before then new objects were thrown into the pyre and in front of the dark mass of the jubilant crowd, vivid in white, shone a monumental pile of books. The pages glowed fiercely for a moment almost coming to life in the flames, before crumbling to ash, as if succumbing to some acute disease.

That early summer's evening in Berlin witnessed the public burning of 'un-Germanic' books by members of the SA Sturmabteilung, 'assault division', a Nazi paramilitary organization accompanied by university students. Posters had advertised the event: 'The National Socialist Student Association calls for the public burning of destructive Jewish writing in response to the Jews' shameless incitement of Germany.[3] The list of damned books included the Jewish philosophers Spinoza and Moses Mendelssohn, and also the works of Sigmund Freud, Karl Marx and Albert Einstein. Fuelling the fire that night were also books by Heinrich Heine, the nineteenth-century German lyric poet born of an assimilated Jewish family.

Joseph Goebbels celebrated the fire as the 'symbol of renaissance'. Upwards of twenty-five thousand books were thrown into flames. The crowd roared.[4] Alfred Bäumler, hawk-eyed and jubilant, oversaw the event, crowing with pleasure in a rousing speech. But neither Bäumler nor Goebbels were Hitler's superman.

A few days earlier, on 1 May in Freiburg, southern Germany, there had been more fire. However, this blaze had been one of publicity. With great zeal in an elaborate public ceremony, one of Germany's most highly regarded professors of philosophy had joined the Nazi Party. He had joined on the same day as Carl Schmitt and his membership number was 3,125,894.[5] The date for him was tactical, arranged with the Nazi authorities, and referred to as May Day: the 'national holiday of the people's community'. The philosopher's invitation to university members came 'drafted in the style of a military order'. In his speech this famous professor heralded the Third Reich as 'the construction of a new intellectual and spiritual world for the German nation'. The construction of National Socialism 'has now become the single most important task for the German universities', he declared. He continued in his speech to praise Hitler's goals and hailed Nazification of the universities as 'national labor of the highest kind'.[6]

The local Nazi newspaper wrote with huge respect for this renowned thinker: 'we know that [this professor] with his high sense of moral responsibility, with his attentive care for the fate and future of the

German people has stood at the heart of our movement'. The same newspaper couldn't heap enough praise on this man. It stated that 'for years he has effectively supported the party of Adolf Hitler in its heavy struggle for existence and power . . . no national socialist has ever knocked in vain on his door'.[7]

Martin Heidegger, professor at the University of Freiburg and one of Germany's leading lights, was the philosopher in question. His mind was dynamic, his ideas dazzling – here was a 'superman'.[8]

Heidegger had quickly idealized Hitler and within three months of Hitler's election to chancellor on 30 January 1933, he had been granted the rectorship of the university.[9] His nomination had been cheered as 'the first step in bringing universities in line with national socialism'.[10] These acts of collaboration sent shock waves around the world, for Heidegger was no ordinary man. Indeed, he was no ordinary philosopher. He had the aura of a sage. His student Hans Gadamer tried to capture this charisma, claiming that 'he was the smallest, the weakest, the loudest, the most useless, but *he led us all*'.[11] Heidegger had accrued an awesome reputation. Rumours had spread that 'this uncrowned king of the empire of thought' had created a whole new philosophy.[12] His lectures were packed, students jostled to find spaces, spilling out into the corridors.

Heidegger was catapulted on to the world stage with his dazzling magnum opus, *Being and Time*, which he published in 1927. This was followed shortly afterwards by *Kant and the Problem of Metaphysics* (1929), which served only to enhance his reputation. Later he would complete an extraordinary array of original and ground-breaking works, including *Introduction to Metaphysics* (1935), *Contributions to Philosophy* (1936–8) and others packed with ideas inherited from the Romantics, such as *Hölderlin's Hymn 'The Ister'* (1942).

Heidegger's collaboration with the Nazis was bewildering to his European admirers, but in Germany it proved hugely influential. A puzzling question emerged from all this. Why did a man as brilliant as

Heidegger succumb to an individual as bluff as Hitler? When the famous psychiatrist-philosopher Karl Jaspers, one of Heidegger's closest colleagues, asked him, 'How do you think a man as coarse as Hitler can govern Germany?' Heidegger replied, eyes shining with glee, 'Culture is of no importance. Look at his marvelous hands!'[13] Perhaps Heidegger's past will give us a clue to his impassioned collaboration.

Heidegger was born only five months after Hitler, on 26 September 1889. A painting adorning the church of St Martin in the small Bavarian town in which he grew up was perhaps pertinent to his life. Illustrated in soft browns and gentle fawn colours, the Virgin Mary depicted in smooth, simple robes, her eyes softened in gentle, feminine motherhood, glances down towards the baby Christ. Three men in contrasting affluence, with golden adornment and rich flowing fabric, greet the newborn child. The evidence of their wealth is only present in the detail of the painting, their figures are washed in the same sand-coloured hues as the rest of the picture. Palm trees and stone columns frame the image, *The Adoration of the Magi*, painted by the Renaissance 'Master of Messkirch', c.1538. It would have been a familiar image for this small boy and his family, though none could have guessed that he would himself one day grow up to become a 'Master of Messkirch'.

Messkirch is a small town within an area rich in history, a landscape inlaid with churches, castles and a Benedictine Abbey. This Catholic wealth contrasted with the region's simplicity. A brewery, a bobbin factory and a dairy were the only industry present, for this was a poor area populated only by peasants working in agriculture and crafts.

Heidegger's home town was perched near the Swabian Alp mountains, 'open . . . to the vastness of the sky and at the same time . . . rooted in the dark of the earth', as Heidegger liked to describe it.[14] The high plateau was barren, a harsh forbidding landscape, bitterly cold with no shelter from the wind. Messkirch was perched between the plateau, Lake

Constance and the upper Danube. The fertile lakelands spread west, eventually giving way to a milder climate.

Born into the lower middle class, Heidegger enjoyed a simple, modest upbringing, a lifestyle which he maintained throughout his life. His father was a sexton at the local church, and against the epic landscape around him the boy found refuge in a small, cosy home. Nearby in a farm in Göggingen, the village of his mother's birth, Heidegger's cousin lived, and being of similar age they played together amongst the soil and walled yards, the open spaces and nearby schoolhouse with its own garden.

Heidegger's family couldn't afford to send him to university, so he entered a Jesuit seminary. He then went on to study theology at the University of Freiburg from 1909 to 1911, intending to become a priest. He switched, however, to follow life as a 'philosopher-sage', driven by a need for inward exploration. He completed his doctoral thesis and further studies and then obtained a position the following year as an unsalaried private tutor. He served as a soldier during the last year of the First World War and then took a menial office job – he never left Germany. In 1917 he married Elfride Petri and soon they enjoyed the arrival of two sons.

It was after the war had ended that Heidegger studied with Edmund Husserl and managed to gain a post as a salaried senior assistant to this great man at the University of Freiburg. With no sense of what was to come, Husserl became Heidegger's devoted mentor and personal friend. In 1923 Husserl helped him to obtain a post at the nearby University of Marburg. Heidegger welcomed the opportunity and spent five years there. In 1928 Husserl retired from Freiburg and on 21 January, immediately after a decision by the appointment's committee, he drafted a personal letter to Heidegger: 'My dear friend! The board's decision: unico loco. Not a word to anyone of course.'[15] Husserl had been passionately concerned that Heidegger and Heidegger alone would be appointed to the Chair, so it was that Heidegger became Husserl's successor.

Remaining at Freiburg for the rest of his life, Heidegger even turned down prestigious offers including one from Berlin, the most highly regarded German university of the day. He was rooted in his home, and he always looked to family and place of upbringing for inspiration, to 'blood and soil'.[16] He wrote of Messkirch: 'I am wonderfully calm . . . up here. The solitude of the mountains, the quiet routine of the mountain people, the elemental closeness of the sun, storm, and sky, the simplicity of a trail on a wide slope covered deep in snow. . . . This is the homeland of pure joy. Here there is no need for anything "interesting", and the work takes on the rhythm of a man chopping wood in the distant forest.'[17]

Heidegger loved nature. In order to dwell on the riddles of his fore-bears such as Kant, he had a wooden cabin especially constructed for himself high up in the mountains in Todtnauberg. He often retreated to write there, without electricity and with water pumped from the nearby well; he called it 'die Hütte'. Over the years, Heidegger produced many of his most famous writings in this hut, from his early lectures to his final enigmatic texts. He claimed an intellectual and emotional intimacy with the building and its surroundings, and even suggested that the landscape expressed itself through him, the spirit of the mountains speaking through his voice. Along meandering tracks, Heidegger would climb high into the fir forests, breathing the crisp, cool mountain air. Away from the urban bustle, he became sensitized to the delicate sounds of nature, the mist clearing, the wind rising gently in the trees, and the native birds. Peasants in their folksy knickerbockers and waistcoats, wearing thick knee-high woollen socks, completed the picture that he cherished.

Of ramshackle appearance, single story, painted green and with blue-framed windows, was how his abode appeared from the outside. Inside were dark wooden walls. The furnishings were very basic, and from outside came the rustic smell of a campfire, fir trees and the moist, damp earth. The study where Heidegger worked was dark, with small panelled windows looking out on to the emerald forest. A meadow stretched to a gurgling water trough – of special significance for him. The building also contained a tiny kitchen where Elfride would cook, with a black stove and chimney, stark against the whitewashed kitchen wall. The family spent every Christmas up there, in the snow, with hats and skis. Heidegger wore peasant-style clothes, chopped his own wood, and adopted a Black Forest way of speaking.

Throughout the 1920s Heidegger worked hard, sometimes before a large audience teaching and lecturing, other times alone in his forest retreat, wrestling with both Kant and Nietzsche. His undisputed charisma translated into *Being and Time*, which read like an occult text, mesmerizing and written in cryptic language. Its mission was to unravel the mysteries of everyday experience. 'What is meant by to "be"?' Heidegger asked. 'Do not let the familiarity of the word blind us to the great mystery of existing.' Always a notoriously vague and difficult thinker, Heidegger's quest to understand the meaning of 'being' lent itself to the elusive tradition of existentialism.[18] This began with the idea of time itself.[19] 'Being', Heidegger argued in profound tones, is a process of 'becoming'. We humans are constantly on the move, we project ourselves into the future with hope and purpose. For example, the farmer making a tool extends himself ahead into the future, the completion of the project, the purpose of the tool. In traditional communities, Heidegger believed, we had a sense of absorption in our tasks. He declared that this was 'authentic existence'. Threatened with ruin, however, this life had been overridden by modern progress, with the advent of cities, the conformity to mass behaviour which led to 'inauthentic' lives.

In the early 1920s, before *Being and Time* was published, Heidegger had already accrued quite a reputation. In Marburg his lectures were celebrated and a number of esteemed philosophy students were already in thrall to him. These would come to include Hans-Georg Gadamer, Hannah Arendt, Karl Löwith, Leo Strauss, Günther (Stern) Anders, Hans Jonas and Herbert Marcuse, many of these being Jewish. All would create formidable oeuvres of their own and thereby ironically perpetuate their teacher's reputation and legacy. During the Marburg years one student especially would stand out.

To women, Heidegger was mesmerizing. He had the looks of the era, a sort of combination of Leslie Howard and James Mason. His allure was partly sinister, perhaps the erotic draw of a tyrant. In contrast, his philosophy was romantic, enchanting, and this combination of mystery and power made him irresistible to both male and female students alike. In an echo of the Renaissance painter from his childhood home, 'the Master of Messkirch', Heidegger became known as 'the magician of Messkirch', and one female student was possibly so enthralled by his enigmatic charisma that she took her own life.[20]

Heidegger's charisma impacted upon his personal life, and one particular individual fell for his charms. Heidegger became involved in an extramarital affair, something which jarred with his private life, for Heidegger's wife was notoriously stern and possessive. With their two sons they lived an outwardly devoted and traditional family life, typical of that of the conservative Black Forest region. His young lover was a student – although not necessarily the first young woman Heidegger had seduced during his marriage:[21] 'I daydream about the young girl who, in a raincoat, her hat low over her quiet, large eyes, entered my office for the first time, and softly and shyly gave a brief answer to each question.'[22] Heidegger recalled his first meeting with Hannah Arendt. She had just attended one of his lectures, and intrigued by her in the audience, he had invited her back to his office in private. She was a mere teenager, eighteen years of age compared to his thirty-six. She was demure, with thick dark hair, a slim Jewish nose and ponderous eyes. A note had summoned her to his room and with deference she had obeyed. Their affair began.

10.11.25

Dear Miss Arendt!

I must come and see you this evening and speak to your heart.

Everything should be simple and clear and pure between us. Only then will we be worthy of having been allowed to meet. You are my pupil

and I your teacher, but this is only the occasion for what has happened
to us . . .'[23]

Be happy, good girl!

Your M. H.

Heidegger always placed much emphasis upon the need for secrecy:
'So I have to be available for unanticipated meetings in the evening –
hence it will be hard for us to see each other this week. In any case,
definitely Tuesday the 26th. You'll still be here, won't you? But only after
9 o'clock . . . Destroy this note.'[24]

The time and place of each rendezvous was, unsurprisingly, decided
by him: 'My dear . . . I would like to ask you to come and see me Sunday
(28.VI) evening after 9, Much Love, Your M . . .' and 'My dear Hannah!
Do you want to come and see me this Sunday evening (19.VII)? . . . .
Come around 9 o'clock!'[25] He warned, 'if a lamp is lit in my room,
though, I will have been detained by a meeting. In this . . . event, come on
Wednesday . . .'[26] The lamp becomes a signal to tell Hannah whether or
not to enter. Heidegger wrote on 31 August 1925: 'Dear Hannah. . . . Do
you want to come to see me at 8.45 tomorrow? If no light is on in my
room, ring the bell.'[27] He also visited Hannah's room – she lived in a
student attic.

The affair must have been exciting to them both, not least because
of the concealment. And the town in which it was conducted added
an air of mystery. Marburg with its narrow, winding streets, its crooked,
toppling buildings, and intricate, medieval alleyways offered a hidden
world.

Heidegger took great care to hide his liaisons from his possessive wife
and the conservative world of the university. To Hannah, however, he
evinced some clarity: he spelt out that she would only ever fulfil
the role of mistress. He explained: 'The path your young life will take is
hidden. We must be reconciled to that. And my loyalty to you shall only
help you remain true to yourself.'[28] He promised her loyalty but only in

the context of where she was 'true to herself' and followed her own 'path' in life.

The hierarchy in their relationship manifested itself from the very beginning. He determined that her role for him was as his muse: 'But just once I would like to be able to thank you and, with a kiss on your brow, take the honour of your being into my work.'[29] Throughout her time in Marburg, while Hannah worked at her studies, the affair continued. However, when he felt the risks were too great he requested her to leave and study elsewhere. He arranged for her to transfer to Karl Jaspers so as not to compromise his position. She was hurt and dejected, but he managed to soften the blow and eventually coax her back into continuing the affair.

Heidegger was fascinated by Hannah as a girl on the threshold of womanhood. He wrote in a letter dated 10 February 1925: 'I cannot and do not want to separate your loyal eyes and dear figure from your pure trust, the honour and goodness of your girlish essence.' And again he reiterated these sentiments in a letter a few days later, on 21 February: 'it has happened now, when your life is silently preparing to become that of a woman, when you will take intuition, longing, blossoming, and laughter of girlhood into your life and keep it as a source of faith, of beauty, of unending womanly giving'. Her potential as an intellectual was less exciting to him. He stated that: 'the opportunities for womanly existence open to you are completely different from what the "student" in you believes, and much more positive than she suspects. May empty criticism fall away from you, and arrogant negativity recede.'[30]

Heidegger's erotic drive was at times barely suppressible. He exclaimed on one occasion, 'dear Hannah, the demonic struck me ... nothing like it has ever happened to me.'[31] And on another occasion he wrote: 'But my longing for you is becoming less and less controllable.'[32]

They also shared a poetic sensibility. In the midst of his infatuation (he always fell shy of calling it love) in the winter of 1925, Heidegger dreamt of her:

Lilac will leap over the old walls and tree blossoms will well up in the secret gardens – and you will enter the garden gate in a light summer dress. Summer evenings will come into your room and toll the quiet serenity of our life into your young soul. Soon they will awaken – the flowers your dear hands will pick, and the moss on the forest floor that you will walk on in your blissful dreams.[33]

Hannah came from a more urban background, but like Heidegger she was both a dreamer and spiritually sensitive. Her own poems showed the same porousness to mood, the same immersion in the mood of landscape. 'And soon on a solitary climb, I will greet the mountains whose rocky stillness will meet you someday, and in its lines what I have kept of your essence will return. And I will visit the Alpine lake, and look down from the steepest steepness of the precipice into its silent depths.' Heidegger's words couldn't have found a more receptive being.[34]

Their affair continued for several years. During this time in Marburg, Heidegger often retreated to walk in the Black Forest. He loved the dappled light from the sun falling through the branches of the pines, pools of green light lying on the forest floor, punctuated by the dark tree trunks. An unexpected clearing would reveal a vertiginous drop, where the white rock cliffs fell away suddenly from the forest.

Heidegger always acknowledged a reticence about love, even if this were couched in his usual vague, philosophical terms: 'Thank you my good girl! . . . I am not strong enough yet for your love. Love as such does not exist of course . . .'[35] Then he was elected to a Chair at Freiburg and suddenly Hannah became a liability. His letters became increasingly opaque, with excuses about not being able to meet, and delays on account, he alleged, of being busy. Finally, after waiting, Hannah wrote from Heidelberg on 22 April 1928: 'So you aren't coming now! – I think I understand. But still I have been anxious in the last few days, suddenly overcome by an almost baffling urgent fear.' Accepting that the affair was

over and that she represented a risk to Heidegger, she continued:
'I would lose my right to live if I lost my love for you, but I would lose
this love and its reality if I shirked the responsibility it places on me.'
She ends the letter: 'And if God choose, I shall love thee better after
death.'[36]

Throughout the 1920s Heidegger had been an intellectual, a poet, a lover
and a family man. Although his romanticism had parallels with the gloss
of National Socialism, his public life was as a sage, not a politician. All
that, however, was about to change.

On 27 May 1933, three weeks into his membership of the Nazi Party,
Heidegger as the new Rector of Freiburg University delivered his inaugural address.[37] In a theatrical public ceremony with red and black swastika flags that swept across the stage, he declared himself the new Führer
of the academic establishment. Dressed in full military attire he echoed
the sea of Nazi uniforms before him: Party officials were ubiquitous, they
had even been given front-row seats at the expense of elderly academics'
wives. The new Rector's address, the Rektoratsrede, was entitled 'The
Self-Assertion of the German University' and was to become notorious
for its praise of Nazism. Heidegger rose to the platform, giving a full Nazi
salute, and began:[38]

> The assumption of the office of rector is an obligation to the spiritual
> leadership of this university. The allegiance of teachers and students
> awakens and gains strength only from its true and common roots in
> the spirit of the university. But this spirit achieves clarity, distinction
> and power only and above all when the leaders, Führer, are first led
> themselves – led by the relentlessness of that spiritual order that
> expresses its history through the fate of the German nation.[39]

His speech was long and covered many points, but concluded with the
following plea to the assembled crowd:

it is entirely up to us whether and how extensively we mean to make a fundamental effort toward . . . self-determination . . . we just mean to change old institutions and add new ones. Nobody will prevent us from doing that . . . but we can only completely understand the glory and greatness of this uprising if we carry in us that deep and ample level-headedness of which the old Greek wisdom spoke the words: 'all greatness stands firm in the storm' . . .[40]

Professor Heidegger had the words of the 'Horst-Wessel-Lied', the anthem of the Nazi Party, printed on the back of the programme notes that accompanied his inauguration ceremony.[41] Also printed were the directions that the words were to 'be sung following the address by the leader, Führer of the university'. The song went:

'Raise the flag, stand rank on rank together!
Storm troopers march with firm and valiant tread,
Comrades gunned down by Red Front and reaction
March on in spirit, swelling our ranks.'

Raising hand, shout, Sieg Heil.[42]

Not long after this address, Heidegger was one day making his way to the university. He always woke early. Across Freiburg he joined the dark-suited men with walking canes and the many other pedestrians who populated the streets and city squares. He dodged his way past the bicycles that wobbled over the cobbles, and past the occasional car, then he wove through the emerging bustle of a crowd of flitting pedestrians. That morning Heidegger was lost in thought. He was composing a telegram to his new mentor. Impatient to put his reflections down, he hastened to his office. Once there he seated himself quickly before the large walnut-veneered desk and began to write. In a telegram he explained how he was enthusiastically supporting 'bringing the University into line'. It was addressed to Adolf Hitler. A second telegram was also dispatched, post-haste, to the Nazi Robert Wagner on his appointment as *Reichsstatthalter* (mayor) of the region of Baden: 'I am happy about your nomination as *Reichsstatthalter* of Baden and salute the Führer of the province of the fatherland with a fighting "Seig Heil!"'[43]

Heidegger's predecessor had previously resigned from his post as rector in view of a deeply distasteful task he had been assigned to carry out. Heidegger, keen to prove his mettle, embraced this task now himself. One of Hitler's first measures was to remove all non-Aryans from universities and public life. Heidegger issued this 'Baden Decree' and all non-Aryan professors and senior members of the university were suspended. Included among them was Germany's then most famous philosopher, Edmund Husserl. Husserl, as noted earlier, was Heidegger's devoted mentor, responsible for most of Heidegger's career opportunities.[44] Husserl received a letter in April 1933 notifying him of his enforced 'leave of absence' from his emeritus position. Heidegger had the power to retract this, but did nothing. (The decree went further and also suspended Husserl's son, Gerhart, from Kiel University.)

From the Rector's office with its tall panelled windows framed with carved wood Heidegger set about penning a series of damning letters about various colleagues to the Nazi police. Among these, he instigated an investigation into one of the world's most distinguished chemists, Professor Friedberg Hermann Staudinger, who later won a Nobel Prize. His crime was that he had 'pacifist' tendencies. Heidegger also invented the spurious allegation that the chemist might be a spy. He informed the Gestapo and recommended that: 'because Staudinger is lukewarm about national recovery. Rather than offering him retirement, we must think of dismissal. Heil Hitler. Heidegger.'[45] Solely due to Heidegger the terrified man was surveyed, interrogated and hounded. Heidegger even requested a meeting with a senior Nazi official, and eventually Staudinger was forced to leave. Rector Heidegger also tried to destroy the careers of other colleagues whom he believed were less than loyal to the Nazi cause.[46]

Solstice day, 25 June 1933, and a long column of students and university staff marched through Freiburg town and on to the sports stadium. There to greet them was an enormous fire in front of the stadium, and on a podium, Heidegger. He spoke: 'Solstice feast of 1933. The days pass by. They grow shorter. But in us grows the courage to pierce the approaching shadows. Let us never be blind to struggle. Instruct us, flames, enlighten us. Show us the road from which one does not return! Let the flames leap, let hearts burn.'[47]

In the immediate summer following Heidegger's election, a code of honour for the university staff based on the regulations of the officer corps was drafted. Student SA units were also set up at Freiburg and these 'Brown shirts' patrolled the campus. Under Dr George Steiler, associate professor of philosophy and a former naval commander, they enacted military exercises on campus with dummy weapons while Heidegger looked on approvingly. Not satisfied with merely training and playacting at battle, these SA student units began a campaign of targeting local opposition politicians and staging 'public disturbances' outside their homes in order to fabricate their arrests. The aim was to 'soften up', by use of violence, local political opposition. Heidegger was notified of these activities and replied: 'I have noted your remarks . . . you appear to be unaware of the dubious conduct of the local resident concerned, which apparently prompted these scenes of public disorder. . . . I would in future be obliged, for the sake of the "realization of the Third Reich", if some of the suggestions submitted to me were of a more constructive kind . . .'[48]

Meanwhile participation in militaristic field sports at Freiburg also became a requirement for every student. When professors objected to these activities as 'wasting time', Heidegger, in a notorious speech of 30 June 1933, exploded: 'How can we speak of "wasting time" when it is a question of fighting for the state? It is not in working for the state that the danger lies: the danger lies in indifference and opposition.'[49]

A few months later, in October 1933, Hitler made his ominous speech to the Reichstag in Berlin signalling Germany's withdrawal from the League of Nations. Soon afterwards, Heidegger spoke: 'after these words by our chancellor, other peoples may decide the way we do . . . we will march down the most arduous road . . . we already know what this requires . . . BE PREPARED FOR EXTREME SITUATIONS AND REMAIN COMRADES TO THE END . . .'[50]

The following was from an article in a student newspaper by Heidegger as Führer-Rector of Freiburg at the beginning of the winter semester in 1933/4:

> May you ceaselessly grow in courage to sacrifice yourselves for the salvation of the nation's essential being and the increase of its innermost strength in its polity. . . . The Führer himself and he alone is the German reality, present and future, and its law . . . Heil Hitler.[51]

Heidegger had glorified Hitler, of that there was no doubt. But many of his disciples looked for excuses and explanations for their hero's behaviour. While his love of nature, nationalism and initial zeal for Nazism were never in doubt, his feelings about Judaism were perceived to be more complex. But even here he had willingly executed the Baden Decree and had taken part in various unpleasant activities. Also, even before Hitler had come to power there is evidence of Heidegger's anti-Semitism. Not long after his affair with Hannah ended, Heidegger had made the acquaintance of Viktor Schwoerer, a councillor to the government and the director of the Bureau of Universities of the Ministries of Public Education of Baden, 'extremely friendly and like one is with one's fellow countryman' Heidegger commented to Jaspers. A year later in 1929 Heidegger had written to Schwoerer with regard to appointments at the university: 'Either we restore genuine forces and educators emanating from the native soil to our German spiritual life, or we abandon it definitively to the growing *Jewification*.' The term Heidegger used was *Verjudung*, an anti-Semitic term used in *Mein Kampf*.[52] Against 'Jewification' Heidegger had advocated 'the fundamental possibilities of the essence of the originally Germanic race'.[53]

Why was Heidegger against the Jews? Hitler promised elimination of Jews from their role in society and the preservation of the Germanic nation – this nationalism would have appealed to Heidegger. He longed to see the preservation of a more simple, rural life, and the National Socialist image of peasants marching with spades was enchanting; it was his philosophical dream sprung to life. But was this folksy nationalism so alluring to Heidegger that he would even sacrifice his own friends?

From his cabin in the woods, perhaps Heidegger dreamed that the inauthenticity of modern life would finally be overcome. On long walks through the Black Forest, along its wooded paths, in glades and clearings, skiing down its slopes, and in long hours poring over books in his hut, did Heidegger regard Hitler as the voice of authenticity? And perhaps Heidegger crafted for himself a special role: Hitler's guide, the envisioned philosopher-king.

Heidegger's relationship with anti-Semitism remained fraught. His mistress had been Jewish and many of his students and friends were too. Surely a true Hitlerite would not become intimate with a Jew? Possibly, therefore, Heidegger was simply an opportunist, drawn to power and status, seizing a chance for promotion and grandeur under the Nazis. If his move was careerist, however, it did not lead to a straightforward victory.

From the beginning of his time as Rector of Freiburg in 1933, Heidegger taught that Germany should put its faith in Hitler. Nevertheless, in spite of his allegiance, his time as Rector encompassed many trials. Stiff competition arose from amongst the ranks of the Nazi professors, for all ambitiously pursued becoming the Führer's chosen one. Erich Jaensch and Ernst Krieck in particular were hostile to the new Rector.[54] They jealously intervened with Alfred Rosenberg to undermine Heidegger's rising star. And further problems beckoned.

Heidegger's philosophical position was thought to conflict with certain elements of National Socialism. He was supposed to be old school, an advocate of the romantic, cultural nationalism espoused by Fichte and others, not the new pseudo-Darwinian biological race. Baden's education minister even accused Heidegger of pursuing a kind of 'private national socialism'. In return, Heidegger claimed that the political leadership of the university proved to be false to 'the inner truth and the grandeur of national socialism'.[55] Ironically, recent evidence has shown that Heidegger did in fact advocate race, that he actively lobbied the provincial minister of culture for a new Chair in 'race studies and genetics'[56] and advocated that 'in order to preserve the health of the state', 'questions of euthanasia should be seriously contemplated'.[57]

Whatever his allegiance, Heidegger felt hard done by. He complained that his Rectoral address had been 'spoken into the wind', that 'during the whole of my time as rector none of my colleagues ever discussed the address'.[58] His discontent grew, 'the Rectorship address, which was not printed in larger numbers ... was still not sold out in 1934'. In his own view, he had spoken words of truth but his listeners had failed to understand. If Heidegger was careerist, then his Rectorship had failed miserably. He had the skills of philosophy but not those of political manipulation – for these he should have heeded the words of his hero who had honed them in *Mein Kampf*. In frustration, after only one year Heidegger handed in his resignation as Rector.[59]

'The failure of the Rectorship – a thorn in my flesh' was how Heidegger later referred to this episode. However, even in such a short space of time this influential professor had proved invaluable to the Nazis. He had elevated the Führer to superhuman status and had contributed to the legitimacy of the Third Reich. How would Hitler's 'superman' feel about the Nazis now that he had resigned from the Rectorship? Had he become disillusioned?

At the beginning of May 1934, right after his resignation from the Rectorship, Heidegger participated with Alfred Rosenberg, Hans Frank,

Carl Schmitt and Erich Rothacker in the 'Days for the Commission for the Philosophy of Law of the Academy for German Law', organized in the buildings of the Nietzsche archives. The theme was the 'Realization of German Law' – the archives had become sacred for German philosophy. Around this time Heidegger took charge of editions of Nietzsche's work prepared by the archive and sent these to Hitler, Rosenberg, Bäumler and even Benito Mussolini. Recommending Bäumler and Kurt Hildebrandt, the two Nazi interpreters of Nietzsche's works, later in 1938 Heidegger would go on to affirm the political need for the Nazi censorship of publications.[60]

In the summer semester of 1935, Heidegger embarked on a series of lectures entitled 'An Introduction to Metaphysics'. In these he described the 'inward truth and greatness of the *movement*'.[61] Nobody had any doubt in the context of the National Socialist state of 1935 which *movement* Heidegger was referring to. The lectures were only published later when this evidence of Heidegger's continuing allegiance came to light.

The following year, in the spring of 1936, Heidegger undertook a lecture tour in Italy. He travelled to Rome where he was overwhelmed by the beauty and magnificence of the nation's cultural achievements. He lectured on the poet Hölderlin and also on Germany's finest academic works. During the tour, one of Heidegger's colleagues and a former friend, the Jewish philosopher Karl Löwith, was banned from speaking at the Kaiser Wilhelm Institute – which was ironic considering that the institute owed its very existence to an endowment from a Jewish organization. How would Heidegger respond now that he was no longer the Rector and no longer obliged to perform certain duties? Would he support his friend? Heidegger stepped forwards and with great panache gave a talk on the topic of 'European and German philosophy'. Unflinchingly before an admiring audience, he enthused about his subject, utterly unperturbed by the anti-Semitic rejection of Löwith. Wearing the insignia of the National Socialist Party throughout, he continued on his lecture tour.[62]

When confronted by Löwith after his speech, Heidegger excused his actions by dissociating the Führer from other more repugnant Nazis such as Julius Streicher. Heidegger's admiration for Hitler remained intact. Löwith believed that Heidegger's National Socialism was not extremely short-lived but was a deeply held allegiance and indeed was fundamental to his very philosophy. Löwith argued that Heidegger's idea of 'being' was already metaphysical Nazism.

If Löwith felt disappointed with Heidegger's refusal to back his Jewish former friends, this was nothing compared to Husserl's disillusionment. Heidegger willingly agreed with his publisher to remove the dedication to his former Jewish mentor and close friend Husserl from *Being and Time*. Moreover, he did not visit his old friend and teacher, even during the latter's terminal illness, and he failed to attend Husserl's funeral in 1938.

A 'Party comrade and pioneer of National Socialism' was how the author of a letter from the Scientific Society of the Freiburg League of National Socialist University Lecturers referred to Heidegger. Heidegger himself remained a member of this institute until its dissolution in 1945.[63] He also continued his close connections with Rosenberg and other Nazis philosophers such as Rothacker, Heyse, Bäumler, Krieck and Schmitt, even if at times some of these relations were fraught.[64]

Although no longer rector of the university, Heidegger continued unabated with his intellectual mission. Indeed, an entire generation of students was called upon to abandon Christian and humanist ideas. 'A "Christian" philosophy is neither fish nor fowl, a fundamental misconception,' Heidegger declared. He chastised the faith and its values as often as he could and helped block teaching appointments by Christian academics.[65] 'No committed Christian of any denomination should in future be admitted to a university lectureship.'[66] Morality, human rights, pity, these were bygone notions. They should be expelled from philosophy lest Germany be weakened.[67] And while he denounced Christianity, as late as 1942 in his lecture on Hölderlin's

Der Isther he continued to rate National Socialism and 'its unique historical status – not that it stands in need of such favours'.[68] He also continued to defend Hitler's regime and its war activities between 1940 and 1944.[69]

Heidegger remained Chair of philosophy at the university and continued to teach, publish and research. *Being and Time* was published quite freely by Max Niemeyer, in a series of editions, the last appearing in 1941, and the Rectoral address was republished and printed throughout the occupied zones until 1944:

> Heidegger's good relations with the regime are confirmed by a note held at the Berlin Documentation Centre. In January 1944, a time when publications were curtailed or suspended because of the serious lack of paper, the Ministry granted the Klostermann publishing company a delivery of paper to print Heidegger's works.[70]

Paying his dues regularly and maintaining his Nazi Party membership until 1945,[71] more poignant even than his relationship with the regime, the meaning of Heidegger's intellectual project has recently been thrown into darkness. It has been argued that his masterwork *Being and Time*, far from offering an account of individual existence, is in fact a doctrine of radical self-sacrifice where individualization is allowed only for the purpose of heroism in warfare. Indeed Heidegger's entire oeuvre has been interpreted as founded upon Nazi beliefs.[72]

If Heidegger was an ideologue, what of his family and friends? Heidegger's wife Elfride had become a National Socialist activist before Heidegger and fully endorsed Nazi racial and anti-Semitic ideology. Her neighbours apparently were afraid of her and never dared to discuss the Party in her presence for fear of being reported if they let any small criticism slip. Later, after the war, the de-Nazification committee would issue a report written by Friedrich Oehlkers in which it would be revealed that Elfride was widely distrusted. As late as autumn 1944 she had been 'brutally mistreating the women of Zähringen involved in the digging of entrenchments' and had 'sent sick and pregnant women to dig'.[73]

There is no evidence that Heidegger suffered sleepless nights in his native Germany while millions of Jews were sent to the slaughterhouse. Under Hitler, his family flourished and he enjoyed a splendid career with abundant glories. His professional experiences in many ways paralleled those of Krieck, Bäumler, Rosenberg and Schmitt, and indeed the myriad other philosophers working during the chancellorship of Hitler. Whether committed Nazis or opportunists, whether mediocre or brilliant, they all reaped the fruits of collaboration.

But Heidegger was special. Not in spite of his genius but because of it. For all the ambiguities and subtleties of his intellectual rapport with the Third Reich, the deed was done. Heidegger had helped glorify the Führer. He had provided the icing on the cake of Hitler's dream: for here was the intellectual Nazi superman for all to see.

PART 2

Hitler's Opponents

From 1933 and for the remainder of the decade Hitler's dream was realized. By transforming himself into the 'philosopher' Führer, convincing the country of his genius, and sifting the past for its poisonous strands of thought, Hitler had paved the way for a new reality to underpin his world order. The German mind was his. Most of the institutions of education, the universities, their teaching, research and the tranche of philosophers within them, supported his vision. Racism, war and tyranny were studied, endorsed and enshrined in law. And the ultimate glory was provided by a charismatic genius.

Meanwhile, the targets of Hitler's wrath, the Jews, were now unemployed, impoverished, rendered powerless and vilified. Violence against them was officially sanctioned and legally enshrined. Jews who remained in Germany were reduced to a beggarly existence, threatened with annihilation of their entire people. Could any survive?

Those Jewish philosophers who were Hitler's self-declared enemies were, in the main, a subtle and sophisticated group. What the likes of Rosenberg, Bäumler and Krieck, along with their often crude-minded and obedient hacks, were obliterating were some of the most gifted minds in European intellectual history. These Jewish thinkers now had to respond to a force that had no ability or desire to accommodate them, a force that was increasingly dedicated to the annihilation of Jewry.

Jews in Germany in the 1930s were a loosely identifiable group, as Hitler categorized Jews on the basis of race. A majority of German-Jewish thinkers, although racially Jewish, had been assimilated into German culture and were not actively practising Jews. Many did, however, retain certain distinctive sensibilities that were indebted to their cultural heritage, and these infused their philosophy. Three scholars in particular are of interest here: Walter Benjamin, Theodor Adorno and Hannah Arendt.[1] They were intuitive and imaginative thinkers, and as they observed and interpreted the world around them they saw what others failed to see. Their distinctive intellectual stance as a result of confronting Nazism, their cultural affinities, and the fact that their lives were interconnected – both with each other and also with Heidegger – make them with hindsight a natural community of three. They should be as well known as Kant, Nietzsche or Heidegger, for their stories are really quite unique. So who exactly were they and what became of them when the Third Reich hung its swastikas in the university halls?

CHAPTER 6

Tragedy: Walter Benjamin

One of the Jewish literati unfortunate enough to witness the first rampages of the Nazis was an extraordinary figure.

Winter in Berlin, 1933. A well-dressed family in warm coats walked across one of Berlin's many grey cobbled streets. Two young girls wearing beautifully polished shoes, thick woolly tights and woollen hats pulled down over their ears, carried large bundles as if they were about to embark on a long journey. They walked, one with the mother, the other with the father, the parents clasping their daughters' hands so tightly that you could see the fingers of the little girls turn pale. The mother wore elegant shoes and a soft hat that followed the curves of her dark-brown wavy hair. She was quite tall, about the same height as her husband, who in his long overcoat was bespectacled, had a slight moustache, and wore a bowler hat. He too had dark hair. The children glanced about them, distracted, nervous, bemused. The mother looked down, ashamed or frightened. The father gazed directly at a news reporter's camera which pointed at him; his face was blank, not registering the lens. Behind the family stood a large mob of young men dressed in military attire, staring aggressively. Two had motorbikes. The couple moved hurriedly past. This young family were some of the first Jews to be expelled from Germany after Hitler's election as chancellor in January 1933. Their fate would be replicated by many others.[1]

A tenement block sat at the intersection of two cobbled streets and the road here widened, accommodating the mob who watched the Jewish family leave. From a top-floor window the scene below had been observed.

If one had been able to see through this top-floor window, the occupant would have been revealed to be a rather stout, heavily built man in his early forties, with short, greying hair, a slightly Jewish profile and dark moustache. The man held a large, curved pipe and stooped over a table. He walked ponderously back and forth, the golden hue of the interior holding out against the darkness outside. The lamplight evoked a memory:

> In our garden there was an abandoned, ramshackle summerhouse. I loved it for its stained-glass windows. Whenever I wandered about inside it, passing from one coloured pane to the next, I was transformed; I took on the colours of the landscape that – now flaming and now dusty, now smouldering and now sumptuous – lay before me in the window. . . . While considering the sky, a piece of jewellery, or a book, I would lose myself in colours.[2]

But the man inside the Berlin apartment wasn't able to lose himself in colours now. From his movement and gestures one could discern that he was very agitated.

From the secrecy of his interior the man was trying not to dwell on his own family, his younger sister Dora, brother George and his son Stefan, still a schoolboy. He pictured Stefan as a small boy, plump knees protruding from beneath white shorts, large curious eyes, hands alert and twitching, holding a teddy bear in his arms.[3] 'There is hardly anyone among those touched by the events who can look . . . into the future. All of this . . . would be bearable if only Stefan weren't where he still is', he confided to a friend.[4]

This man witnessing the first expulsions of the Jews from Berlin in early 1933 was Walter Benjamin. He was the Jewish-German writer and

philosopher who even at this time was a budding star: 'the editors
are already referring to him as "the best living writer in the German
language" – although only those who happen to be Jewish', a leading
journal claimed.[5] A friend captured Benjamin's singular appearance
at around this time in 1933:

> Benjamin's physical stoutness and the rather German heaviness he
> presented were in strong contrast to the agility of his mind, which so
> often made his eyes sparkle behind his glasses. I can see him in a small
> photograph I saved, with his prematurely grey, closely cropped hair
> (he was forty years old at the time), his slightly Jewish profile and
> black moustache, sitting on a deck chair on the front porch of my
> house, in his usual posture: face leaned forward, chin held in his right
> hand. I don't think I have ever seen him think without holding his chin,
> unless he was carrying in his hand the large curved pipe with the wide
> bowl he was so fond of and which in a way resembled him.[6]

In addition to his heavy build Benjamin had a nervous disposition and
felt that he 'hardly dared step outside his own four walls'. He had hoped
to avoid being in Germany at this time as he was keenly aware of the
impending political events: the rise of the Nazis was apparent everywhere and he had no illusions about their power and intentions.[7] But in
November 1932 he had been forced to return from a journey abroad,
back to Berlin, the city of his birth.

Benjamin watched the inaugural celebrations of Nazis springing up
like toadstools across the city. He heard of the likes of collaborators such
as Heidegger, Bäumler and Krieck, who were enjoying their newly found
prestige, and everywhere he could see groups of threatening figures on
the street, the mob, swaying in and out of the shadows.

As the winter of 1932 progressed into the early spring of 1933,
Benjamin stayed hidden in the small world of his apartment. But he soon
learned of the fate of his close friends. Some who had seen the writing on

the wall had already taken flight, including the Marxist playwright Bertolt Brecht, the German-Jewish Marxist philosopher Ernst Bloch, and the writer Siegfried Kracauer. Others, less fortunate, disappeared during the nights of 27–28 February, the time of the arson attack on the Reichstag. They vanished into the hastily erected concentration camps and torture chambers of the SA.[8] Brecht wrote in response to these events:

> '*To the fighters in the Concentration Camps*'
> You who can hardly be reached
> Buried in the concentration camps
> Cut off from every human word
> Subject to brutalities
> Beaten down but
> Not confuted
> Vanished but
> Not forgotten![9]

In contrast to Brecht, however, Benjamin was not given to a fighting spirit, but a contemplative one. Hence he was more despairing. To one of his closest friends, the Jewish philosopher Gerhard Scholem, he wrote: 'The air is hardly fit to breathe any more'; this fact 'of course loses significance as one is being strangled anyway'.[10]

Benjamin was sure that the Third Reich was no passing phantom. Others waited, hoping for it to pass, but he urged his family to leave. In particular he was anxious to get his son Stefan out of Germany but was dependent upon his ex-wife Dora Sophie, who had custody. She was one of the optimists, waiting, hoping that the tide of fascism would abate. This situation caused Benjamin sleepless nights and in a letter to his great friend Scholem he confided about the:

> heighten[ing of] my desire to know that Stefan is safely outside
> of Germany: ... I encouraged Dora along these lines while I was in

Paris. Judging from her reply, she seemed then to want to wait and see how things developed. In the meantime, the regulations about the numerous clauses for Jews in high schools and middle schools have been published. I do not yet know if Stefan is affected by them. But more germane is the fact that he is squarely on the Left and does not possess the constant prudence that a Jew has to have to leave Germany today if he wants to have a chance of saving his own skin.[11]

And again, 'A week ago I urged Dora once again – insofar as is possible in a letter – to send Stefan out of Germany'.[12] Whatever his anxieties for his family, Benjamin knew that his time was up. He was a Jew closely linked to political activists; his own ideas would be seen as subversive. Benjamin considered his options. Flight was essential. But where to and how? His problem was that his various means of livelihood were now cut off by the Nazis. He had eked a meagre living, not by way of a formal academic post, but through journalism, working for radio, for the broadcasting company Funkstunde in Berlin and the newspaper *Frankfurter Zeitung*. In 1933 the Nazis assumed control of the radio station so quickly and completely that he lost his position immediately. And the *Frankfurter Zeitung* said to him 'wait and see' while the publication of his works was suspended.

Unemployment and destitution were even more terrifying for Benjamin than harassment or direct violence. He had an absolute horror of starvation: 'The terror against every attitude or manner of expression that does not fully conform to the official one has reached virtually unsurpassable heights. Under such conditions, the utmost political reserve, such as I have long since practised, may protect the person from systematic persecution, but not from *starvation*.'[13] This apprehension of poverty 'transform[ed] [his] ill-defined wishes to leave Germany into a hard and fast decision'.[14] Closing his shutters one last time, Benjamin packed his things. He was now, like other thousands of Jews, on the run.

An exile. Where to go? He decided to head via Paris for Spain, Ibiza, where he had friends and felt he might be safe.

The journey was arduous and he soon missed the familiarity of his home, but he learnt that he had left not a moment too soon. As he arrived in Ibiza, news reached him of his brother Georg. Georg Benjamin had been taken into 'protective' custody by the Prussian police on 8 April 1933. He was under arrest, first in the police gaol at Alexanderplatz, from where he was soon transferred to Plötzensee 'prison'.[15] Georg was politically active and his left-leaning activities might cost him his life – others who had been arrested had been taken immediately to the concentration camps run by the SA or SS. In a letter written from Ibiza to Scholem, Benjamin expressed how he heard news of Georg:

> Fonda Miramar
> San Antonio, Ibiza
> May 7, 1933
>
> Dear Gerhard,
> Just a few lines, even without having heard any news from you.
> I have learned, from a serious, but not necessarily infallible source, that my brother Georg, who practices medicine in Berlin N[orth] Brunenstrasse, fell into the hands of the SA, was severely brutalized, and lost an eye. He is presumed to be in a state hospital, either as a prisoner or in preventative detention, and is most likely cut off from the outside world . . .
> Yours, Walter.[16]

Going on to depict how he came by this news: 'The story was told in Zurich by Reni Begun, a Jewish doctor, who is said to have left Berlin ten days ago. She is now in Paris; I am trying to establish direct contact with her, but this will take some time.' Benjamin explained his fear:

My brother's predicament has given us reason to fear the worst. The matter is too serious – and the prospects of being able to help too futile – for me to return to Berlin for information, since such an enquiry could endanger either the recipient or the person giving the information. Perhaps you can extract some information about my brother from the people who have just arrived. Please try this and inform me at once. My sister meanwhile is back in Berlin . . .

A couple of months later, Benjamin would write: 'Did I write you that I have meanwhile received grim confirmation of the news about my brother? Yet, I am still in the dark concerning the nature of his injuries.'[17] Eventually, during several arrests, imprisonments and interrogations, the Nazis would torture Georg Benjamin. He would be imprisoned in a concentration camp where the brutal treatment was so horrific that he would choose to end his own life by electrocution on a live wire rather than endure more.

Meanwhile a long period of exile in Ibiza was Benjamin's fate. Arriving on the Spanish island in April 1933, he had taken lodgings first in a rudimentary room in a decrepit hostel. This hostel room, and others like it, were to be his home for the next few months. There in the stifling heat the dirt clung to his sweat and gnawed at his skin, bringing him out in sores. The sores became constant afflictions, so too loneliness and anxiety punctuated only by correspondence and the activity of thinking.

Nostalgia for happier times overwhelmed Benjamin and from his cramped dwelling he began to reminisce. Fairly soon ruminations blossomed into purposeful activity and he started work. From the filth of his surroundings, Benjamin worked on what would become one of the most inspirational accounts of childhood ever written. *Berlin Childhood Around 1900* began with:

In 1932, when I was abroad, it began to be clear to me that I would soon have to bid a long, perhaps lasting farewell to the city of my birth.

Several times in my inner life, I have already experienced the process of inoculation as something salutary. In this situation, too, I resolved to follow suit and I deliberately called to mind those images which, in exile, are most apt to awaken homesickness: images of childhood ...

He continued:

For a long time, life deals with the still tender memory of childhood like a mother who lays her newborn on her breast without waking it. Nothing has fortified my own memory so profoundly as gazing into courtyards, one of whose dark loggias, shaded by blinds in the summer, was for me a cradle in which the city laid its new citizen.

And as Benjamin sat in his Spartan room furnished with little more than a bed, table and chair, he recalled the splendid city of his birth:

The rhythm of the metropolitan railway and of carpet beating rocked me to sleep. It was the mould in which my dreams took shape – first the unformed ones, traversed perhaps by the sound of running water or the smell of milk, then the long spun ones: travel dreams and dreams of rain. Here, spring called up the first shoots of green before the gray façade of a house in back; and when, later in the year, a dusty canopy of leaves brushed up against the wall of the house a thousand times a day, the rustling of the branches initiated me into a knowledge to which I was not yet equal. For everything the courtyard became a sign or a hint to me. Many were the messages embedded in the skirmishing of the green roller blinds drawn up high, and the many ominous dispatches that I prudently left unopened in the rattling of the roll-up shutters that came thundering down at dusk. ... Coachmen were accustomed to hanging their capes on the railing while they watered their horses, first clearing away the last remnants of hay and oats in the trough by drawing water from the pump that rose out of the pavement. To me, these waiting stations, whose peace was seldom disturbed by the coming and going of carriages, were distant provinces in my backyard. . . . Later, from the perspective of the rail-road embankment, I rediscovered the courtyards. When on sultry summer afternoons, I gazed down on them from my compartment, the summer appeared to have parted from the landscape and locked itself into those yards. And the red geraniums that were peeping from their boxes accorded less well with the summer than the red feather mattresses that were hung over window sills each morning to air . . .[18]

Benjamin was born on 15 July 1892 in Berlin 'at a time half way between the founding of the Empire and the First World War – when the capital of the new German Empire was developing into a metropolis'. Developing at breakneck speed, encapsulating the industrialization of the modern era, Berlin was regarded as the most modern of cities. Benjamin witnessed all this, the 'steaming, snarling monsters of the Ringbahn and Stadtbahn; then the electric trams, whose poles and overhead conductors spread like a lattice of wires and iron over the city'. He loved this urban environment – it was home. His birthplace at Magdeburger Platz 4, in the old western part of Berlin, was a district inhabited by the genteel and the well-to-do. As the city developed and shops and businesses grew up in the area, Benjamin's family, like so many others, moved even further westwards into the newer areas to escape the urbanization.[19]

The family were able to move on account of the sizeable wealth of Benjamin's father, a highly successful businessman: 'A particularly nice and sociable man.'[20] He was, however, obsessed with judging every activity through the lens of business, submitting all enterprise to financial logic – a character trait that was hardly sympathetic to Benjamin's own disposition. The boy's mother, too, although not overly preoccupied with financial matters, was a practical and resolute person,

who structured the family's world, leaving little space for either the development of responsibility or rebellion in her eldest son. Benjamin's every
need was provided for by an father, administered by his mother, and all
the little details were accomplished by an army of household servants,
typical for a family of their affluence and standing at this time.

Benjamin was educated at home until the age of nearly nine, so he
enjoyed the personal attention of a governess and was surrounded by the
opulent intimacy of his family world. When at Easter time in 1901 he was
sent to Kaiser Friedrich School in Charlottenburg, institutionalization
came as a shock. He hated the 'compulsion incessantly to remove my
cap . . . when another of the teachers passed' and the 'school discipline in
the lower forms – caning, change of seat or detention'. He detested the
'excursions to the country' and games on the field at Tempelhof or on 'a
drill ground in the vicinity of Lehrter Station'.[20] During this, the era of
Kaiser Wilhelm, militaristic drill was the order of the day.[21]

As a schoolboy, Benjamin was frequently ill:

> It would begin with a few spots on my skin, with a touch of nausea. It
> was as though the illness were used to waiting patiently until the
> doctor had arranged for its accommodations. He came, examined me,
> and stressed the importance of awaiting further developments in
> bed. . . . I saw in my imagination the spoon whose edge was colonised
> by the prayers of my mother, and how, after it had been brought close
> to my lips with loving care, it would suddenly reveal its true nature by
> pouring the bitter medication unmercifully down my throat. As an
> intoxicated man sometimes calculates and thinks, merely to see if he
> can still do so, I counted the ringlets of sunlight that danced across the
> ceiling of my room and rearranged the rhomboids of the carpet in ever
> new groupings.[22]

Schooldays, whether in good or ill health, were not all misery. They had
hidden riches too; he wrote with relish of *Boy's Books*:

My favourites came from the school library. . . . The teacher would call my name, and the book then made its way from bench to bench; one boy passed it on to another, or else it travelled over the heads until it came to rest with me, the student who had raised his hand. Its pages bore traces of the fingers that had turned them. . . . Hanging on its pages, however, like Indian summer on the branches of the trees, were sometimes fragile threads of a net in which I had once become entangled when learning to read.[23]

In 1904 for health reasons Benjamin's parents removed him from the hated Kaiser Friedrich institution and after a few delicious months at home without schooling he was finally sent to a country boarding school in Haubinda, Thuringia. He was only there for two years, but the experience left deep impressions on him. It was his first encounter with an intellectual environment. Theodor Lessing, the philosopher, university teacher and journalist who was later murdered by the Nazis, had taught at the school until 1904. Numerous other writers, musicians, theatrical talents and thinkers had attended the same boarding school.

By the age of fifteen Benjamin had developed interests in philosophy, literature and aesthetics. He was eventually sent back to his original, loathed school at Kaiser Friederich, but now with ammunition to fight for his newly gained autonomy. By the age of seventeen he had successfully completed his exams and continued over the next few years reading Goethe, Schiller, Shakespeare and Ibsen. He also wrote journalistic and creative prose for the school magazine. In 1911 he left this institution and put the largely unloved experiences behind him. He was about to embark on a new adventure:

The strip of light under the bedroom door in the evening, when the others were still up – wasn't it the first signal of departure? Didn't it steal into the child's expectant night, just as, later, the strip under the stage curtain would steal into the audience's night? I believe the dream-ship that came to fetch us then would often rock at our bedside on the breaking waves of conversation and the spray of clattering dishes, and in the early morning would set us down, feverish as though we'd already made the journey that was about to begin.[24]

Since early childhood, Benjamin had journeyed inwardly through sounds, scents and impressions. Imagine his delight and freedom when that same sensuous thirst could quench itself on travel and the riches of Europe! After leaving school he went first to Italy, and then in later years he came to know France, Germany, Spain, Lithuania, Russia and Norway.

After these travels he returned in April 1912 to provincial Freiburg im Breisgau, and attended the Albert Ludwig University. Here the atmosphere was dominated by the philosopher Heinrich Rickert, and alongside Benjamin in Rickert's lectures sat Martin Heidegger. While Heidegger might have been inspired by the atmosphere of Freiburg, Benjamin, the urbane, upper middle-class Jew was disappointed. He found the scholarship unimaginative and the environment stuffy.

During his student years Benjamin had his first contact with Zionism, but kept his distance from the zealous extremes of the movement. He was more inspired by intellectual and literary friendships such as those with Gerhard Scholem and with the Austrian poet Rainer Maria Rilke. These affinities developed and Benjamin resided in a cocoon of these invigorating friendships as 1914 saw the outbreak of the First World War. Throughout the war Benjamin avoided being called up to fight and continued his life first in Munich and then in Switzerland.[25] He wrote to Scholem on 30 July 1917 from St Moritz:

We have been here for a week; I found this spot – I may say – after years of struggle, and finally set foot here after my last relationship . . . had died away in Zurich. I hope to have absorbed the two years before

1 Adolf Hitler's room in Landsberg, 1923.

2 Hitler reading a book in SA uniform, Munich, 1931.

3 Leni Riefenstahl's inscription to Hitler in the first edition of Johann Gottlieb Fichte's *Sämmtliche Werke* (1848).

4 Hitler viewing the bust of Friedrich Nietzsche, 12 April 1931.

5 Hitler meets Elizabeth Nietzsche at the Nietzsche Archive, Weimar, 1935.

6 Carl Schmitt on the podium, 1930.

7 Book burning, Berlin, 10 May 1933.

8 Heidegger at a public demonstration of support for Nazism by German professors, 11 November 1933.

9 Walter Benjamin in the Bibliothèque Nationale, photograph by Gisèle Freund, 1937.

10 Adorno at his desk in Yale Street, Santa Monica, 1949.

11 Hannah Arendt, *c.* 1930.

12 Kurt Huber, *c.* 1941.

13 Roland Freisler, President of the People's Court, 1942–5: 'Hitler's Hanging Judge'.

14 Interior of the Nuremberg courtroom, 30 September 1946.

the war like a seed and everything since then has purified them in my
spirit. When we see each other again, we'll talk. .... Everything was in
decline, except for the little that let me live my life, and here I find
salvation in more than one sense: not in the leisure, the security, the
maturity of the life here, but in having escaped from the demonic and
ghostly influences, which are prevalent wherever we turn, and from the
raw anarchy, the lawlessness of suffering.[26]

Relieved to have escaped the trenches which he regarded as perpetuating
total and meaningless conflict, he constantly sought out oases of quiet.
One of these was personal. In 1917 Benjamin married Dora Sophie
Kellner. She was the 'we' to whom he had referred in his letter to Scholem.
A friend described her thus: 'Dora Sophie Kellner "was very beautiful"[27]
and she had striking looks which alone gave her a "presence". But there
was more to her than that. A blonde Jewess with slightly protruding eyes,
a heart-shaped mouth with full red lips, she excluded vitality and joie de
vive.'[28] Dora was reputed to be an engaging, socially confident, intellectual, musically talented, and exceptionally beautiful woman. Benjamin's
friend since childhood, Herbert Blumenthal, however, did not agree with
this opinion. Instead he referred to her as 'nothing but an ambitious
goose who had already thrown herself at her first husband simply because
he was the cleverest and richest man in [their] circle'. And then when
Benjamin appeared on the horizon as the 'coming man, she left [her first
husband] without giving the matter a second thought'.[29] These words
marked the end of Benjamin's friendship with Blumenthal and the beginning of a new life with his wife. The latter began in fact in a rather
secluded fashion and, as Dora explained, he lived 'up to his ears in
books'.[30]

   A year into their marriage in 1918, Benjamin's son Stefan was born
and the young family continued with a peaceful intimate life. Benjamin's
delight in his son can be evinced from the many pet names he invented.
He recorded in his private jottings:

Stefanze Stefanserich Houselion (when he was laying on his stomach after bathing in Berne) Mr Silly Mr Treasure (after a wooden doll that I had named in the same way) . . .

One foot is called Felefoot (Philip foot) the other is Franz Foot. When he was brought in the room in swaddling clothes he was called Babysausage . . .[31]

Fascinated by Stefan, an interest emerged in the ways that his little boy acquired language. Benjamin noted Stefan's expressions, like 'image pig' for a wild pig which he had seen as a picture, 'kiss' for anything damp that touched his face; or 'letter' for any piece of paper; 'oulish' for ugly or evil, derived from 'ghoulish', but co-determined by 'owl'; and 'bagschool for satchel'.[32] He also noticed his child's mimicry. When Stefan tried to say 'quiet' he raised his finger in the air, imitating his mother. Benjamin's tenderness is obvious in his recordings: 'After Stefan had been undressed he was left alone in the room and he cried. When Dora came in to see him after a little while he said: Wipe nose and dry tears all by self.'[33]

Stefan's doting father worked long hours pursuing his writing. After a spell of such studiousness he would be away for a short time. When he returned, Dora recounted how his son had missed him: Stefan had gone to the nursemaid Grete and told her to be very quiet for 'he must do his work now'. Then he had climbed the stairs and opened two doors to enter his absent father's room. There he waited patiently in the dark, imagining his father still present, and when Grete entered he ordered: 'Grete do not disturb him. He really has to work.'[34]

Benjamin's fascination with childhood was evident in his notion of mimesis which ran throughout his philosophical oeuvre, especially in 'Doctrine of the Similar' and his theories of 'mimetic capability'. Language, imagination, the development of the relationship between the external world and the mind, were woven into the many layers of his work. But his intellectual analysis was always gentle, founded upon personal and often humorous observation: 'Mammy, the cat is laughing.

It is really laughing. But I don't know why it is laughing. It is laughing even when I don't say anything funny. But perhaps cat jokes are different.'[35] Benjamin noted this night-time conversation with his son: 'He is lying in bed, pulls his pyjamas up. I ask: why? "It is modern, you know. . . . One has to see the stomach, the navel, at all times, because then one knows what holds one together." ("It is modern, you know" has been one of his turns of phrase for a while.)'[36]

During these early years of fatherhood, Ernst Bloch, by now a close friend, observed: 'Benjamin was rather whimsical and eccentric, but in a very fruitful way. . . . we spent long nights in conversation.'[37] But aside from whimsy and parenthood, Benjamin's life encompassed a number of struggles. Financially, his writing did not secure enough income to support the needs of a growing family and he was still dependent upon his wealthy parents. However as the family's allowance became ever more necessary, it also became ever more precarious. Finally, after many painful negotiations with his father he was advanced some of his inheritance to tide him over until he could establish a profession. Nevertheless, throughout the 1920s Benjamin's world held together and he embarked on a period of immense creativity.

Long hours were spent in quiet and solitude, punctuated by energizing conversation. He worked on his periodical *Angelus Novus* (summer 1921); a translation of Charles Baudelaire's *Tableaux Parisiens* (1923); his essay on Goethe's *Elective Affinities* (1924). During this time his first publications appeared in the *Frankfurter Zeitung* as well as in the *Literarische Welt*. Benjamin also began one of his greatest works, the *Arcades Project*. He completed a first volume of a translation of Proust (*A L'ombre des jeunes filles en fleurs* (1927) and published both *One Way Street* (1928) and the *Origin of German Tragic Drama* (1928). He was sowing the seeds of some twentieth-century literary-philosophical classics.

What was unique about Benjamin was a sensitivity to his surroundings that would normally be associated with a 'Romantic', writing about nature.

Appreciation of a city's cultural riches, of architecture or art, however, was usually steeped in an urbane sophistication, often coupled with a degree of pomp or snobbishness. At the very least it was a *worldly* appreciation. Romantic poetry, on the other hand, was a realm where one could discover more innocent, unguarded sensitivities, as in the poems of Keats and Wordsworth. Benjamin was unique in that he brought a sense of childlike spontaneity and unguarded sensual unity with the world around him with regard to his observations of the city – not only as far as its architecture and formal culture was concerned, but also apropos its day-to-day mouldings. Domestic, functional or even business and industrial aspects of the city were experienced by him through a mood of mysticism. Everything had a presence for Benjamin, whether the sound of a roller blind in the window, the shadow of a terracotta plant pot in a courtyard, a distant train, or a cobbled street. And the presence, the mysterious, spiritual presence of the city was part human – human history in the things made by unknown hands, touched, used, felt, experienced – as if things themselves had memories of the fingers that had made them, the people who had used them and the eyes that had beheld them over the centuries.

The kind of sensitivity with which Benjamin was equipped was one he had retained since childhood, honed by articulateness into thought and language so that he could bring to life an urban landscape. No hard-hitting prose, no 'modern' shock, no tough, self-conscious stylized urbanity, but an innocent wonder at the presence in all things. That was his gift. Wonder, a rite of passage into a new and magical world underlying what was usually taken for granted; a reopening of the gates of paradise in the form of untarnished, unguarded spontaneity. Benjamin explained:

Early on, I learned to disguise myself in words, which really were clouds. The gift of perceiving similarities is, in fact, nothing but a weak remnant of the old compulsion to become similar and to behave mimetically. In me, this compulsion acted through words. Not those that made me similar to well-behaved children, but those that made

me similar to dwelling places, furniture, clothes. I was distorted by
similarity to all that surrounded me. Like a mollusc in its shell, I had
my abode in the nineteenth century, which now lies before me like an
empty shell. I hold it to my ear. What do I hear? Not the noise of field
artillery or of dance music à la Offenbach, not even the stamping of
horses on the cobblestone or fanfares announcing the changing of the
guard. No, what I hear is the brief clatter of the anthracite as it falls
from the coal scuttle into a cast-iron stove, the dull pop of the flame as
it ignites the brass mantle, and the clinking of the lampshade on its
brass ring when a vehicle passes by in the street. And the other sounds
as well, like the jingling of the basket of keys, or the ringing of the two
little bells at the front and back steps. . .[38]

The nineteenth century had witnessed the blossoming of Romanticism
as a reaction against increasing industrialization. Benjamin turned those
sensibilities that were usually directed against modern civilization
towards it instead. He felt aspects of the Romantic in what human hands
were creating. Man the maker was not Benjamin's enemy; he was not the
destroyer of a meaningful world. Other mystical philosophers such as
Heidegger used Romantic arguments to denounce modernity. Heidegger
even built on the Jewish philosopher Husserl's ideas to develop these
views, regarding modernity as the vanquishing of a more natural past, a
form of violence that needed to be met with equal violence.

In a letter to Theodor Wiesengrund-Adorno, Benjamin voiced his
concern about the Nazi philosopher:

Paris

10.6.1935

Dear Herr Wiesengrund,

. . . in the meantime I am much looking forward to receiving more
information from you concerning your critical destruction of the
'intuition of essences'. Would not Husserl himself welcome such a

destruction now that he has been able to see what has become of this instrument at the hands of someone like Heidegger?[39]

Cordially yours,

Walter Benjamin.

In a desperate attempt to negate Heidegger's views, Benjamin also wrote vitriolically that he needed: 'to initiate a small reading group in order "to demolish Heidegger" '.[40]

But Benjamin was no fighter, not even intellectually. His way of being was not to assert or advocate a point of view, but to delve into the secrets of everyday life. For this he needed quiet, to silence the busy human voices around him and to listen to things themselves. Hence, Benjamin was drawn to solitude and to wandering. Not to escape from people as an aim, but to escape from noise and distraction so that he could enjoy the rich melodies of the myriad of treasures revolving around him. The world was an Aladdin's cave for Benjamin, a trove of exciting secrets which he eagerly sought out. Solitary wanderings, on foot in the street, in a café, or longer journeys – all held the same delicious reward for him. He claimed his desire for travel was kindled by his grandmother's postcards from far-flung places.[41]

During his life in Berlin, as the seasons changed, Benjamin's curiosity about the world would resurface each spring. Berlin was his home, his roots, the place around which all things pivoted. But, lured by the treasures of Europe, when the spring came, like a child drawn to an enchanting book of fairy tales, he was eager to turn to, and devour, the next page. In *Berlin Childhood*, Benjamin described the inspiration for one of his adventures. Drawn to every 'winter morning' and 'winter evening' where, as he put it, 'I meet with the memory of a wintry Berlin', he had a fascination for icy landscapes.[42] So one summer in 1930 he undertook a lonesome journey to the frozen North. In July he boarded a boat in Hamburg and set off for several weeks on a voyage across the North Sea to the Arctic Circle and northern Finland, returning to Germany via the Baltic

Sea.[43] In his *Berlin Chronicle* he wrote: 'the dunes of the Baltic landscape have appeared to me like a fat morgana here on Chausseestrasse, supported only by the yellow, sandy colours of the station building and the boundless horizon opening in my imagination behind its walls.'[44] The northern sea – 'a series of halls, stretching northwards, filled with the sound of waves, and on their walls seagulls, towns, flowers, furniture, statues and always, day and night, light streaming through the windows.'[45] In this manner Benjamin wrote a piece entitled the 'Northern Sea Cycle' until his ship docked at Sopot in August 1930.[46]

The 'Northern Sea Cycle' shone with Benjamin's characteristic style of philosophy: the *Denkbild*, or thought-image.[47] This comprised a unique form of philosophy, not the imposition of a theory upon the world but a way of letting objects themselves reveal their secrets. It was a sensuous philosophy, not the controlled, clinical observation of the scientist, but the abandonment of the poet or mystic. Look, touch, smell the object and let it speak for itself: the world will reveal its riddles if you only abandon yourself to the gentle act of listening.

Books, of course, were favourite items for Benjamin to 'listen to'. With all the gluttony of a child before a box of sweets, when he returned from his travels he approached with delight the task of unpacking his book collection:

> I am unpacking my library. Yes, I am. The books are not yet on the shelves, not yet touched by the mild boredom of order. I cannot march up and down their ranks to pass them in review before a friendly audience. You need not fear any of that. Instead I must ask you to join me in the disorder to crates that have been wrenched open, the air saturated with the dust of wood, the floor covered with torn paper, to join me among piles of volumes that are seeing daylight again after two years of darkness, so that you may be ready to share with me a bit of mood – it is certainly not an elegiac mood, but rather, one of anticipation – which these books arouse in the genuine collector....

Now I am on the last half-emptied case and it is way past midnight. Other thoughts fill me other than the ones I am talking about – not thoughts but images, memories ... memories of rooms where these books had been housed, of my student's den in Munich, of my room in Bern, of the solitude on the Lake of Brienz, and finally of my boyhood room, the former location of only four or five of the several thousand volumes that are piled up around me. O bliss the collector ...

... ownership is the most intimate relationship that one can have to objects. Not that they come alive in him [the collector]; it is he who lives in them. So I have erected one of his dwellings, with books as building stones, before you, and now he is going to disappear inside, as is only fitting.[48]

Benjamin's bliss in his world of travel and books couldn't last. By the early 1930s the storm clouds were gathering over Weimar Germany and he was about to be driven from his private sanctuary by their inexorable force. Only a few years after he had unpacked his library in Berlin, his friend Scholem would write to him on 26 July 1933:

... the latest Berlin laws are of course designed to usher in the final campaign of plundering. Have you actually taken steps to rescue at least your library from confiscation as property of an 'enemy of the German people'? ... We are appalled to hear that valuable libraries have been sold off for absurdly trifling sums, in the rush to emigrate – because what cannot be taken along has simply lost all value.[49]

A pain in Benjamin's right leg jerked him uncomfortably back to the reality of his room on the Spanish island of Ibiza, 1933. From his dirty mattress amidst the unbearably hot summer, he reached out, grabbing the only stationery that was available, to write to his dear friend Scholem. The letter was drafted on irregularly sized, greyish-blue paper, of a kind Benjamin never normally used.

Fonda Miramar

San Antonio, Ibiza (Baleares)

July 31, 1933

Dear Gerhard,

The mere sight of this stationery should suffice to make you, as the unchallenged authority on my letter writing, realize that something is amiss. And the fact exonerates me at least part of the three weeks I let go by without thanking you for the beautiful letter you sent me for my birthday. In particular, it covers me for the continued non-appearance of the notes on language you are entitled to.

You see, I have been ill for about a fortnight now. And because the outbreak of illness – not very serious in itself – coincided with the fits of July heat . . . I had my hands full to keep myself somewhat going under such difficult circumstances.

. . . With regard to my poor health, I have a very unpleasant inflammation of a wound on my lower right thigh. Luckily it started up just when I happened to be in the town of Ibiza for a few hours. In San Antonio, my situation would have become grotesque. I live here in a hotel room at one peseta a day – the price indicates what the room looks like – and I drag myself through the town for unavoidable errands. If the situation doesn't improve in the next two or three days, I will be forced to keep myself completely immobile. A German doctor whom I have unearthed here delights in painting daily pictures of my chances of dying, should a complication arise. So much for today. With kindest regards,

Yours, Walter.[50]

Benjamin's misery did not abate. He spent the long summer and autumn of 1933 bedridden. Working with difficulty, his financial situation deteriorated, together with his health. Far from the town, far indeed even from the nearest village, his worst fears were coming true.

Fonda Miramar

San Antonio, Ibiza (Baleares)

September 1, 1933

Dear Gerhard,

Nearly a month has gone by since I received your last letter. But this time I don't have to search for reasons for my long silence, even though I would gladly trade actual reasons for such embarrassment. First, I have hardly emerged at all from poor health over the last two months. It is nothing serious. But periods of exhaustion and complications in the external circumstances of my life are meshing so perfectly into a chain of mishaps, that I am held in check for days or weeks . . .

Regarding my condition, I am once again lying sick in bed, suffering from a very painful inflammation of the leg. Doctors, or even medicine, are nowhere to be found, since I am living in the country, thirty minutes away from the village of San Antonio. Under such primitive conditions, the fact that you can hardly stand on your feet, hardly speak the native tongue, and in addition even have to work, tend to bring you up against the margins of what is bearable. As soon as I have regained my health, I will return to Paris. But I do not know how long [it] will take. In any case, you should keep writing to this address . . .

A fond farewell, and let me hear from you soon,

Yours, Walter.[51]

Struggling not only to obtain food but also with 'the incredible difficulties endured in obtaining any water', his living conditions were shocking, 'if you knew how bad the worst mattress in the world is (I am lying on it) . . .' he wrote.[52] Having always dreaded a beggarly, cut-off existence, the Nazis were consigning Benjamin inexorably to both – from friends to isolation, from riches to rags.

He determined to make it back to Paris, to a world with which he was familiar, as close to Berlin as possible. For if he were to die, and he feared doing so, he would at least be surrounded by an environment that had meaning:

> I do not know when I will be capable of making the trip to Paris. I am bedridden here in the countryside, virtually without help, with no doctor, and unable to take a few steps without the greatest pain. . . . many sores, small ones, that have become infected, and – whether from the heat or my problematic diet of recent months – an obvious shortage of recuperative powers.[53]

He begged, borrowed and sold possessions to raise money for travelling and finally managed to haul himself to the French capital, where he wrote on 16 October 1933 the following to his friend Gerhard Scholem:

> . . . let me just sketch out my situation. I arrived in Paris seriously ill. By this I mean that I had not recovered at all while on Ibiza, and the day I was finally able to leave coincided with the first in a series of very severe attacks of fever. I made the journey under unimaginable conditions, and, immediately after my arrival here, malaria was diagnosed. Since then a rigorous course of quinine has cleared my head, even though my strength has yet to be fully restored. I was considerably weakened by the numerous hardships of my stay on Ibiza – not least of which was the wretched diet.
>
> You won't be surprised to learn that I am faced here with as many questions as there are street corners in Paris. . . .
>
> I have hardly been out of bed, and hence have been unable to activate my local contacts . . .[54]

Benjamin did finally recover and make contact with friends. Mostly, he spent the rest of his exile in Paris, which although an expensive and difficult environment, gave him access to great libraries and the intellectual atmosphere that he craved. In France he met other German artists and intellectuals who had also become refugees, including Hannah Arendt and her partner Heinrich Blücher. However, Benjamin continued to live in poverty and spent the next few years in hotel rooms, boarding houses, and occasionally a begged or borrowed apartment across Paris or in other European cities. He sometimes found shelter with friends such as Bertolt Brecht, staying with him in exile in Svendborg, Denmark, and he also managed to spend a short but precious time with his ex-wife Dora Sophie and beloved son Stefan when they were safely ensconced in San Remo, Italy.

During the mid-1930s Benjamin also managed to eke a living from his writings. These included a few last publications for the German *Frankfurter Zeitung*. His financial situation, however, continued to deteriorate, until relief came in the form of the Frankfurt Institute for Social Research. This was a group of German-Jewish, left-leaning philosophers of awesome reputation who by this time had relocated to New York. They even paid him a regular stipend and he strengthened his ties with the most eminent of these, Theodor Adorno and Max Horkheimer. In 1936 they published what was to become one of Benjamin's most famous essays, 'The Work of Art in the Age of Mechanical Reproduction', in their journal, *Zeitschrift für Sozialforschung*.

But these were tough years, and time was running out. In February 1939 the Gestapo were on to Benjamin as an opponent of their regime, and in a letter dated 26 May the German Embassy wrote to inform him of his expatriation: Benjamin was stripped of his German citizenship. He wrote that 'the nightmare that oppresses people in this situation' was 'not so much the upcoming day in prison as the concentration camp that threatened after years in prison.'[55]

The threat of the concentration camp began to loom ever nearer when on 1 September Hitler invaded Poland and Britain and France were now at war with Germany. Benjamin had already lost his home, his livelihood, his country and his citizenship – now if he wasn't careful he would lose his liberty. As one commentator put it:

La drôle de guerre between France and Hitler's Germany, did not begin with fighting on the Maginot Line or in any other location, but internally: against French Communists and socialists as well as against despised foreigners, above all German-speaking emigrants who, regardless of whether they were anti-fascists or not, were now regarded indiscriminately as Hitler's Fifth Column.[56]

With the advent of war all Germans, Austrians, Czechs, Slovaks and Hungarians aged between seventeen and fifty were immediately rounded up in France. These foreigners were 'interned' in temporary camps. Those in Paris were sent to the Stade de Colombes, a football stadium that was not adequate to house hundreds of thousands of refugees. Benjamin was among them. 'Lying on the terraces, huddled up in stone benches, strolling along the cinder track, killing time playing cards or chess, racking their brains over how the French government could act in such defiance of international law', they were then bundled into buses like prisoners of war and transported to the Gare d' Austerlitz under military escort, and thence in sealed carriages to formal internment camps. Benjamin was finally incarcerated by the French authorities in a camp near Nevers, a small town in the Loire valley roughly halfway between Paris and Lyon.[57]

Held for three months, Benjamin was finally released at the end of November 1939. He returned to Paris where he wrote in an understatement to his friend Scholem, on 25 November 1939, 'I was obliged, after war was declared, to go to an internment camp, like all German refugees.'[58] However, the experience of internment was so horrifying to him that it determined the course of later events and pushed Benjamin towards a fateful end.

In the French capital, in spite of the war, Benjamin worked determinedly and completed his theses 'On the Concept of History'. Calm, but still isolated and lonely, he composed his last ever letter to his friend Scholem on 11 January 1940, writing: 'The isolation that is my natural

condition has increased owing to present circumstances.'[59] His return to
Paris had been dangerous and by May 1940 he had more than solitude to
concern him. Hitler's armies opened the offensive on the Western Front
and broke through the French defences, forcing their way through the
Ardennes and pushing deep into France. They converged on Paris, where
Benjamin had mistakenly believed he was safe.

Once again, as he had done in 1933 in Berlin, Benjamin looked down
from an apartment window in a European capital on to cobbled streets
teeming with families fleeing for their lives. But this time it was Paris
1940 and the situation was even more urgent. A mass exodus was
underway and over 2 million people were fleeing by car, horse-drawn
carriage, or on foot, taking with them what little they could rescue of
their belongings in wheelbarrows, children's carts or simply tied onto
their backs. They trudged with 5 to 6 million Belgians and French
from the north and east who were also fleeing the Nazis. These
refugees formed a never-ending caravan of bundles of clothes, piles
of possessions and human misery traipsing towards the south of
France.[60]

Benjamin joined the exodus. He fled first to Lourdes, a small market
town lying in the foothills of the Pyrenees, which was already overrun
with refugees. He did not feel secure and was becoming increasingly
convinced that he had to get out of France altogether. In a letter to
Theodor Adorno, 'Teddie', written in Lourdes on 2 August 1940,
Benjamin expressed his anxiety:

My dear Teddie,

I was delighted to receive your letter of 15 July for a number of
reasons – for one, because you kindly remembered my birthday . . .

. . . as you know, things currently look no better for me personally
than they do for my works. The circumstances that suddenly befell me
in September could easily be repeated at any time, but now with a
wholly different prospect. In the last few months, I have seen a good

number of people who have not so much simply drifted out of their steady . . . existence as *plunged headlong* from it overnight . . .

The complete uncertainty about what the next day, even the next hour, may bring has dominated my life for weeks now. I am condemned to read every newspaper (they now come out on a single sheet here) as if it were a summons served to me in particular, to hear the voice of fateful tidings in every radio broadcast . . .[61]

In his attempt to leave France, Benjamin went to the Consulate in Marseilles to try to get the necessary permit. But the visit was unsuccessful. Arrangements had been underway for some time, painstaking negotiations having been undertaken by both of Benjamin's philosopher friends in America, Theodor Adorno and Max Horkheimer. They were trying to secure the necessary permit for him to exit France and enter the United States.

Benjamin wrote to Adorno, 'the prospect of hearing from the consulate in Marseilles renewed my hopes somewhat. A letter from the Consulate there would probably get me permission to go down to Marseille.' He continued:

I have heard something about your negotiations with Havana and your efforts concerning San Domingo. I am quite certain that you are doing everything humanly possible, and indeed 'more than humanly possible' . . . to help me. My great fear is that we have much less time at our disposal than we imagined. And although I would not have contemplated the possibility a fortnight ago, new information received has moved me to ask . . . [to] possibly obtain permission for me to visit Switzerland on a temporary basis. I realize that there is much to be said against trying this escape route, but there is one powerful argument in its favour: and that is time. If only this way out were possible![62]

Benjamin felt trapped and his fear was that the net was tightening. In August, he finally obtained a visa to the United States, successfully negotiated by the Frankfurt School. But in spite of the visa the authorities demanded further documents and he simply did not have them. Then his worst fear came true. On 24 September 1940 it was agreed that emigrants in the unoccupied parts of France were to be handed over to the Germans. Deportation would then await them. Benjamin could be picked up at any moment and interned, a transitory move towards a concentration camp.

Now, truly desperate, Benjamin had to get out of France immediately. But without the correct papers, the only way was to cross the French border illegally. This was perilous and he would have to elude the police at every stage. Perhaps he could depart for America from neutral Portugal, which he might reach via Spain?

Lisa Fittko, a friend of Benjamin's residing in southern France, had the following memory:

> I remember waking up in that narrow room under the roof where I had gone to sleep a few hours earlier. Someone was knocking at the door. It had to be the little girl from downstairs: I got out of my bed and opened the door. But it wasn't the child. I rubbed my half-closed eyes. It was one of our friends, Walter Benjamin. . . . Now how did he get here? – 'Gnädige Frau,' he said, 'please accept my apologies for this inconvenience.' The world was coming apart I thought, but not Benjamin's politesse. 'Ihr Herr Gemahl,' he continued, 'told me how to find you. He said you could take me across the border into Spain.' [The friend replied] 'But Mr. Benjamin, do you realize that I am not a competent guide in this region? I don't really know that road, I have never been up that way myself. . . . You want to take the risk?' – 'Yes,' he replied without hesitation. 'The real risk would be not to go.'[63]

On 25 September 1940, Benjamin began an escape from southern France across the Pyrenees. Lisa agreed to be his guide, but it was too risky to accompany him, a stranger, through the village, so she arranged to meet him in a special place halfway up a mountain. Benjamin had to find his own way to the arranged rendezvous.

Benjamin joined a hiking tour and hid amongst a group of tourists. Together they climbed through the grassy paths at the lower reaches of the Pyrenees. Then, when he arrived close to where he was to meet Lisa, Benjamin hid among the early autumnal foliage of the mountainside while the rest of the group descended back down to the village without him. He prayed that they would not notice his absence, and he was relieved as they disappeared out of sight. Then as the dusk spread, as if from the mountain itself, the shadows rising from beneath the rocks and from under the trees, he hid, hoping that Lisa his guide would make it, past the police in the village, to meet him. And as darkness descended and the red-browns of the September leaves faded, replaced by the more dramatic hues of the evening stars, Benjamin found a comfortable resting place and slept out in the open, under the slowly revolving night sky.

Early the next morning Lisa and a friend, Henny, with her son Joseph, who were both Jewish, began their perilous journey to meet Benjamin. The group mingled with the locals as they passed through the village. To escape detection by the police, they were carrying small canvas bags, 'musettes', and were even dressed like farmers. They made it safely out of the village and began their steep trek through the countryside. Benjamin waited from his hiding place in the mountains, senses alert, his heart beating faster at the bark of every dog or the footsteps of a possible passer-by. At last, by early afternoon he saw his guide and her friends. Such warm relief flooded over him. Now surely they would escape. They continued to ascend the mountain. The group were forced to walk for ten minutes followed by a one-minute break, because Benjamin's heart was weak and his health altogether poor. Nevertheless travelling in this fashion with many small rests, by afternoon they reached Portbou. This was a French-Spanish border town in the Pyrenees; a dramatic place, with the mountains behind and steep cliffs leading down to the ocean before them. It was a fitting image for a place of salvation.

Then the sublimity of the landscape was interrupted by a flash of a uniform. Spanish police intercepted them. Benjamin tried not to panic, they had the necessary permits he reassured himself. But his heart was racing inside his chest as the police pored over the measly paperwork. The whole group had transit visas to Spain, which were valid when they started the trip. However, the police pointed out that these had been made null and void overnight on orders of the Spanish government. Refugees were no longer allowed to cross through Spain. As if this were not bad enough, the government had also ordered that all refugees from France had to be sent back at once. Benjamin gazed disheartedly at the trampled grass on the path lying behind him and at the long way he had come.

Benjamin and his friends were escorted by the police to spend a night in a hotel, the Fonda de Francia in Portbou. Having been refused entry to Spain, they were to be taken back to France the next day. They were under observation in the hotel: 'and we were introduced to three policemen who were supposed to escort us to the French border in the morning', his friend explained. The hotel owner of the Fonda Francia had close connections to the Gestapo, and was renowned for sending back fleeing refugees to the Nazis. Benjamin had to eat in the presence of this owner and the Gestapo in the dining room that evening.

After dinner Benjamin went out into the corridor where it was cooler. He made a number of desperate last-bid phone calls, pleading for help. All to no avail. Evicted from his home, driven from a life of comfort to one of poverty, Benjamin had been made destitute, and had already been interned once before. He knew that the persecution would continue. He was in the Nazis' hands now and would eventually be sent from France back to Germany. Like all Jews, he knew what awaited him on his home soil – a concentration camp.[64]

After his failed phone calls, Benjamin retreated to his room. There, behind the heavy wooden door, he remembered a childhood game – hiding.

I already knew all the hiding places in the house, and would return to them as to a home ground where everything is sure to be in its familiar place. My heart would pound. I held my breath. . . . The child who stands behind the doorway curtain himself becomes something white that flutters, a ghost. The dining table under which he has crawled turns him into the wooden idol of the temple; its carved legs are four pillars. And behind the door, he is himself the door, is decked out in it like a weighty mask and, as a sorcerer, will cast a spell on all who enter unawares. Not for a fairy kingdom would he be found. . . . Whoever discovered me could hold me petrified as an idol under the table, could weave me as a ghost for all time into the curtain, confine me for life within the heavy door.

As a child, when Benjamin was bound to be caught, rather than cowering in fear, he would take the situation into his own hands and shout to reveal himself.

Should the person looking for me uncover my lair, I would give a loud shout to lose the demon that had transformed me – indeed, without waiting for the moment of discovery, would anticipate its arrival with a cry of self-liberation.[65]

To shout now when the Gestapo entered his room would be to no avail. Benjamin had only one option. So that evening, while the Gestapo enjoyed after-dinner drinks in the dining room downstairs, Benjamin took out a small phial he had been carrying in his pocket. It was, in his own words, a dose of morphine, enough 'to kill a horse'.

Benjamin swallowed the poison, his magic potion of 'self-liberation'.

In the Portbou register of deaths, a listing for a 'Walter Benjamin' was made. The death was recorded at 10 p.m. on 26 September 1940.

CHAPTER 7

Exile: Theodor Adorno

Benjamin's plight was just one example of a great intellectual destroyed by the Nazis. Persecution, poverty, flight, suicide, all these were common enough experiences for those hounded by the Third Reich. However, although in great danger, not all the German-Jewish philosophers lost their lives under Hitler. Some managed to escape their homeland and as books went up in a crackle of flames, a few lucky individuals found sanctuary abroad.

Theodor Adorno was one such person. Like Benjamin, he was quirky and charming. With equal intellectual insight and sensitivity, he was however, on the surface at least, a lot less of a tragic personality. Indeed this philosopher and musicologist, one of the most complex, abstract and formidable thinkers of the twentieth century, was often regarded as a comic figure, and was known in England as a dandy – a Charlie Chaplin of the philosophical world. He was also more able to survive, and his story tells the highs and lows of a genius in exile.

Escaping Germany, Adorno lived out the decade of the mid-1930s to the mid-1940s with his wife and fellow refugees on the West Coast of America. In a series of letters to his parents he described the charms and horrors of exile. In one particular letter, written on 8 February 1944, Theodor – Teddie – at that time forty years old, recounted an amusing incident involving the film star Greta Garbo.

My dears, . . .

On Sunday at Salka's for tea. Aside from the family (with old Frau Steuermann) there was only a sportily dressed woman who was vaguely familiar. I had only noticed that Salka told her our own names, but not vice versa, from which I inferred that she must be so famous that she expected us to know who she was anyway. It was only after having this thought that I recognized her as Garbo. . .[1]

Adorno went on to mention his pet dog Ali Baba:

Ali Baba waited in the car. He cropped up in the conversation, and Miss Garbo, who loves Afghans, requested that he be brought in. Now, Salka has three dogs of her own, two highly nervous setters and an enormous German shepherd that had just bitten Miss Garbo (it bites everyone). But the three monsters were locked away. So Ali was then allowed in. He smelled his colleagues, stormed about like mad – I have never seen him so beside himself – and suddenly, before we knew it, he had lifted his little leg by a book shelf and made his mark upon a book . . . in the presence of the supposedly most beautiful woman in the world . . .[2]

The joke of his dog peeing in front of a cinema icon was a glimpse of the absurd glamour typifying Adorno's displaced life. Residing on the West Coast of California, this Jewish-German émigré fraternized with many Hollywood stars. On several occasions he even met Charlie Chaplin:

One of the guests came up to say goodbye early while Chaplin was standing next to me. Unlike Chaplin, I extended my hand a little absent-mindedly and then jerked it back violently. The man saying goodbye was one of the main actors in the film *The Best Years of Our Life*. . . . He had lost one of his hands in the war and wore an artificial

claw made of iron, but very effective. When I shook his right hand and
responded to the pressure, I was very taken aback, but realizing at once
that I should not let Russell see my reaction under any circumstances,
I instantly transformed the shocked expression on my face into a
winning grimace which must have looked even more shocking. Scarcely
had the actor departed than Chaplin was already mimicking the scene.
So close to horror is the laughter that he provoked . . .[3]

The event was telling, for the chic social life that Adorno and others were
encountering in America was a far-flung world from that of Europe at
war. The iron claw of the wounded actor was not just a shock in itself but
a sudden reminder for Adorno of the horror that was happening abroad.
Through the handshake, Adorno felt with his flesh the sudden physical
presence of violence.[4]

Raised in Frankfurt am Main amidst the sophisticated architecture of
an old European city, Adorno and his wife Gretel now found themselves
living in California. Gretel described, in a letter to her parents-in-law, a
typical Los Angeles apartment:

> Today I would describe to you what our apartment looks like . . . one
> immediately enters the living room with a large window to the
> West . . .. The pieces of Biedermeier furniture stand next to the
> fireplace (which we do not use, however) facing the entrance,
> the grand piano is in the diagonal corner that slopes into the
> room . . .. books, sheet music, records manuscripts etc. still have to be
> ordered. . . .[5]

How incongruous the old European furniture must have looked in its
shiny, modern environment.

Old fashioned and as out of place as his furniture, in America,
Adorno must have seemed quaint. By 1944 he was middle-aged, his hair
thinning considerably and with dark, square-rimmed glasses breaking up

his otherwise rounded head and countenance. He was typically to be seen in a dark suit, this formal attire giving him a somewhat severe appearance, but it was softened by his elegant manners and the careful, thoughtful expression in his eyes. Short and somewhat stout, he was something of a stranger to physical exercise, though he more than compensated for this with his mental exertions. And his elegant, formal manners were no doubt out of kilter with his new Californian environment.

Many other Jewish émigrés lived in Los Angeles, including celebrity names such as the Hollywood film directors Max Reinhardt and Fritz Lang. Adorno socialized with them, as well as with the Nobel prize-winning writer Thomas Mann and the composers Arnold Schönberg and Béla Bartók. In a letter to his parents, Adorno mentioned: 'On Saturday evening we had dinner with the Dieterles, where Max Reinhardt was Gretel's dinner partner.'[6] Reinhardt was of Jewish ancestry – he had been born Maximilian Goldmann in Austria-Hungary – and after the *Anschluss* of Austria in 1938, he emigrated first to England, then to the United States. His films were banned by the Nazis. Among his many successes he directed *A Midsummer Night's Dream* with a cast that included James Cagney and Mickey Rooney. He ran the prestigious Reinhardt School of the Theatre in Hollywood, on Sunset Boulevard.

The Adornos' lives were interlinked with these iconic émigrés, not only socially but also domestically. For instance, when they moved house in California they had a very distinguished man to help them arrange their furniture. Adorno recounted in a letter to his mother:

Mumma, my animal,

So we moved house smoothly, without incident and very comfortably, without even a gramophone record or a glass being damaged; and the packers were perfectly charming. . . . The plans enclosed will give you an idea of the furnishings – *Fritz Lang* drew them up for us, so that we knew exactly where to put every piece of furniture.[7]

It was not everyone who could boast that the person who helped them to plan the arrangement of the furniture in their new home happened to be one of the most famous film directors in the world, Fritz Lang. His best-known film, *Metropolis*, had led him to be dubbed the 'Master of Darkness' and he had become synonymous with film noir. In Hollywood Lang went on to make dozens of silent and sound films, numerous classics, starring such greats as Spencer Tracy, and, in later years, Marilyn Monroe. Lang was a Jewish-German émigré of Austrian descent – it was on account of his mother's Jewish ancestry that he had been forced to flee the Nazis.

Both Reinhardt and Lang had directed their fellow German actress, Marlene Dietrich. An interesting moment had occurred for this actress. She had been approached by representatives of the Nazi Party to return from America to Germany, but had turned them down flat.[8] (She hated the Nazis and recorded a number of anti-Nazi records in German). She also raised funds for war bonds and entertained American troops on the front lines. Adorno became familiar with Dietrich through Reinhardt and Lang. In a letter to his parents he referred to her 'beauty of great radiance'[9] and also could not resist a mention of her 'famous legs'.[10]

In this Hollywood company with Fritz Lang and Lang's partner and later wife, Lily Latté, Adorno and his wife spent their Christmases. Perhaps Adorno was told the famous story circulated by Lang, in which Lang claimed that Joseph Goebbels had called him to his office for a meeting in which he banned the film *The Testament of Dr. Mabuse* (1933). However, because Goebbels was so impressed by Lang's film-making he offered him a position as the head of the German film studio UFA. Unbeknownst to Goebbels, however, Lang had already been planning to leave Germany for Paris, but the meeting with Goebbels ran on for so long that by the time it finished the banks were closed – Lang fled that night without any money. The story was not believed by everyone, but even so made entertaining listening for Lang's friends.

Meanwhile Adorno's wife bonded closely with Lang's partner Lily, as Adorno noted in a letter to his mother:

Gretel and Lily are inseparable; I am not involved with her, so you need not get any silly ideas. The best of company, very elegant; and yet totally unpretentious. You must know only that she is the partner – virtually the wife – of Fritz Lang, the most famous German film director, who is also incredibly successful here.[11]

Gretel herself wrote of Lily Latte, 'it turned out that she went to the same school as I did, and that all of us there fancied the young Latin teacher Rommel (!)'. *'Truly* a very close friend of ours' was how Adorno referred to Lily. She:

is thinking of going to N. Y. in the first days of October. If she does, it goes without saying that she will call on you. She is one of the very few friends in the true sense that we have found in America. An enchantingly graceful and personally *absolutely* reliable person whom I am sure you will like a great deal. . . . So receive her kindly and you will enjoy yourselves.[12]

As the philosopher from central Europe mingled with the Hollywood elite of Los Angeles, this home away from home had a fantasy feel. Adorno described it as:

a land of such plenty one can surely live in paradise . . . have you ever eaten alligator pears? If not you must buy some in the nearest fruit shop for a few cents. One takes out the stone, and fills the hole with a dressing of vinegar, oil, salt and pepper and possibly a little Worcester sauce. It is one of the most delicious things one can obtain in America.[13]

But for all its chic, the German Jews were in America not out of choice, but necessity. Writing to his parents, Adorno explained how he had been fired under the Nazi legislation: 'I am fully aware of what you went through in Germany, and had myself, incidentally, been thrown out of the university and robbed of any opportunity for work already about five years beforehand.'[14]

For all the opulent escapism of his social life Adorno was homesick. Initially he was ill at ease with the climate. 'There is an altogether inhuman heat here . . .'[15] he explained, and he often complained of 'the unwavering sunshine.'[16] The landscape also left him feeling alien:

> On Monday we drove through the Nebraska – very monotonous, nothing but cornfields (Who eats all that corn?) We traveled through the Rockies in the state of Wyoming on Monday night, and did not see a thing or even notice the difference in altitude. Tuesday through snowy Utah with the big salt lake. The landscape seems strange, with those mountains that suddenly shoot up out of the plains like pyramids, and increasingly disappear as one approaches Nevada.[17]

> One actually has the feeling that this part of the world is inhabited . . . by gasoline stations and hot dogs.[18]

These seemingly trivial observations masked a deeper unease. Adorno sensed danger. One: 'should be *extremely careful*, especially when going out alone. For America is not a land of walkers, but of drivers; on foot, one is hopelessly in the minority and one has to look both ways *at least three times* whenever crossing the street. . . . Furthermore, I would avoid leaving large sums of money in the house . . . the safety standards are particularly unsatisfactory . . .'[19] But Adorno's anxiety went deeper than mere homesickness. He had an underlying, constant worry for the life of his friends left behind in Germany. He also suffered another more sinister anguish, a glimpse of which could be seen in a letter to his family:

> I still believe we should not take the attitude of the cigarette salesman who walks about saying 'In my heart, I have given up on Germany'. . . .

Not because I have any illusion about Germany, but rather because I have none about the *world*. Fascism in Germany, which is inseparable from anti-Semitism, is not a psychological anomaly of the German national character. It is a universal tendency. . . . The conditions for it – and I mean *all of them* . . . are at least as present here [America] as in Germany, however, and the barbaric semi-civilization of this country will spawn forms no less terrible than those in Germany. . . .[20]

He trembled at the idea of the encroachment of fascism into his erstwhile refuge America:

I consider that the solution . . . that the Jews should mingle with the others, out of the question. It is too late. Essentially I am convinced that one is hopelessly trapped, regardless of where one may be. And it was this conviction that was the root of my resistance towards emigration. . . . If one is definitely going to be struck dead, I thought, then at least in the place where one belongs. . . . The only chance to survive the horror, and by no means one that I rate highly, is for fascism to collapse in Germany before it breaks out here. Aside from that fact I would prefer not to die amidst fear and horror. . .[21]

He confessed his horror in a private letter to his parents:

I consider the war lost . . . even the most dreadful fear fantasies are still surpassed by reality. I am now unable to regain my balance even to a moderate degree, which has never happened to me before, am barely sleeping at all, and stare as if paralyzed into the black abyss sucking everything into its eddies and destroying it.[22]

Although confiding in his family, Adorno hid his terror from his fellow exiles. As he stoically continued with the outer appearance of a normal life, his number of friends grew each day. They came to include William

Dieterle, a previously famous German actor and director who made films for Hollywood. There were many mentions of dinners in Adorno's correspondence: 'the Dierterles will be coming on Monday'[23] and 'Our evening with the Dieterles yesterday was a very pleasant one'.[24] But however great their prestige, no amount of success could protect the Jews from the rise of international fascism.

Adorno was not simply paranoid to imagine fascism brushing against American shores. The German Consulate under the Nazis was active in Los Angeles from 1933 to 1941 and arranged rallies of the American Nazi Party close to where Adorno was living. The conservative German-language press including the *California Staatszeitung*, the *Sued-California Deutsche Zeitung* and the *California Demokrat* all gave support to Nazi Germany. An outspoken Nazi paper the *California Weckruf* was published from 1935 to 1938 by a central Nazi organization on the West Coast called the German-American Volksbund. The film industry itself was not immune from the threat. The German Consulate arranged the visit of the collaborator Leni Riefenstahl, the National Socialist film director, who had travelled to America with her film of the 1936 Berlin Olympics and visited Los Angeles in 1938. Whereas Adorno's film friends refused to meet this friend of Hitler's, there were those within the film industry who were only too keen – for instance, Walt Disney.[25]

Nazi rallies sprung up amidst the sanctuary of the exiles. On 30 April 1939 two thousand German American Bund members came to hear West Coast Bund leader Hermann Max Schwinn and the 'American Führer' Fritz Kuhn. The stage was draped in swastika banners.[26] For Adorno and his Jewish friends, it felt as though the net was closing in and that soon there would be no place left to hide.

Hanns Eisler, born in Leipzig, the son of a Jewish philosopher, also became a great friend of Adorno. Eisler was a composer who had worked closely with Brecht and had been forced into exile along with Brecht on account of his Jewish ancestry. In New York City, Eisler taught composition at the New School and wrote experimental chamber and documentary music. Moving shortly before the Second World War to Los Angeles, Eisler composed several Hollywood film scores, two of which – *Hangmen Also Die!* and *None but the Lonely Heart* – were nominated for Oscars. Also working on *Hangmen Also Die!* were Brecht himself, who wrote the story, and Adorno's director friend Fritz Lang. The films expressed the hope that besides the innocent, the brutal were also mortal. The only hope for Adorno and his friends seemed to be that the fascists themselves would succumb to death, before they destroyed every living Jew.

Adorno and Eisler worked together and later co-authored the book *Composing for the Films*. One day Adorno wrote excitedly:

Los Angeles, 21.12.1942
[and]
429 West 117th Street
New York
21 December 1942

My dears,
We have something pleasing to report: Hanns Eisler, with whom I am on very good terms (and Gretel and his very charming wife), and who, as you probably know, is director of the Rockefeller Film Music Project, and now has to write a book about it, has asked me to write it together with him. The official confirmation from the publisher (Oxford University Press) came yesterday, stating that we both have the status as authors and will split the royalties 50:50. As I had made the preparations long in advance, I will be able to manage it comfortably in my spare time. I think it will be a very substantial external success. Eisler is being extremely loyal. Fond regards once again.[27]

While war raged in Europe the exiles continued with their creative endeavours. They worked with a passion, attempting to fight the forces of destruction with those of creativity. Eisler composed his two most notable works of the 1930s and 1940s, the monumental *Deutsche Sinfonie* (1935–57), a choral symphony based on poems by Brecht, and the *Hollywood Songbook* (1938–43) which, with lyrics by Brecht, Hölderlin and Goethe, established Eisler's reputation as one of the twentieth century's great composers. Meanwhile Adorno continued with his philosophical work. Beneath the apparently innocuous and slightly comic spectacle of this quaintly closeted European gentleman, was a man attempting to come to grips with the horror of fascism. While he relaxed in company, with impeccable manners and sentimentally indulged his pet dog, he used his intellectual skills to understand the horror of his own country. 'And as I am fated to be a seismograph, and in a certain sense think more with my nerve ends than with a calculator faculty, I am at present disorientated by shock.'[28] To his parents he wrote: 'I cannot tell you how much I enjoyed your letters. They are a true ray of hope in these immeasurably horrific times, and I am not exaggerating when I say that the present time is worse for me than anything previous . . .'[29]

Labouring to understand the brutality that lay lurking beneath the surface of apparent civilization, Adorno dwelt upon his subject minute by minute, hour by hour, day by day for weeks, months, years. He worked with a frenzy to the point of exhaustion and illness, 'I am in such an exhausted and overworked state as I have never experienced before'. 'I am keeping my head above water by working desperately.'[30] Unravelling how supposedly civilized people could embrace barbarism became his life's work. And he wasn't going to flinch in the face of what he encountered. He wasn't going to excuse his generation, his country, the human heart or mind. No simplistic, mechanical explanation of poverty, social change, historical occurrence was going to suffice for him. He was going to dig deep into the roots of the human psyche and the very essence of the modern Western world. He built a new philosophy to explain Nazism by drawing upon the philosophical canon from the ancient Greeks to the eighteenth-century thinkers of the Enlightenment. Immersing himself in Kant, Hegel, Nietzsche and Freud, he put together the ideas for the modern philosophical classic, *Dialectic of Enlightenment*.[31]

As well as Adorno, other intellectual refugees confronted the horrors of fascism in their work. Some were of the eminence of Arnold Schönberg. Adorno wrote that his wife Gretel 'got on splendidly with [the wife of] Schönberg. She too is much nicer than she used to be. It would be superb if this relationship were to remain untroubled.'[32] Schönberg in fact became a regular part of Adorno's small group. Writing to his parents, Adorno described how apart from work there was 'nothing new, we work mostly in the garden, go to bed with the chickens and meet with a small, and as Else would say, "select" circle of people, aside from the Institute ... Eisler, Schönberg, Brecht ... that's about all.'[33] Schönberg, an Austrian Jew connected to the expressionist movement, was the leader of the Second Viennese School – he went on to pioneer innovations in atonal composition. But during the rise of the Nazi Party in Austria his music had been labelled, alongside swing and jazz, as degenerate – he had been forced to flee. Adorno was mesmerized by him: 'On Sunday we heard Schönberg's latest work, a piano concerto, broadcast from New York. ... It is [a] quite extraordinary, indescribably convincing and mature work that can only be compared to Beethoven's late style. The performance and transmission were excellent. I called the old man afterwards and he was very happy.'[34]

Other musical heavyweights such as Béla Bartók, the Hungarian composer and pianist, regarded along with Franz Liszt as his country's most eminent musician, also emigrated to America under the threat of Nazism. Adorno wrote:

I am introducing a concert broadcast by [the city radio station] tonight, involving a conversation with Béla Bartók about his music. (The second violin sonata will subsequently be played by Rudi and Eduard.) I prepared this conversation yesterday with Bartók. He is the most curious person one could imagine, a cross between a child and an old man, a quite extraordinary musician, but so naïve and obstinate that every word, even about his own music, has to be put in his mouth for him.[35]

Soirées became an established feature of Adorno's life. His 'pretty friend Lisa Minghetti',[36] was a violinist born in Vienna who performed across Europe.[37] Adorno often played the piano at recitals with Lisa: 'My dears, such a shame that you were not here on Christmas Eve, for it was quite splendid, and I played a great deal of chamber music with the excellent violinist Maaskoff and his wife (Lisa Minghetti).'[38] His letters to his parents make frequent mention of Lisa, who 'will be coming to make some music this afternoon'.[39]

But it felt as though any moment the bubble would burst. Adorno and his colleagues were condemned men. They were perched on the furthermost edge of the Western world with their backs to the Pacific Ocean. They had nowhere to run. Annihilation, Adorno believed, was not just possible but inevitable. Referring to the Allies, he had this to say: 'by the time they are armed and ready, Hitler will presumably have pocketed the rest of Europe. We are trying to keep a cool head and not be dumbed down by horror. But this horror has meanwhile taken on such proportions that even that is no easy matter, and one falls into a sort of frozen state, like the bird staring at the snake.'[40]

Beyond film and music Adorno's passions extended to literature. As already noted, the poet and playwright Bertolt Brecht was also in exile – although not Jewish, his Marxist convictions had led to persecution by the Nazis. He had reached California via Vladivostok in July 1941 and settled in Santa Monica.[41] Adorno and Brecht were friends and worked together. Brecht penned a poem entitled 'Hollywood':

Each morning I earn my daily bread
By going to the market where lies are bought
Full of hope
I take my place among the sellers.[42]

Adorno explained to his exiled parents, '[I] continue to relax, and hold on to what Brecht, in a beautiful poem, calls the refugee's occupation: hope.'[43]

Other émigré writers were even more notable. Adorno wrote: 'Tonight at Max's place with a few bigwigs, including Thomas Mann and his dear lady wife.'[44] Adorno recalled: 'We were Thomas Mann's guests on Tuesday, unfortunately with music, otherwise very nice.' And later Adorno and his wife returned the invitation and concluded: 'Our dinner with the Thomas Manns was a great success.'[45] Mann enjoyed immense fame and authority as *the* German novelist of the day. His work was modern, but synthesized ideas from the past. He was awarded the Nobel Prize for Literature in 1929, principally in recognition of his popular achievement with the epic *Buddenbrooks* (1901), *Der Zauberberg* (1924) (The Magic Mountain), and his numerous novellas and short stories. When Hitler came to power he was forced to flee to Switzerland, then when war broke out he emigrated to the United States in 1939. During the war, he made a series of anti-Nazi radio speeches, *'Deutsche Hörer!'* ('German Listeners!'). They were taped in the USA and then sent to Great Britain where the BBC transmitted them, hoping to reach German listeners.

When the Mann family moved to Pacific Palisades, in west Los Angeles, they lived not far from Adorno. Adorno writes of their initial friendship: 'We were invited to a premier ... as prominent refugees, without knowing why, along with Max, Thomas Mann, the Brechts and very few others ...'[46]

tomorrow we are invited, by ourselves, to the house of Thomas Mann. He read my *Philosophy of New Music* and was so impressed that he wants to discuss it in detail with me and read me parts of his new novel, about a musician (the protagonist is somehow based on Schönberg), on which he would like to know my opinion. Well, perhaps he will become Reichspräsident. ... He is very pleasant, friendly and cultivated, in any case, even if he is no longer at the height of his intellectual powers, and we enjoy his company.[47]

Meanwhile, on 27 September 1943, Mann noted in his diary:

> In Adorno's text.
>
> He came to dinner with his wife.
>
> At the table discussed details of the philosophy of music.
>
> Afterwards reading of the chapter of lectures.
>
> Intimacy with music confirmed with praise.
>
> Objections to details, some of which can easily be taken into account, others hardly at all. On the whole, served to reassure me.[48]

Soon after, Adorno and Mann worked avidly together. Mann was writing *Doktor Faustus* (1947), the story of the corruption of German culture in the years before and during the Second World War. The novel focused on the composer Adrian Leverkühn, who was based upon Schönberg. Mann sought detailed advice from Adorno on this and all the other musical aspects of the novel.

The European culture that all these iconic refugees represented was deeply under threat. According to Adorno:

> I am quite certain that the madness of fascism once it has taken hold of the earth ... [will leave little to] be salvaged of those things on which a meaningful existence for us once depended. I do not like to use such grand words, but what is going on here is not simply a world at war anymore, but rather the collapse of [a] form of culture ...[49]

Others had more optimism. His fellow philosopher in exile Max Horkheimer, Adorno wrote: 'entertains the hope that one will perhaps find a hiding-place after all to survive the end of the world – for that is what it is, I have no illusions.'[50] But what hiding place would be left if the entire Western world were to succumb to fascism? The only hiding place most of the Jewish intelligentsia could imagine was their work. As

Adorno wrote: 'To survive not purely cling to life at all costs, although that is of interest too, but in order to secure some of our insights, which might in future times prove not entirely worthless for humanity.'[51] They worked to try to preserve European culture itself.

The philosophers in Adorno's circle were, in the main, part of the 'Frankfurt School'. This consisted of thinkers, critics and social scientists who had formed the Frankfurt Institute for Social Research in 1929. When it had become impossible to operate as a Jew in Germany, Max Horkheimer had moved the institute to America. Horkheimer was the School's first prominent thinker. He had grounded philosophy in social reality and demanded an ethical dimension to all theorizing. This combination of philosophy, ethics and social science generated 'critical theory', an intellectual movement that became very influential across the world. Horkheimer, like the other Frankfurt School members, drew upon Marx and Freud, but also upon the same German traditions that Hitler and later Nazi thinkers worshipped. In spite of the anti-Semitic strands running through both German Idealism and Romanticism, Jewish-German philosophers were heavily indebted to these movements.[52]

'Soft head' became Adorno's nickname for Horkheimer. As he explained, in America 'we have now adopted the names of Indian chiefs: Max is called "soft head", Gretel, in keeping with an older tradition is called "three lamb-vultures", and I am simply "Big Ox". As you see, I shall soon have lost my wits, and if I carry on like this I will surely be given the professorship in Oxford for which I was previously too highbrow.'[53] Adorno had worked fanatically beside Horkheimer: '[I] completely revised, i.e. rewrote, a long essay by Max on the Jewish question together with him and Gretel. We spent the last week working literally day and night on this most interesting piece of work, at such a pace that Max broke down immediately after its conclusion and went to bed with fever.'[54]

Another prominent member of the Frankfurt School was Herbert Marcuse, born on 19 July 1898. Heavily influenced by Freud as well as Nietzsche, Hegel and Marx, Marcuse's best-known works included *Eros and Civilization, One-Dimensional Man* and *The Aesthetic Dimension*. Poignantly, back in the early days of his career, his thesis had been rejected by Martin Heidegger. While in America, Marcuse provided valuable information against the Nazis, undertaking work for the American intelligence agency, what would later become the CIA. Adorno kept up an excellent correspondence and working relationship with Marcuse, though Adorno met him less frequently than other intellectuals.

Frederick Pollock was also one of the earliest members of the Institute for Social Research before it became an adjunct to the University of Frankfurt. Born to a factory worker, he went on to study philosophy in Frankfurt am Main where he wrote his thesis on Marx's labour theory of value. Pollock was a lifelong friend of Horkheimer and always an intimate of the Institute. They had a mutual enthusiasm for a 'good Apricot Brandy'.[55]

These working friendships with Horkheimer, Marcuse and Pollock were essential to Adorno, to help him try to save 'the sinking ship of European culture'. In addition to his émigré community, Adorno had another, more private, way of retaining the past. Out of nostalgia for his youth, his childhood and his family he tried to preserve *his* Germany. This was facilitated in part through close contact with his parents, wife and old friends, and it was also aided by his penchant for memory and reflection.

Since earliest childhood, Adorno had grown up surrounded by beauty. He was born in Frankfurt on 11 September 1903 and christened Theodor Adorno Wiesengrund. Later he would come to refer to himself only as Adorno, using his maternal family name to avoid the discrimination associated with the Jewish Wiesengrund. He was raised as the only child of his musician mother Maria and affluent wine merchant father. Adorno therefore grew up in a world of wine and song. He learnt to play the piano from a very young age. His mother's close sister, Agathe, going under her pre-marital name of Calvelli-Adorno della Piana, was, like Adorno's mother, a successful singer and would become a second mother to him. His mother and aunt would sing him to sleep with Brahms's 'Lullaby'. The words were sacrosanct to him:

Sleep in gentle ease
little eyes shut please,
hear the raindrops in the dark,
hear the neighbour's doggy bark.
Doggy bit the beggar-man,
Tore his coat, away he ran,
To the gate the beggar flees,
Sleep in gentle ease.[56]

Horkheimer recorded the atmosphere of Adorno's childhood home:

Anyone who entered the house in Seeheimer Strasse in Oberrad in which Adorno spent his youth experienced an environment to which he owed a protected childhood in the best sense of the word. The traditions that came together in his parents' house, the commercial spirit of Oscar Wiesengrund, his Jewish father from Frankfurt, and the aura of music that surrounded his mother Maria . . . the shining eyes of her sister Agathe who was like a second mother to him, are all preserved . . . in Adorno's thought and feelings.[57]

For Adorno, life, love and music were inextricably linked. He described 'lying in bed at night and pricking up my ears to listen to a Beethoven sonata for violin and piano when I was supposed to be asleep'.[58] Developing a delicate and detailed sensitivity to his environment, nothing harsh ever entered Adorno's world:

there was very little symphonic and chamber music that was not introduced to the family circle. This was thanks in part to the large volumes.
. . . They seemed to have been made for the express purpose of turning
their pages, and I was allowed to turn the pages long before I could
read the notes, just following my memory and my sense of hearing.
They even included Beethoven sonatas in curious adaptations. I have
internalized many pieces, such as Mozart's G minor symphony, so
deeply that it still seems to me today that no orchestra can ever reproduce the excitement of that introductory quaver movement as perfectly
as the questionable touch of the child on the piano.[59]

Pampered and indulged, Adorno had the quintessence of a happy
childhood. His philosopher friend Leo Lowenthal remembered that
Adorno had 'an existence you just had to love – if you were not dying of
jealousy of this beautiful, protected life – and in it Adorno had gained the
self-confidence that never left him his entire life'.[60] The memories
of this contentment Adorno forever cherished – it was his most precious
refuge.

There was a downside to Adorno's dreamy upbringing. He was left
unarmed for brash encounters with the world. As a child he suffered at
school, beginning with his teachers: 'From the outset there is a dishar-
mony of the soul between teacher and pupil.'[61] The disappointments of
the teacher–pupil relationship were soon outweighed by the playground.
A friend recalls:

He was the pampered child of his family. . . . At home he was called
Teddy [sic] and his nickname had somehow become known at school.
. . . During break the older boys would wander round slowly in a circle,
while we, the younger ones, played our boisterous games. Teddy had a
few close friends who, like him, failed to notice that some enemy or
other had stuck a piece of paper on his back with the word 'Teddy' in
large letters. In a trice there was a howling mob shouting 'Teddy' at

their unsuspecting victim. At the time, Teddy was a slightly built, shy boy who simply did not realize what was going on. We all knew that he was Jewish. But the uproar in the playground was not an anti-Semitic demonstration. Its target was this unique person who outshone even the best boys in class. It was a stupid boys' trick, nothing more.[62]

Adorno didn't regard anti-Semitism as separate from anti-intellectualism. For him these forms of prejudice were cut from the same cloth, and having suffered at the hands of the school bullies he perceived in their behaviour the latent seeds of National Socialism. Both groups sensed and reacted to difference.

Genius comes in unusual guises. As a child, Adorno's musical sensitivity was so acutely developed that throughout his life he could hear beyond the ordinary range. Likewise he could 'see' what others could not. Adorno's vision was apparent in his reading, and he was able to understand profound and difficult concepts from an early age. He possessed an uncanny ability to think and pursue complicated ideas beyond the capacity of all other children, and indeed beyond the stamina of well-educated adults. Adorno might have been spoilt, closeted, pampered, but he had intellectual grit. He did not squander his privilege. He worked hard, very hard, so much so that in later life he would continue until mentally and physically exhausted. He would work until he was trembling and ill, especially when seized with an absorbing project. But Adorno was not puritanical, for his family had also taught him how to relax and enjoy pleasures. So he could endure the extremes of mental exertion over long periods of time sustained by periods of relaxation, indulging in opulent surroundings, with good company, music, wine and food. It was a pattern of behaviour he retained all his life.

Aside from school, the outside world had little impact upon Adorno's closeted childhood. The horrors and hardship of the First World War meant only a change of address to a more prosperous part of Frankfurt. Even the post-war Depression from 1929 failed to touch the affluent

Wiesengrund household. During this time, while many other families struggled with the mundane practicalities of existence, Adorno devoured every kind of music, composed, and engaged in a voracious reading of philosophy, classics and literature. And while children of his age socialized with each other in the classroom and the neighbourhood, Adorno became friends with an adult male, fourteen years his senior. This was Siegfried Kracauer, the eminent German-Jewish intellectual, writer and critic. Kracauer describes his first impression of Adorno:

> He wore a green jacket made from loden cloth which, together with his red tie, was a rough cloak in which he looked like a little prince. Leaning on his mother's chair, he answered the questions I put to him in a dull tone that contradicted the large, mournful eyes that gazed out from beneath long lashes. Their expression hinted at a mystery that lay hidden in the youth . . .[63]

And while other boys muddied their knees in the playground, an eminent composer of the Second Viennese School, famous for adapting the twelve-tone technique originated by Schönberg, became Adorno's 'play mate'. Alban Berg, eighteen years older and his teacher, also became his close friend, and Adorno enjoyed the company of other members of the Schönberg circle too. Walter Benjamin, eleven years Adorno's senior, became a close companion. Years later Adorno referred affectionately to Benjamin as 'one of the most peculiar indeed possibly "*the* most peculiar" person' he had ever encountered in his life.[64] Leo Lowenthal, destined to become one of the world's most eminent sociologists, also joined the Adorno circle. Lowenthal described Adorno as the 'classical image of a poet, with a delicate way of moving and talking'.[65]

Margaret Karplus, or Gretel as she was better known, had been Adorno's sweetheart from youth and belonged to the family of old friends of his parents. She was elegant with an athletic build and a highly intelligent face. She had moved in scholarly circles herself, knowing

Walter Benjamin, Ernst Bloch and Bertolt Brecht. Theodor and Gretel shared many memories and she provided Adorno with the support he needed all his adult life. Since his early childhood, Adorno's empathetic and playful nature had given him a natural affinity with women. One student would later recall:

No sooner did he encounter a woman than he began to flirt with her. This sometimes seemed arbitrary, as if he were 'colour-blind' to the individual nature of the particular woman – he was aroused, seemingly automatically, by 'woman as such'. To be sure, erotic permissiveness was no male monopoly in his view – he conceded the same rights to women. But in my opinion Adorno was neither chauvinistic or sexist. And I can say that because I felt close to him personally and I do not wish to deny the presence of an erotic undercurrent in our relationship. His approaches had nothing macho or virile about them, they were instead uninhibited and childlike – much as in other spheres of life Adorno always preserved a natural kind of spontaneity that went back to his childhood. But he could also be extremely timid, something that does not fit the image of the ruthless lady-killer at all. Moreover I always found Adorno to be very dependable and affectionate in his behaviour towards women. The decisive factor for me was. . . . That I was able to be friends with both him and Gretel, I felt that relationship between them was marked by the same tension, loyalty despite everything, reliability, an almost symbiotic mutual attachment on the one hand and the ability to preserve one's freedom on the other.[66]

Gretel was necessary for Adorno and tolerated his flirtatious nature. Indeed in later life she indulged him, just like his mother and aunt had done when he was a child.

The contentment that characterized Adorno's childhood continued into early adulthood. He was not restricted by post-war poverty, by an

authoritarian father or a judgemental mother. He had no need to rebel
and showed no interest in student politics. A brilliant pupil at the Johann
Wolfgang Goethe University in Frankfurt, he read philosophy, psychology
and sociology. In 1924 at the age of twenty he received his doctorate. The
drab academic world, however, took its toll. As a musicologist, composer
and dazzling thinker, the run-of-the-mill academic staff in Frankfurt
regarded him with suspicion. Resentful, they often relegated him to the
status of an exotic ornament. Relief came in the form of the composer
Alban Berg, and Adorno left his home to study in aristocratic Vienna.
This was in 1925, two decades after Hitler had wandered its streets.
Other parts of Europe, including Italy, were explored by the young
Adorno before he was forced to return to Frankfurt in search of a stable
career. He attempted to combine life as a composer with philosophy,
working first on Freud and then studying for his habilitation with Paul
Tillich on the subject of the Danish existential philosopher Søren
Kierkegaard.

In 1931, after several years struggling to find a career, Adorno eventually found some success and gave his inaugural lecture as a new young
academic in Frankfurt. He became a prolific writer, publishing, teaching
and organizing seminars.[67] After two years in his newly found and hard-
earned career, the book version of his Kierkegaard thesis was published
in March 1933 by Mohr-Siebeck. It appeared 'on the very day that Hitler
seized dictatorial powers'.[68]

While Adorno had been struggling with trying to build a career, the
world around him had been caught up in turmoil. With steeply rising
levels of unemployment, the Weimar Republic from 1918 to 1933 had
been massively unstable. Both economic inflation and political extremism
were spiralling out of control. When the Nazis entered the Reichstag,
many of Adorno's fellow assimilated Jews fled, but Adorno clung on. He
couldn't believe that the German people would give any long-term
backing to this Führer who seemed to him to be 'a mixture of King Kong
and a suburban hairdresser'.[69]

After the Reichstag arson attack of 27 February 1933 and the book burnings in May of the same year, racist witch-hunts began. As a great swathe of Jews were fired from Frankfurt University, on 8 September 1933 the 'Prussian Minister for Science, Art and Education' wrote to Adorno with the following words: 'On the basis of article 3 of the Law of the Restoration of the Professional Civil Service of 7 April 1933, I herewith withdraw your license to teach at the University of Frankfurt am Main.'[70] Adorno's colleagues, Max Horkheimer and his old tutor Paul Tillich, and indeed the registrar of the university himself, were all fired. The Frankfurt Institute was forced to close. Adorno found that his mail was being tampered with – he suspected surveillance by the Gestapo. Then in July his home in Seeheimerstrasse was searched aggressively by the police.[71]

Composers such as Berg, Schönberg and Anton Webern were silenced, and Adorno's friends – Kracauer, Bloch and Benjamin – fled. Whereas in Adorno's words 'everyone who counted' left, he still obstinately persisted in trying to remain. He tried to re-qualify as a music teacher but was told he was only allowed to teach 'non-Aryan pupils'. Then he was forced to apply for membership of the Reich Chamber of Literature if he wished to continue to publish. His application was rejected as he was not considered a 'reliable member of the Volk', that is, 'persons who belong to the German nation by profound ties of character and blood. As a non-Aryan you are unable to feel and appreciate such an obligation. Signed Suchenwirth. Certified as correct: Nowotny.'[72] By 1934 Adorno had no means to earn a living and began to witness the increasing persecution. For him it was unbearable to leave his native Frankfurt, but finally it was clear he had no choice. He joined the myriad of others in taking flight.

The wind, wet and sudden, gusting in all directions, the sky peppered with white and grey clouds, the shrieking of the gulls and noise of the ship's machinery – Adorno was overwhelmed by his senses. The sea spread in every direction, its massive waves impermeable to thought.

From rooms and furniture, still, warm air and the ticking clock, suddenly Adorno was buffeted by the outdoors. And no mere streets with winding alleys or tall buildings were there to surround him; he was exposed to the absence of a human environment, emptiness in all directions. To a man who spent much of his time seated at a desk in a study, poring over texts and music scores, the sudden vastness of the ocean must have made him agoraphobic. This is where Hitler had led him, to the edge of the European mainland, to a flight across the sea.

His ship brought him to the shores of Britain, which in 1934, was attempting to appease Hitler, so that refugees were hardly welcome. A strict asylum policy under the Aliens Restriction Act kept German Jews away from British shores unless they had a sponsor and could show private means of economic subsistence. It was Adorno's task to find such a sponsor. His father intervened and wrote to an old acquaintance, the economist John Maynard Keynes.[73]

Adorno's uncle, Bernhard Wiesengrund, lived in London with his wife and three children. There he had successfully assimilated into British society, even changing his name to Wingfield. His children were all educated at good English schools including St Paul's School, Hammersmith. His son, Bernhard T. Wiesengrund, or Wingfield, went on to study at Merton College, Oxford – although his career was undistinguished, to say the least.

Through the Wingfield family, Adorno's father tried to establish the connections his son would need, but in the end it was through Theodor Adorno's own efforts that opportunities arose. His endeavours led him to Adolf Lowe, an economist at Manchester; Karl Mannheim, a sociologist at the London School of Economics; Ernst Cassirer, a German-Jewish philosopher, himself struggling at the time to obtain a post at Oxford, and Edward Dent of Cambridge. Dent sent an unhelpful reply[74] and Cassirer, too, would not vouch for the quality of Adorno's work. However, he was eventually granted a place at Merton College, Oxford.

From the outset Adorno was treated with condescension at Oxford. He wrote after dining in Merton that it was 'a nightmare come true ... like having to return to school, in short, an extension of the Third Reich'.[75] He was denied a position of status with any stipend attached and was demoted from being a lecturer, as he had been in Germany, to once again becoming a student, and had to repeat his qualification for an English institution. Enrolling as an 'advanced student', he worked on Edmund Husserl's philosophy with Gilbert Ryle, who was the tutor at Christ Church College.

Adorno's colleagues soon began to ridicule their new German-Jewish colleague. These baiters, oddly enough, included two English-born academics with Jewish ancestry, A. J. Ayer and Isaiah Berlin. Ayer described Adorno as a 'comic figure', with a 'dandified manner and [great] anxiety' to be given recognition. Relief from this mockery seemed to come in the form of Isaiah Berlin, the historian of ideas, who presented himself as a friend. However, later correspondence in the 1980s reveals a number of telling remarks. In a letter to the philosopher Bernard Williams, Berlin wrote of Adorno that:

> ...he was short, bald, ludicrous in appearance, looked like a Kindermörder – Peter Lorre – & largely – tho' clever – bogus: but he knew it, didn't mind, & just scribbled on: at times he wondered – as such persons often do – whether what he was saying was not, after all, very profound: at other times – when drinking with Syme or telling me about beautiful women he admired – he knew he was just a jolly con-man who meant no harm & had some wit ...[76]

In another letter, Berlin continued in the same deriding tone: 'I knew the egregious Wiesengrund ('Adorno' was a somewhat specious addition, which I could explain, naturally with a vague reference to the Doges of Genoa, as if any Jew could be descended from them) ...'[77] Earlier letters also confirm these disparaging feelings:

28 October 1965

Dear Robert Craft,

... in order to confuse matters further [I] have asked Dr Adorno to contribute something to one of the publications about Moses and Aaron that Covent Garden is about to put out. Not a word will be understood, and it will be comical to see how our critics react to his profundities. Do you know him? You must know him well. I knew him well in Oxford and cannot help thinking him a marvellously comical figure. I propose to invite him to Oxford to deliver a lecture, and that too I shall enjoy, though perhaps not in quite so direct a fashion as I should.[78]

Others were less supercilious about this 'survivor of the sinking of the great ship of European culture by Hitler to wash up on the shores of Oxford, or, more precisely, to come to inhabit remote bedsitters in the northern part of the city'.[79] Maurice Bowra, the Oxford classicist, tried to engage with the work of the Frankfurt School and liked Adorno tremendously. The admiration was mutual and Adorno wrote, 'He is one of the most intellectual and cultivated men I know.'[80] Bowra at Adorno's request wrote an article for a journal that Horkheimer was editing in New York. However, Adorno was disappointed with the result. 'In fact, the piece . . . is much too general and has only the tone of good journalism . . . there is hardly any evidence offered,' he complained. 'Bowra uses ideas,' he continued, 'without relating them to the underlying social reality.'[81] Bowra was forced to admit he found Adorno rather severe and that he found the Germanic style quite unfathomable.

Easier relationships came to Adorno through music. He joined the Oxford University Musical Society and befriended Redvers Opie, who was then vice president of the society and bursar at Magdalen College. Their friendship seems to have been sincere and they enjoyed many musical soirées which his daughter, Helen Opie, then aged only four, recalls:

. . . being a 'proper' 1930's upper middle class home (or aspiring upper class, I'd guess), I was kept apart with a nanny while the adults were in the Forbidden Room known as the parlour. I did go in there to listen to my father and his friends play chamber music, probably where I gained my everlasting love for this form.[82]

Testimony to the closeness of their friendship was that Redvers Opie acted as a witness to Adorno's marriage to Gretel, which took place on 8 September 1937 in the registry office in Paddington, London. Along with Horkheimer, Adorno's and Gretel's parents, Opie was the only other person present.

Suffocated by the small-town life of Oxford, Adorno developed a penchant for London. When his friend Alban Berg planned to visit London, Adorno wrote excitedly, promising to show him the streets he knew quite well, 'from the Whitechapel streets where Jack the Ripper met Lulu, to the best restaurants in Piccadilly, from the Bloody Tower to Hampstead, London's *Heitzing*'.[83] However, Adorno was haunted by home: 'In London a precise dream from my childhood came true, too late and almost painfully.' He described a dream about ticket colours on buses and ended sadly with 'it is no more possible for me to salvage anything than it is possible for the London colours to restore the bliss and nostalgia of childhood'.[84]

While many of the Oxford elite enjoyed the sport of observing refugees wash up with their 'foreign' culture on to British shores, Adorno battled with no income to support himself or his family. It had been difficult to get into England, but now, faced with no job opportunities and the prospect of none until he could become naturalized, which would require a minimum of five years' residence, he began to panic. Meanwhile Nazism was encroaching deeper into Europe. Adorno wrote to Horkheimer:

the European situation is completely desperate; the prognoses in my last letter seem to have been confirmed in the worst way possible:

Austria will fall to Hitler and in a world hypnotized by success this will enable him to stabilize his position indefinitely and on the foundation of the most appalling terror. It can scarcely be doubted any more that the Jews still living in Germany will be wiped out . . . for once they have been expropriated, no country in the world will grant them asylum. And once again nothing will be done: the others fully deserve their Hitler.[85]

Unable to return to the continent and with no prospects in England, his situation began to look very bleak. Then suddenly it all changed – an opportunity for a position arose in New York. Relieved, anxious, excited, feeling a cascade of emotions, he made plans with his new wife and on 16 February 1938 they set sail for America. They crossed the Atlantic on the huge passenger ship *The Champlain*.

After running the gauntlet of old-boy snobbishness in Oxford, facing destitution and the ever-increasing threat from the Nazis, Adorno embraced America with a sigh of relief. Gone was the old world and in its place a brave new one that was as opulent as it was unfamiliar. Soon after his arrival, the Nazi regime intensified its hostile measures against the Jews. Europe seemed to be passive and helpless before the spread of violent anti-Semitism and rumours began to be whispered about the Jews in America. Three years later, in 1941, living in Los Angeles, with his back to the furthest edge of the Western world, with nowhere to go but into the Pacific itself, Adorno could still feel the breath of fascism upon him. In his own words, he was 'like the bird staring at the snake'.[86]

CHAPTER 8

The Jewess: Hannah Arendt

Back in 1933 Hitler was recasting the streets of the German nation in his own image. Amidst all this turmoil, some German Jews such as Walter Benjamin would flee, others such as Theodor Adorno were preparing for the worst, while many simply continued as best they could. The young Jewess Hannah Arendt, like Benjamin and Adorno, was destined to become a legendary figure. She would emerge as one of the leading political thinkers of her generation. Her oeuvre would eventually include classics of the twentieth century and her dedication to the Jewish cause, which would later become controversial, was only just beginning. Her life was to read like a thriller as she would duck and dive past the mounting array of hazards and pitfalls thrown at her by the Third Reich. Through her story we witness the intellectual and emotional disruption caused by a head-on collision with Hitler's dream.

Early spring 1933, Berlin. The first crocuses were beginning to bloom – flashes of purple amid the grey dawn in the sprawling industrial city. Long-distance trains travelled through the suburbs before arriving at their stations, citizens threaded their way around the Rykestrasse Synagogue with its beautiful towering ceiling and massive arched roof. Nearby an increasing Nazi presence trampled the pavements. Smelling rank with garbage, coal dust and industrial grease, the city exhaled its first morning breath.

In the centre of Berlin, the imposing stone columns of the grandest state building in Berlin, the Reichstag, were smouldering from a devastating blaze and the facade was charred beyond recognition.[1] The communists, fighting to empower the ordinary working people, were blamed for the fire, and a state of emergency was declared with decrees issued by Hitler suspending freedom of speech and assembly. The only relief to the grim shadows on the streets were the flickers of red: scarlet flags rippled in the chill, damp air as the SA units (the National Socialists' paramilitary force) marched through the streets, parading their political victory. They carried official documents, political-party registers allowing them to identify the addresses of all members of the left-wing opposition. Their mission was to enact the new legislation – to round up and arrest all communists.

During 1933 Hitler would withdraw from international peace agreements, including the League of Nations, and anti-Semitic policies would be on the increase. Dachau, the first concentration camp, would be set up in an abandoned munitions factory northwest of Munich in Bavaria.[2] The Nazi dawn was just beginning. By May, Jewish shops would be vandalized, windows smashed, and in parts of Berlin fires were started as students joined the Gestapo in the burning of books.[3]

At this time the city was still blooming with cultural riches, from theatres and opera houses to universities, museums and libraries. Hannah Arendt, aged twenty-seven, emerged from one of these magnificent buildings, the Prussian State Library. She had been working determinedly all morning and was now hurrying home, carrying papers and documents demonstrating the full extent of the Nazis' anti-Semitic activities through non-governmental organizations and professional societies. She was working covertly for the German Zionist Organization (the largest institution for Jewish activists in the country), finding evidence to smuggle abroad. Her findings were to be disseminated across the world to alert democratic countries to the tide of racism sweeping across Hitler's new Germany. Her work was illegal and dangerous. She would eventually be arrested and imprisoned.[4]

Arendt had not always acted on behalf of the Jewish cause, indeed throughout most of her young life she had not even really considered herself to be particularly Jewish. To understand how she came to take this particular path we need to go back to the beginning and follow her journey from its roots, witnessing how her early emotional experiences would later interact with Nazism.

Hannah Arendt had been born in 1906 in Königsberg, now Kaliningrad, a city no stranger to philosophers. Crowned by its Prussian castles overlooking the lake, Arendt's intellectual forebear Immanuel Kant also came from this city. Unlike Kant, however, who had led a quiet life, Hannah's was to be fraught with danger. Königsberg had always been a refuge for Eastern European and Russian Jews. Nestling between south-western Russia and the Baltic Sea, the city formed a natural gateway between Russia and Europe, with the main stretch of railroad taking exiles onwards to German cities and thence to England or America. During the last years of the reign of the great Czars in the nineteenth century, long, straggling lines of these outcasts could be seen, tired, dirty, burdened by the heaps of their possessions, fleeing Czar Nicholas I's anti-Semitic policies and forced conscription to fight in the Crimean War (1853–56).[5]

Jacob Cohn, categorized by the Czarist regime as a 'non-useful' Jew, was himself one of these dishevelled wanderers. From Lithuania he emigrated in 1852, just a few years before Czar Nicholas handed down power to his son Alexander II.[6] The same year that Cohn died, 1906, his granddaughter Hannah Arendt was born. Hannah's other grandfather, Max Arendt, was also Jewish.[7] But it was not this Jewish ancestry that was to cast a long shadow over her early life. Indeed, it is possible that the most powerful emotional drive in Hannah's life derived not from anti-Semitism but from disease. Her father, Paul Arendt, had syphilis.

Paul Arendt's appearance was rather severe, with a black, waxed moustache and pince-nez spectacles. He spent his spare time reading from leather-bound volumes on ancient Greece and noting in a some-what abstract fashion his daughter's development. The child 'is very curious and shows inclination to raise upper torso; has been lifting head for a while. Shows fear reaction to sounds, loud voices, etc. very easily.' But he also wrote affectionately: 'The smile looks loveable to us. Gay songs get a joyous reaction, sentimental ones incline her to tears.'[8]

Paul Arendt received treatment at Königsberg University Clinic, but by the spring of 1911 the disease had spread and Hannah's scholarly father was covered in lesions, paralyzed and partially insane. Grandfather Max was kindly and initially he proved a substitute for her sickly father. This kept Hannah buoyant and she thrilled to wake up and find it was the weekend. That meant a visit to the Arendt's house with walks in the park and stories. Max was a fabulous storyteller and used to narrate fairy tales and poems. Grandpa, as she fondly called him, took her and Meyerchen the dog through the *Glacis*, the remains of medieval fortifications and green space in the city, as the Baltic mists swept in from the sea. He recounted tales of czars sweeping through forests on horseback and old rabbis with secret spells. After their enchanting walks came the solemnity and ritual of the synagogue when she would join her grandparents for Shabbat services. Hannah tried to tell stories and perform too, developing an early interest in theatre and spectacle. This penchant for the dramatic would hold her in great stead in her later years when she became an internationally known philosopher who would travel the globe to deliver prestigious lectures. But for now, within the spontaneity of childhood, she amused and entertained the doting audience of her family.

Hannah was only seven when tragedy struck. Her beloved grandfather Max Arendt died in 1913. Later that same year, Hannah's father died in the psychiatric hospital to which he had been admitted. Hannah had seen and experienced the entire horrible transformation of her father from dignified scholar to immobile lunatic, infested with syphilitic sores. Her father's illness and death haunted her all her life. She would suffer insomnia, nightmares, melancholic mood swings and a perpetual sense of unease in day-to-day life. And she would always yearn for a father figure, a yearning that would lead her into a deadly and treacherous relationship.

But there was little time for mourning. Within months of her father's death the First World War broke out, and Hannah's mother became panic-stricken as she feared the advancing Russian army would occupy Königsberg. They fought for a place on a train to escape to Berlin. Nauseated by the thick cigarette smoke, the dirt and putrid fumes from a mass of German trench coats, they were crammed in behind the soldiers in a corner of a carriage. The German troops who had fought the Russian First Army to the east were being transferred to meet the Russian Second Army to the south. Hannah and her mother were nearly separated in the chaos, as farmers and ordinary citizens fled the Russian advance. Terrifying tales of pillaging, burning, rape and violence were told.

Within the space of a year, Hannah had lost not only her father and grandfather but also her beloved home. In response perhaps to this tragedy, she developed a poetic, sometimes even melancholic, temperament. In later years she had a heightened sensitivity, alert to the strange images of the city. In a youthful poem about a train on the Berlin subway she wrote:

Coming out of darkness,
Snaking into light,
Rapid and bold,
Slim and controlled
By human powers,
Attentively riding
The drawn-out paths;
Indifferently sliding
Above the haste.
Rapid, slim, and controlled
By human powers
It does not heed;
Into dark it flows.
What's above, it knows;

Winding it flies,

A yellow beast.[9]

From early on Hannah sought out intellectual friendships. One in particular, with Anne Mendelssohn – descendant of the famous Jewish thinker
of the Enlightenment, Moses Mendelssohn – was a bond that would last
a lifetime. Hannah developed a circle of older friends and was introduced
to some of the most difficult German philosophical texts. She read
Immanuel Kant, Enlightenment and Romantic German thinkers, and
unconventional Christian philosophers.

From 1922 until 1923 Hannah studied classics and Christian theology
at the University of Berlin. She was preparing for the German university
entrance examination known as the *Abitur*. Her success came in 1924,
and under a grey autumnal sky she entered Marburg University to study
philosophy. Her mentor was the charismatic young 'magician of
Messkirch', Martin Heidegger.

One of Heidegger's students, Karl Löwith, described Heidegger's
infamous charisma over his audience. 'He was a small dark man who
knew how to cast a spell in so far as he could make disappear what he
had a moment before presented. His lecture technique consisted in
building up an edifice of ideas which he then proceeded to tear down,
presenting his spellbound listeners with a riddle and then leaving them
empty-handed.'[10]

To some he seemed 'like an eagle soaring in the sky', to other
students, like 'a man in a frenzy'. One wondered 'whether this philosopher was not some Aristotle gone berserk, arousing attention because he
was pitting the greatness of his thinking power against his thinking, and
because in that thinking he claimed not to be thinking at all, but to be
existence'.[11] When Hannah encountered this captivating, egoistic and
authoritarian man, he dissolved her self-confidence into awe. She was
awash with his power and mystery, and in reverence she described
him as 'the hidden king who reigned in the world of thinking, which,

although it is completely of this world, is so concealed in it that one can never be quite sure whether it exists at all.[12] Hannah had found the object of her desire – a paternal god to worship – upon the altar of the lectern.

Hannah was ready for total devotion. Her young philosophical ardour was ready to succumb not only to ideas themselves but also to the embodiment of these ideas in a man. Heidegger tempted her both mentally and physically. Her sexuality took shape through him. This was no surprise, for Heidegger was famed for his erotic influence over his students: 'A seducer of youth' he was called.[13]

She was aware that through this covert, sexual awakening, her image might be tainted. Others would think her 'uglier and more common, even to the point of being dull and licentious'.[14] But for her, Heidegger reawoke her childhood, where life seemed wondrous, everyday observations were tiny miracles, and a mood of lyrical vagueness encompassed all concrete experiences, rendering them misty, opaque. All this she expressed later in a piece sent to Heidegger entitled 'Shadows'.[15]

After a year of secret liaisons, perhaps fearing discovery, Heidegger encouraged Hannah to leave Marburg. He arranged for her to find an alternative tutor and study with his friend Karl Jaspers in Heidelberg. She consented to leave 'because', as she expressed it, 'of my love for you, to make nothing more difficult than it already is'.[16]

Karl Jaspers was a thin, keen man, a psychiatrist and philosopher who taught from a study piled high with papers and manuscripts, so dense that it was as though the walls themselves were composed of books. Hannah worked with him on the thesis that she had begun with Heidegger, which was based on St Augustine. At this point in her life, still devoted to her former lover and mentor, she was following the Catholic tradition in which Heidegger had been so deeply rooted. Her language also was distinctly Heideggerian. However, feeling somewhat humiliated by her displacement, she focused on Augustine's concept of love, something that she argued – no doubt with personal lament – was missing from

Heidegger's own approach.[17] *Der Liebesbegriff bei Augustin* was published in 1929 by J. Springer in Berlin.

A year after the completion of her dissertation, determined not to give in to her humiliation but still on the rebound from Heidegger, she felt she had found a cure for her loss of self-esteem and heartache. While the January frost was crisp underfoot, Hannah, behind a jewelled veil, wrists and ankles decorated in gaudy bangles, stepped carefully through the doors of the Museum of Ethnology to attend the masked ball. She was dressed provocatively as an Arab harem girl, and in this guise she met the handsome young Jewish philosopher Günter Stern. Within the year, they were married.[18]

They moved to Frankfurt where Hannah wrote a number of articles such as 'Augustin und Protestantismus', which was published in 1930 by *Frankfurter Zeitung* – the same journal Walter Benjamin had worked for. She also co-authored a piece, 'Rilke's Duineser Elegien', with her husband. His career meanwhile encountered its first trial. Günter, eager to make headway into academia, submitted his thesis to the illustrious Frankfurt School of Philosophers. Theodor Adorno read Günter's thesis with disappointment. It was rejected and as a consequence Günter's hopes of an immediate university career lay in tatters. Hannah Arendt never forgave Adorno, and the repercussions were such that these two powerful intellectual Jews, with so much in common, were never to be reconciled.

Rahel Varnhagen, a beautiful, romantic Jewess whom Hannah called 'her closest friend', became a focus for her soon after her rejection by Heidegger. Rahel had also been involved in an illicit love affair with an older man, the gentile Count von Finckenstein. This love 'had been slowly and painfully refused'.[19] Hannah identified with Rahel and published articles for *Kölnische Zeitung* and *Judische Rundschau* about her life. These would become the subject of a later biography entitled *Rahel Varnhagen: The Life of a Jewess*.[20]

In Rahel Varnhagen, Hannah not only found a kindred spirit who had been rejected in love but also encountered a new identity. Hannah quoted Rahel, who on her deathbed claimed, 'The thing that all my life seemed to me the greatest shame, which was the misery of my life – having been born a Jewess – this I should on no account now wish to have missed.'[21] Hannah, whose interest until this point had been German philosophy and Catholic thought, through an emotional identification with Varnhagen discovered Judaism. Hannah's identity as a Jew now became the centre point of everything in her life.

Hannah's new Jewish awareness was infused with abstract fore-boding, expressed in her youthful poetry and writings of her dreams. She continued to be influenced by Goethe, Fichte, Schelling and the German Romantics, not as a way of assimilating into German society but as an expression of cultural ambiguity. She also joined Zionist activists in Berlin. Foreseeing the worsening crisis for Jews in the city, although not predicting how extreme this crisis would become, she grew intolerant of the passivity of her Jewish friends. Anne Mendelssohn she scolded as 'crazy' for continuing to live in a relaxed manner. Hannah's husband was less sympathetic to her impassioned activities than she would have liked, and others she scolded for a foolish lack of vision.

A rift was widening in her marriage. The undercurrent behind it was all too clear. In a letter to Heidegger she wrote:

Sept. 30

Martin,

When I saw you today – forgive me for how I reacted. But at that moment the image of how you and Günter would stand together at the window flashed through my mind, and how I would be alone on the platform, unable to avoid the diabolical clarity of what I had seen. Forgive me.[22]

And if she was decidedly feminine and subservient to Heidegger, her behaviour towards her husband was in stark contrast. The problem for Günter was that she was too assertive. For instance, when she was

presented with a gift of black Havana cigars by an old friend of her grandfather's, her husband protested at her 'mannishness'. She ignored Günter
and smoked them anyway. In her letter to Heidegger meanwhile, she
continued with a deference that she had never shown towards her
husband: 'So many things that had left me utterly confused came together.
Not just, as always, how the sight of you always rekindles awareness of my
life's clearest and most urgent continuity, of the continuity of our – *please*
let me say it – love'.[23] In spite of her increasingly Jewish identity, her insecurity about Heidegger had grown ever greater since their separation,
and she pleaded with him like a child to a father:

> But: I had already stood before you for a few seconds, you had actually
> seen me – you had briefly looked up. And you did not recognize me.
> When I was a small child . . . that was the way my mother once fright-
> ened me. . . . I still recall the blind terror with which I kept crying: but
> I am your child, I am your Hannah.[24]

Events overtook Hannah and Günter. Hannah was just twenty-seven
when Hitler was elected chancellor by the German people in 1933. After
the Reichstag fire in Berlin in February, leftists were rounded up and
arrested. Hannah's husband became fearful. He knew that his name was
in the address book of Bertolt Brecht, which had now been taken by the
Gestapo. Günter fled to Paris.

Hannah, whose name had not been included amongst Brecht's
contacts, remained to fight. Overnight she converted her Berlin apartment into a safe house for those fleeing Hitler's campaign against the
Jews. She, her mother and a female friend kept a communist outlaw in
their apartment and narrowly escaped detection by the police – on one
occasion the communist, with a wink, implied he was entertaining three
'desperate' women.

Eventually, the headstrong Hannah was arrested by the police on
account of her activities, and whereas in the spring of 1933 Martin

Heidegger was promoted to the position of Rector at Freiburg University, both she and her mother were imprisoned. They were interrogated for over a week. Heidegger had vanished from her life and with Günter's departure, Hannah, left to fend for herself, managed to hoodwink her guard and she and her mother escaped. Fugitives with inadequate clothes, few possessions and little food, they not only had to flee gaol but also Germany.

Their getaway was surprisingly direct. A sympathetic family lived in a house with a front door in Germany and a back door in Czechoslovakia, so after a warming meal and under cover of the night, they slipped out the back and across the mountains to safety. Thick green forests led them to Czechoslovakia. This same route used by leftists and Jews through the Erzgebirge Mountains eventually became recorded in popular legend as the 'green front'.

In the autumn of 1933 Hannah found Günter in Paris. She had brought with her his precious first novel, a satire on fascism, which had been left behind in his hurried exodus. It smelt rank of bacon, because she had hidden the novel in the attic in a greasy cheesecloth hung up with many slabs of bacon and had then smuggled it safely through Prague, Geneva and finally to France.[25]

Hannah was now an exile and was to remain so for most of her life. Under any other circumstances the Paris streets would have tempted her. They were teeming with refugees among the city's architectural gems and grand historical monuments, and a dazzling array of displaced artists, intellectuals and writers lived there. Jean-Paul Sartre, Bertolt Brecht, the prize-winning author Raymond Aron, and a host of other Jewish thinkers crossed her path at meetings, social events and in the street. But Hannah was bent upon her Zionist project and befriended Walter Benjamin, who was at that time an exile in France like herself.

She also met Heinrich Blücher, a dazzlingly attractive political activist. With his brown, tousled hair carefully parted over a smooth brow, his wide mouth and his gentle, relaxed demeanour, Heinrich was not simply a clever and alluring man; he was also an antidote to Heidegger. First, he quickly came to adore and worship Hannah. Second, he was a strong, solid character who could offer her the fatherly support she had always craved. Fiery and political, an outspoken opponent of Nazism, he was equipped with a range of values, ideas and language to counter not only Hitler but also all that the Nazis stood for. Finally, she could put her demon to rest. Hannah had loved with a passion. Now she hated with an equal vehemence, and through Heinrich found a ready-made vocabulary with which to articulate it. In her quest for political activism Hannah found in Heinrich her soulmate. They were soon lovers and she amicably divorced Günter.[26]

Hannah admired the songs of Heinrich's friend, the popular song-writer Robert Gilbert, who captured the mood of the 1920s and 1930s:

Not a penny in my pocket
Just my clothes for the dole
My clothes they got holes
The sun peeks through.[27]

This was Hannah's favourite; she walked with Heinrich through the streets of Paris, cold and penniless, but defiant.

As the 1930s drew to their close, the mood among the fifteen thousand refugees in Paris darkened. When Hitler annexed Austria in 1938, a new wave of Jews fled into the French capital. The increasingly fearful, expanding Jewish population wanted to seek refuge in a return to the ghettos. Hannah, however, stood out against this. With her new-found confidence in the face of the ever more brutal Nazis (and against Heidegger), she declared that the Jews had to become not *less* powerful but more so. They must fight.

And she did. In Christmas 1938 she worked for a Jewish agency helping refugees in Paris. She, Heinrich and her mother stayed and laboured for their cause, whispering their mantra:

... that the soft water's movement will

conquer the strongest stone, in time.

You understand: the hard ones are undermined.[28]

But in 1939 Heinrich was arrested and interned in a camp in Villemalard, near Orléans as an 'enemy alien'. The orders were banally specific. The 'enemy aliens' were to carry food sufficient for two days, their own eating utensils, and suitcases weighing no more than 30 kilogrammes. Hannah referred to this as the 'new kind of human being created by contemporary history', those who are 'put into concentration camps by their foes and into internment camps by their friends'.[29] Two months later Heinrich was released and, with a sense of impetuous relief, he and Hannah were quickly married. Almost immediately, however, Hannah and her mother were themselves arrested and then detained. This time Hannah was not so lucky. She could not simply trick her guard.

The huge glass roof of the palladium captured the bright Parisian summer sky. The Velodrome d'Hiver was the venue in Paris for concerts and spectacles, so its associations were of luxury, pleasure and relaxation. Not so for Hannah and the crowd of women now huddled inside. They were deemed 'enemy aliens' and were taken here for quite a different reason, to be sorted, assessed and then moved on to an internment camp somewhere else in France. Inside, the walls reflected the blue of the sky, the sickly colour bounced on to the shiny, concrete floor, shadowed by the coarse, brown Hessian sacks littered everywhere. Stuffed with horse-hair, these were the women's beds for the ensuing week.

By day, the heat was stifling, by night they cowed in terror as airplanes roared overhead. They feared a German bombardment, with nothing but darkness and a large plate of glass over their heads for protection. Finally, arrangements were made and the women were transported along the banks of the Seine, past the Louvre, to the Gare de Lyon, where they were ushered on to stinking, crowded trains headed for the Gurs internment camp down at the very southwestern tip of France.

A total of 6,356 women and some children were to be housed in this camp. They trudged through a thick, pungent sea of mud. Seasonal rains had descended from the Pyrenees and flooded the flat plains surrounding them. Hannah, with the same straw sack for her bed, a bucket latrine that she had to empty herself every evening, and a meagre diet of unappetizing food comprised mainly of dried fish, determined not to give way to despair. She must not feel sorry for herself. She closed her ears to the occasional talk of suicide around her, juxtaposed with a pathological optimism by the same women each morning. Over the long, hot summer, women tried to leave the camp, securing the necessary papers where possible from husbands or relatives outside, returning to Nazi Germany as Aryans, or escaping to live somewhere in France if they were fortunate enough to have family there, or being sponsored to leave Europe for America. Hannah had no such papers and trembled at the shadow of Hitler falling over France.

She awoke, petrified one morning as the news she had dreaded arrived. It was June 1940 and France had fallen. The resulting chaos, however, gave her a very small chance to escape. All communications had broken down, and she succeeded with a group of companions in getting hold of liberation papers and fleeing the camp. There was as yet no French underground movement to turn to, so she had to trek unseen under cover of darkness as quickly as she could to make as great a distance between herself and the camp as possible. Within a day, the camp was reorganized and escape once more became impossible; she had taken her only chance. The women remaining were later joined by six thousand Jews from Baden and Saapfalz who had been smuggled in by the Nazi Adolf Eichmann with the compliance of the Vichy government. Ten thousand in all were held, and those that survived the barbarity of what then became a concentration camp were transported to Germany for extermination. Hannah had escaped the gas chambers by the skin of her teeth.

For days on treacherous roads, cowering from the Nazis, one of the many thousands of wanderers seeking shelter, she hitchhiked and walked.

Finally, Hannah reached her destination and took refuge with her friend Lotte, who lived in Montauban, southern France. Suffering exhaustion and extreme rheumatism from her long days on the road, she had found temporary respite. Then after months of anxiety, miraculously, she literally bumped into her husband the next day on the street. From the chaos of thousands of displaced Jews, communists, peasants and ordinary citizens, there stood Heinrich.

They rejoiced for a while, Hannah taking comfort in his solid presence by night and by day, their spirits so irrepressible that they cycled around southern France, indulging in their freedom and the splendour of the warm, rosemary-scented countryside. But they also lived anxiously in an attic garret and tried to anticipate the actions of the Vichy government. The anti-Semitic measures were forever on the increase – more surveillance, more papers, more ghettoization. France had fallen, England was under threat, the Hitler-Stalin pact remained, thus ensuring the close cooperation of the two most deadly secret police forces in the world. These were, as Hannah expressed it, 'the darkest times' for Europe.[30]

These dark times were perhaps no more poignantly expressed than in the fate of her by now close friend Walter Benjamin. In Paris he had entrusted her with his precious last manuscripts. Little did she realize that these were to be his final works and that he was to take his own life just a short distance from where she had just escaped. Annotating, editing and publishing Benjamin's works would become one of her major projects, and the results of her dedication would lead to his posthumous recognition as one of the cultural icons of the twentieth century.

It was 1941. Hannah was thirty-five years old. Her long, dark wavy hair was cropped short. Her figure became lean, her presence more alert. That dreamlike quality of her youth was gradually replaced by a more acute intellectual engagement, and a pragmatic response to the situations in which she found herself. And that practical nature was activated now. Vichy France was a treacherous place for a Jew. She and Heinrich managed to acquire the papers they needed and with her mother they headed south from France to Lisbon, then boarded a ship across the Atlantic to the United States.

The salt air was infused with the charcoal smell of ships' engines, then eventually there was the rank stench of a busy harbour. A rabble of tired, overwhelmed refugees crowded the docks, haggard and bewildered after their long, fretful escape from Nazi Europe. Gulls screamed overhead, patterning the sky with their incessant circular motion. Among these exiles was Hannah, arriving in New York in May 1941, nearly a century after her grandfather Jacob had himself fled anti-Semitic persecution. With her husband, twenty-five dollars in their pockets between them, and a meagre monthly stipend from the Zionist Organization of America, they began their search for affordable accommodation. A tall, narrow lodging house, crooked under the strain of subsidence, became their home for the next decade. Here on West 95th Street they took rooms for themselves and Hannah's mother. This cramped, poorly lit space, with only the services of an overstretched communal kitchen, was where Hannah was destined to write one of the masterpieces of the twentieth century: *The Origins of Totalitarianism*.[31]

She visited her fellow exiled Jewish philosopher, Theodor Adorno, who had rejected her first husband's thesis. (Adorno disapproved of Hannah's intellectual stance, which he believed was too close to Heidegger's.) On West 117th Street, where the re-established Frankfurt Institute for Social Research was housed, she handed over the contents of a package that she had read with Heinrich while waiting for their ship to take them away from Europe. These were Walter Benjamin's precious unpublished manuscripts, which she had smuggled out. On hearing of Benjamin's death she had written a farewell, simply entitled 'W.B.'

Distant voices, sadness nearby.

Those are the voices and these the dead

Whom we have sent as messengers

Ahead, to lead us into slumber.[32]

Adorno was eventually to publish Benjamin's texts, including his essay, 'Theses on the Philosophy of History', but for Hannah the wait for publication was too long and she fumed with rage, threatening to lecture Adorno on his morality. Instead she waited until Jewish contacts in Palestine could be reached and the whole situation was resolved through tact. The complete collection of Benjamin's manuscripts appeared in 1955.[33]

But that was later. First came the 1940s, when Hannah began to publish for Jewish journals such as *Jewish Social Studies* and *Contemporary Jewish Record*. Her work also became increasingly political, and she wrote on issues of race, German identity and European history in journals such as *Review of Politics*. Many of these pieces would later become part of the backbone for her manuscript of *The Origins of Totalitarianism*. This book exuded emotional energy and would articulate the agonies of a dispossessed people. However, not every intellectual who met Hannah was impressed. Isaiah Berlin met her during the war and she soon occupied a prominent position on his 'most hated' list. Berlin recalled 'when I first met her in 1942 her fanatical Jewish nationalism . . . was, I remember, too much for me. . . . On the subject of the Jews she is a little touched.'[34] Berlin continued, 'in her ideological works, she indulges in a kind of metaphysical free association which I am unable to follow except that the premises seem to me to be inaccurate and the conclusions unswallowable'.[35] Fortunately for Hannah, Berlin's opinions seemed to have been confined to Oxford colleagues.

While in New York in the early 1940s, she began to learn the full story of the Nazi atrocities in Europe. Rumours of the Final Solution were beginning to reach her. She would walk long and often in sad and philosophical contemplation in Riverside Park, among, as she expressed it, 'the rowing boats with their loving couples, like jewels on woodland ponds'.[36] Writing for *Aufbau*, a German émigré paper in New York, she laboured on analysis of Jewish issues, making controversial claims, expressing passionately held opinions and winning as much notoriety as popularity.[37] On 18 December 1942 *Aufbau* reported on the deportation of Jews from the internment camp at Gurs, where Hannah had been held. A long list of names was published – all Jews sent for extermination. Jewish editors proclaimed that the Christian world must act, but the national American press remained reserved in its response, sceptical that reports of the Final Solution were really valid.[38]

Her political analysis might have been met with mute astonishment in America, the ravings of a lunatic Jewess, but in Europe in 1945 Germany was at last defeated. The massacre of the Jews now became apparent to the whole world. But too late; they had been virtually annihilated. Hannah turned to writing furiously, taking only moments to toast the downfall of Hitler.

CHAPTER 9

The Martyr: Kurt Huber

Hitler's dream was to extend his rule not just with force but also with the mind. He would impose his ideas, such as they were, upon the German people. And he appeared to have succeeded. As the 1930s progressed, all Jewish philosophers and other Jewish academics were eradicated from the universities. Exiled, hunted down or dead, all those deemed alien or in opposition to the Nazis had been removed. Edmund Husserl had been swept away along with Walter Benjamin, Theodor Adorno, Hannah Arendt and countless others. By the end of the decade, Hitler, through Alfred Rosenberg, had accomplished his dream. With the Jews gone no one was left to voice opposition, no one to cry out for democracy or even for humanity. Or was there?

The remaining 'Aryan' philosophers by and large put their self-interest, prejudice and ambition ahead of any allegiance to their former colleagues. Rosenberg's initiatives backed by Nazis such as Alfred Bäumler and Ernst Krieck, collaborators like Carl Schmitt and Martin Heidegger, were embraced with zeal. If any small number of professors disapproved of the ethos of the ruling regime, they certainly kept their views to themselves. If dissent could be discerned at all, it was only through omission, so whereas one group of philosophers were rabidly Nazi, others retreated into a realm of abstract scholarship, and as the years went by a silence descended like a thick fog. Only very rarely was this fog pierced by a glimmer of light, as when one brave philosopher and his students dared to speak out. They dared voice opposition to the Nazification of the universities. But the glimmer of their courage was quickly extinguished, and in gruesome fashion.

It was a hot, humid July day in Stadelheim Prison, Munich, 1943. The drizzle that had started to fall earlier that day increased to a light rain. The caretaker cursed – warm, wet weather made his job even more irksome. The executions were scheduled for 5 p.m. and he had been tired, sweating profusely, looking forward to his day's work coming to an end, when news had arrived that several SS officers wanted to observe the last execution. This would cause a delay. Spitting, he thought, How bloody minded can these officers be? Didn't they realise that would add ove̅ hour to his work day? – No extra pay, of course. things would have to be properly cleaned before double over the guillotine, making sure he had blood; hair had got caught up and knotted in the harder to polish. Disinfectant was in short supp remove the dirt and human grime physically, remove the stains. If he didn't get the job done p   ,, the officers would complain and there'd be yet more work. But nobody had thought about him.[1]

The summer rain slanted diagonally across the yard. Opaque light bathed in humidity revealed shattered masonry in one corner, a heap of rubble where the westerly wind gusted through. As the caretaker was locking up, a young SS officer, recently shaved and with sharply swept-back hair, emerged and others soon arrived. The prison warden and the chief executioner came out to meet them. Lots of questions were asked, and the caretaker caught the fragments of conversation across the yard. They wanted to know the details of the method of execution, how long it took for a man to die. Keen to make suggestions about how the process could be improved, they were working on the assumption the prisoners were going to be hanged. When the executioner told them that death was by guillotine, the SS officers were extremely put out, barking that their time had been wasted. The caretaker was glad it wasn't his job to talk to the SS. To compensate for the mistake, the officers visited the guillotine room and received a comprehensive explanation of how the machine actually worked. Again they were concerned about matters of efficiency and the technical details of how fast the blade fell, the weight of the blade, the type of metal, how often it was sharpened and the most effective force required to sever a head from a body. Eventually the men had the information they needed and left. The caretaker could finish his job: two more prisoners to dispatch, then he could clear up and go home.[2]

A tall, lean young man in his twenties with tawny brown hair and his head held high, in a posture of dignity and in a last act of gallantry, crossed the yard.[3] The priest watched from the window in the gaol block until the young man reached the execution room and they closed the door. The caretaker remained outside until he heard the thudding sound: hanging would probably be cleaner and make his job easier, his wife was forever washing his uniform and he wanted no more complaints from her about it. Later, a shorter man of around fifty with a marked limp slowly crossed the yard. He, too, carried himself in a spirit of dignity. After the second thud, the caretaker removed the corpse, its hand slipping out of his grasp, scraping the cobbles as the caretaker carried the body across the yard in a revolting embrace, just as he'd done with the first. Finally, he swept the last of the debris from the stone floor and started to think about his evening meal.

That spring before his arrest, Kurt Huber, the second of the two executed prisoners, had been at home with his family. He had turned the page for his twelve-year-old daughter as she did her piano practice. Afterwards he had caressed his daughter's soft, long locks. It had amused him that when he bent to kiss her head he could always guess what his wife had been cooking for supper – the smells lingered in the child's hair.

He had been no more than five feet six inches tall. When proceeding to the execution he had crossed the yard, dragging his right leg behind him.[4] His hands had trembled as he turned to smile at the prison chaplain. The chaplain was familiar with fear but did not know that the prisoner's hands had trembled all his life, nor did he know that the prisoner had had his throat severed once before.[5]

As a child, Huber had suffered from diphtheria and when the illness had seemed unassailable, surgeons had performed an emergency operation, cutting his throat.[6] The after-effects of the illness and the traumatic treatment had never left him. His hands always trembled, at work, in the street, while meeting friends. Except when he played piano, then he was able to lose himself in the concentration required at the keyboard and with nothing formidable or demanding other than the audible world he created, rising up around him, with his hands stretching back and forth across the keys.

On a winter's day in southern Germany, 1943, the Auditorium Maximum at Munich University reflected the bright light off the wooden panelled walls. The hand that had been pulled across the coarse stone of the executioner's yard had, seven months earlier, been gesticulating before an enthralled audience. Carving out the space before him, the trembling hands belonged to Professor Huber, who had been so immensely popular when he lectured that the largest hall in the university was overcrowded with students jostling for places and spilling out into the corridors.[7] The professor had meticulously prepared his words and began to build with language a world of abstract ideas that was so integral to the nation's pride. Philosophy and music were equally beloved by the German people, they were the breath of the national spirit, and this man had superb command of them both. The young students, hungry to learn from him, were captivated, lost in this world where the senses were quiet and the mind alert. Huber stood before them behind the lectern, his body sloping awkwardly on account of his disability, his speech was slurred; but once given over to his subject, his voice flowed with eloquence and fluidity. Kurt Huber, philosopher and musicologist at Munich University, was a modest man with a brilliant mind, all the more so for embracing both the arts and sciences – besides philosophy he could lecture on mathematical logic and was a leading world authority on folk music. He had a gaunt and interesting face that would have been dazzlingly handsome were it not for his affliction, which resulted in an asymmetry of his features because one side of his face was partially paralyzed. His eyes were quite deep-set and his cheekbones high, and there was an energetic intensity about his countenance, which might have made him seem rather austere were it not softened by an evident sensuousness and frequent expressive gestures. He had thinning hair which emphasized the sculpted cheekbones and a thin, aquiline nose.[8]

Huber had been born in Chur, Switzerland, on 24 October 1893. His parents were both German and they returned to their native land four years after his birth and raised him in Stuttgart in the southwest. He had been well educated and had excelled at school, attending Eberhard-Ludwig-Gymnasium secondary school from 1903 until his father's death, whereupon the remainder of the family moved to Munich. Here Huber studied musicology, psychology and philosophy at the university, and obtained his doctorate in 1917. Three years later he began teaching at the university on a lean salary. He gave highly sophisticated and original lectures on the German Idealist philosophers Kant, Hegel and Schelling, as well as on the seventeenth-century philosopher and mathematician, Gottfried Wilhelm von Leibniz.[9]

Huber married Clara Schlickenrieder in 1929 and they soon had their first child, Birgit.[10] When Hitler was elected chancellor in 1933, Birgit was only two years old. While the storm clouds gathered around them, they nevertheless enjoyed happy years. Clara doted on her first child who was soon joined by another, a boy whom they named Wolf. From their home in Munich during the 1930s Kurt worked long, happy hours annotating and editing an attractive assortment of melodies gathered from his time spent in the southern German mountains.

The spirit of the Alps was natural to him, being a native of Switzerland, and he loved to pick his way through their meandering tracks, climbing

high into the fir forests and breathing the crisp, cool mountain air. Away
from the urban bustle, he craved solitude and his ears adapted quickly to
the delicate sounds of nature. The peasants and their customs were what
really drew Huber up into the mountains. He once wrote: 'A folk melody
is created in the spirit of the community and possesses inherent poetical
and musical qualities which are close to those people.'[11] He had collected
traditional Bavarian folk songs for the German academy in Munich, and
on his return home, after the meticulous work of editing and publishing,
the first collection was so immensely popular that it sold out in three
editions in just a couple of years. Huber was asked to compile more,
which would be published later to equal acclaim in 1936.

That winter's day in 1943, as he stood on the podium of the lecture
hall at Munich University, he was holding forth on Leibniz. The allure of
Leibniz for Huber was his deep concern about the existence of evil and
the way in which he tried to reconcile its presence with an otherwise
benevolent God. Huber followed Leibniz in insisting that evil was a flaw
in an otherwise perfect world, a wrong note in a beautiful concerto.
Huber was also, in fact, working on a definitive book on Leibniz. The
philosopher had profoundly influenced the great eighteenth- and
nineteenth-century thinkers Kant and Hegel, and although these philosophers were revered by Hitler and Heidegger, Huber read their thinking
in a very different way.

Huber's ability to inspire his students was second to none. In his audience that same day was one of his most talented students, a young
woman called Sophie Scholl. Sophie wrote about Huber's lecture to a
friend, fighting at the front:

To Fritz Hartnagel, Ulm, January 1st, 1943.

My dear Fritz,

I'm sharing the little room upstairs with [my brother] Hans. The
silence before we go to sleep is punctuated by isolated remarks uttered
at long intervals, retrospective comments on the day or questions

raised by what we've discussed and read. Last night for instance, Hans said that Leibniz (I'm just reading his Theodicy) had been the first to restrict God's omnipotence on the ground that he can only accomplish good, not evil. I claimed it was a question of volition, not ability, but I soon had to abandon that argument and enlist the aid of a simile: God's inability to be evil is exactly like the inability of the wise to be foolish. . . . His (God's) failing is the inability to have any failing . . .

Yours,

Sophie Scholl.[12]

A student confirmed this inspirational quality of Huber's when he wrote: 'Huber was a kindly little man who possessed the unusual faculty of instilling his own enthusiasm for musical research into the members of his seminars and classes.' Huber possessed 'a brilliance of mind . . . dynamic delivery' and 'was held in high esteem by students and colleagues alike'.[13]

Munich was the ideal home for Huber because of his fascination with folk music. Indeed, by 1943 he was a leading world authority, and he would enthral his students as he talked about the wild landscapes from whence this music derived. He was a man who loved this land and its mountains with an intensity that shined through all his teaching. His great delight in wandering through the Bavarian Alps, writing about the singing of stalwart young peasants in leather breeches and feathered hats, inspired his students.[14]

Huber was conservative, nationalistic and a romantic, perfect fodder for the Nazis. Furthermore, folk music was a subject matter fervently sought after by Hitler. So much so that Huber was chosen to represent Germany in the 1936 International Music Congress in Barcelona. In 1938 he was offered the exciting opportunity to take up the prestigious new Chair for the Institute of Folk Music at the University of Berlin. Needing the money to support his family, Huber accepted the Chair, but he soon found himself expected to produce Nazi propaganda. This was a dilemma, for if he resisted the Nazis he was bound to lose his post and the family would then struggle to make ends meet. Yet submitting to the demands of the Nazis would mean that his life's most cherished values, both moral and intellectual, would be compromised, rendered meaningless. After prolonged discussions with his family, he acted in the only way he could and followed his convictions: refusing to belittle his subject matter and turn authentic folk songs into Nazi national anthems, refusing to falsify the spirit of the German peasants and invent pantomimes for political gain. Huber had done what very few other philosophers were prepared to do, and for this he was immediately dismissed from his post.[15]

After his dismissal, Huber was allowed to return to his professorship at his beloved Munich, but only because 'National-Socialism generously grants a means of livelihood even to those who have forfeited their official positions through ideological insufficiency.' However, his career was in tatters. Alfred Rosenberg's bureaucrats immediately brought pressure to bear upon German editors to prevent further publication of his writings. His doctoral dissertation on Renaissance music, *Ivo de Vento*, referred to by scholars as a brilliant 'classic', was allowed to go out of print, and his last article on 'The Folk-loristic Method in Folk Song Research', which had a second part 'to be concluded in the next number', was never printed. He was unable to gain any recognition for his past work in any field, whether philosophy or musicology, and was unable to publish anything new. Even his musical talents were overlooked. It is clear that the Nazi authorities had undermined his career on account of his resistance to their tyranny, but there was another factor too. They also refused to recognize him because of his disability. Due to his limp and his speech impediment, the Nazis regarded Huber as a cripple; he could never be one of the envisioned 'master race'. They stated this to his face when he pressed for a salary increase in order to provide for his family: 'we can only promote officer material'.[16]

In contrast to Hitler's ideological opponents, Huber was neither left-leaning nor Jewish. He was a nationalist conservative, believing in the sanctity of tradition and the importance of the nation. Indeed, he was deeply proud of the achievements of German culture. However, Huber was vehemently opposed to all forms of violence and regarded Hitler as a destroyer of German values, not as their embodiment. In contrast to Heidegger, Huber was not seduced by Hitler's talk and, unlike many of his academic colleagues, he spoke out. Covertly, commenting about the rights of individuals, the importance of religion and compassion to one's fellow man, Huber's resistance was hidden within a dry wit. In spite of the dangers, he couldn't help frequent barbed references to Hitler. If his lectures included anyone Jewish, he would comment with sarcasm, 'careful, he's a Jew! Don't let yourselves be contaminated.'[17] It was dangerous to voice even this subtle level of opposition, but whether word ever reached Nazi officials of his irony or cleverly disguised rhetoric, is unclear.

Huber also tried to keep a Jewish presence alive in the universities. He openly lectured on banned Jewish philosophers such as Spinoza. So after Husserl had been dismissed and while others were imprisoned, executed or in exile, Huber bravely carried the flame for the all but extinguished line of the Jewish intellectual forebears.

Huber's great passions included the Idealists, Kant and Hegel. They formed the mainstay of his courses, but he read them very differently from how Hitler claimed to read them. Huber used his lectures on Kant to get an embedded message across to students to defy Hitler. He emphasized how Kant was a great moralist who believed that all human beings had the ability to reason and ought to have the freedom to exercise this ability. Reason, not kowtowing to any form of authority, was the basis of morality. In his own time Kant had opposed all forms of unthinking obedience, repeatedly claiming that *independent*, rational thought was the basis of all good conduct. Huber drew subtle parallels between the old irrational beliefs that Kant sought to transcend in the eighteenth century and Hitler's ideology. Kant, in fact, was one of Huber's main weapons in his intellectual resistance to Nazism, and Huber lectured on him as often as he could.[18]

Huber's convictions grew in his mind. He also disliked the anti-religious position of the Nazis and when he learned of the atrocities being committed during the war, he became incensed. His teaching was his only outlet, and fortunately for him his dry wit at first camouflaged his rebellion. Also, because of his responsibilities as a husband and father he had always behaved with caution in spite of his seething opposition. But his repressed anger towards a decade of Hitler's rule would surface even on occasion at home, when his patience at some new Nazi outrage snapped and he would begin to shout. Clara, his devoted wife, would run round the house shutting the windows and whispering urgently, 'Kurt stop it, they'll take you to Dachau.'[19] Even so, despite his caution students picked up on Huber's feelings, and their idealistic actions would spell his downfall. One such student was Sophie Scholl.

In 1921, in a valley steep with vineyards, carrying the Kocher river and the old railway line, lay Forchtenberg am Kocher. Sophie was born there, in the same year that Hitler drew crowds of over six thousand for his speeches in Munich. She attended a secondary school for girls near the banks of the river Danube. Owing to her father's business arrangements her family had moved to Ulm, the birthplace of Albert Einstein. During this time, Sophie was required to join the *Bund Deutscher Mädel* (League of German Girls), the 'female division' of Hitler Youth. Sophie's mother, Inge Scholl, recalled later: 'we heard so much talk about the fatherland and comradeship, the *Volk* community and love of one's home – this impressed us, and we listened with rapture ... we were told we should live for something greater than ourselves ...'[20]

Rapture would soon turn sour, as the true sentiments and intentions of the Nazis became apparent. That was later, however, and in 1933 eleven-year-old Sophie would have sung along with the Hitler Youth the anthem:

Forward, Forward!

Resound the fanfares brightly.

Forward, Forward!

Youth know no danger! . . .

We're marching for Hitler through the night without dread,

With the flag of youth, for freedom and bread.

Our flags lead us on,

Our flag is the new age . . .

Yes, the flag means more to us than death!

Youth! Youth!

We are the future soldiers! . . .

Yes, we'll drop anyone with our fists

Who tries to stand against us,

Führer we belong to you,

We your comrades.[21]

Later, Sophie became a student of philosophy and biology at Munich University. By the time she was twenty-one years old she had chosen philosophy as her principal subject. She was habitually in attendance at Huber's lectures. Quietly seated towards the back of the hall, she wouldn't have been noticeable if anyone were to cast a quick glance around. She wasn't noisy and didn't possess striking looks, but if one looked carefully one would have noticed a young woman with large, dark thoughtful eyes and often with a faraway expression in them. Sophie's face retained a childlike charm, her cheeks were still rounded, her complexion smooth, and her soft brown hair was parted at the side and clipped off her face. She was compelling in a quiet, poetic sort of way. She had an innocence about her, and was of course innocent of her own ghastly fate.

Her spirit was evident to her friends. Three years before her untimely death she wrote to her great friend Fritz.

Fritz Hartnagel, Ulm, July 19, 1940.

Dear Fritz,

I came home rich. It's so grand to be able to take things, just like that, without depriving anyone. It's so good that the fields and forests and clouds never change, unlike us human beings. And even when you think everything's about to end, the moon appears in the sky the following night, the same as ever. And the birds continue to sing as sweetly and busily without worrying whether there's any point in it. Have you noticed the way they tilt their heads to the sky and sing with complete abandon, and how their little throats swell? Its good that such things are always with us. You have them too. It's enough to gladden one's heart, isn't it?

Yours,

Sophie.[22]

Her *joie de vivre* did not prevent Sophie from asking complex and disturbing questions about the nature of life. She would dwell on issues of morality, meaning, existence. Her shyness prevented her from ever approaching her professors, but she had a plethora of questions forming inside her. With her brother and their friends they would discuss the butchery being conducted by the Third Reich. They could not understand how their country had fallen into such depravity. Furthermore, in the summer of 1941, rumours were spreading about special secret programmes in mental hospitals and other institutions: rumours about purging 'disease', whether racial, hereditary or criminal. Sterilization programmes began, aimed at the mentally ill and the disabled. Then the euthanasia programme started: 'useless eaters' were being 'weeded out'.[23] The subject entered the school curriculum and covered Jews, gypsies and homosexuals, as well as the sick. Rumours of poison gas circulated in the universities. Sophie and her student friends turned in shock and despair to a deeper German past, to the ideas of Catholicism, to St Augustine and Thomas Aquinas for answers. Around this time, the Catholic Bishop of

Münster, Clemens August Galen, who could no longer turn a blind eye to these atrocities, began to speak out. His sermons appeared all over the country and were mailed through letter boxes. In response, Joseph Goebbels promised that the bishop would be hanged.[24]

For a conservative Catholic such as Huber, these events were undermining not only his sense of decency but also his sanity. His fury spilled forth during his lectures, in rhetorical comments and black humour. Sophie Scholl yearned for a kindred spirit. She invited her brother and his friends to Huber's lectures. Eventually they gathered up courage and approached Huber himself, inviting him to a reading event at the home of an acquaintance, Frau Doktor Mertens in Munich, in 1942. This small gathering consisted of writers, publishers and students from Huber's lectures. The readings included works by Goethe and Nietzsche. In fact, Nietzsche's philosophy was hotly debated. Discussions that evening centred on three points: the interpretation of friendship as a cardinal virtue; the doctrine of the great individuals whose duty it was to resist the de-individualizing tendencies in the era of the herd; and the doctrine 'God is dead'. The latter was not construed as an atheistic slogan, but reinterpreted as a prediction that God would die in a Church that backed an inhuman regime.[25] The atmosphere grew tense. The lights were turned down low and voices began to criticize the Third Reich in whispers. Huber ventured dangerous words: *something must be done, and it must be done now*. He didn't know it, but he was speaking at a clandestine meeting of the Resistance group known as the White Rose.[26]

Soon after this first encounter with the White Rose, student members were conscripted to fight at the Russian Front. They held a farewell party, to which Huber was again invited. In an atelier in Schwabing on the evening of 22 July the party began. It was a bohemian affair, again attended by publishers, writers, artists and intellectuals. Being a rather conservative family man, Huber was somewhat awkward, but he settled amongst the cushions and pillows liberally splashed in dark, rich colours around the floor. Schnapps and wine glistened in candlelit glasses. Cakes and snacks appeared in oriental bowls and orange, red and yellow painted dishes. Huber tried to appear at ease amongst this cultivated urbane crowd. Perhaps he tried too hard, for his tension bubbled to the surface too rapidly when talk turned to politics, his intensity was uncontainable, and he fractured the vague chatter with direct accusations, moral outrage and a call for action.

Shortly after this meeting, Sophie Scholl's brother and his student friends wrote a letter to Huber from the Russian Front.[27]

Kurt Huber, Russia August 17, 1942.

Dear Professor,

Two weeks ago after a long and eventful journey we arrived at this small, shell-torn town east of Vyaz'ma. . . . I meant to send you a post-card from Warsaw, while the whole of the student company was still together, but it all went far too quickly. The city, the ghetto, and the whole setup made a profound impression on all of us. It's impossible to give even a vague picture of what has assailed me in Russia since the day we crossed the frontier. I don't know where to begin. Russia is so vast. . . . War sweeps across the countryside like a rainstorm. The Russians are attacking in strength it seems, north and south of here, but it's uncertain how things will turn out.

With best regards, Yours sincerely,

Hans Scholl and Alexander Schmorell and

Willi Graf and Hubert

Furtwängler.[28]

All the signatures were from student members of the White Rose, and almost all would be executed within a year.[29]

Sophie and her brother Hans Scholl eventually declared their identity as members of the White Rose. Huber joined the organization and the clandestine meetings began. They met in student digs, unheated attics or at Huber's home when his wife and family were out. The White

Rose was a small, close-knit group of mainly student activists with strong philosophical interests. In a letter to his parents from Munich dated 17 April 1939, Hans Scholl wrote: 'At many lectures I'm the only medical student. All the rest are philosophers.' All the members of the White Rose shared a deep love of German philosophy and used ideas from this heritage to vent their loathing of the Nazis. They were especially fond of Nietzsche. In the same letter, Scholl went on to say 'I really ought to have a complete edition of Nietzsche for my Nietzsche studies. Maybe you could get one second-hand somewhere father . . .'[30] Hans Scholl did receive a copy and read all of Nietzsche, but 'found nothing to quench what his sister called the "burning emptiness" inside him . . .'[31]

The White Rose were brave and non-violent, and resisted in the only way they could: with words. They distributed idealistic, romantic leaflets, calling on the German people to stand up against repression and violence. Under Hitler these were difficult and dangerous things to do. To go out and find paper and printing materials, then to carry and distribute leaflets calling for the downfall of National Socialism, was a frightening enterprise and required painstaking determination.

> . . . since the conquest of Poland 300,000 Jews have been murdered in a bestial manner. Here we see the most terrible crime committed against the dignity of man, a crime that has no counterpart in human history. . . . Is this a sign that the German people have become brutalized in their basic human feelings?

This was the second leaflet produced by the White Rose during the third week of June 1942. It ended with the cry 'everyone is guilty, guilty, guilty'.[32] When Huber joined their group, they had already distributed five leaflets across the universities of southern Germany and beyond. They were planning their sixth and Huber was about to commit himself to writing it.[33]

It was early in 1943 and Huber had closed his curtains as usual for the blackout, thrown the last coal on the fire, and shuffled through his papers for some facts and figures. With the oil lamp flickering he began to write.[34] He wasn't afraid, which surprised him. His children and wife were sleeping and he could hear the gentle sounds of the night outside. After curfew there was little noise and the winter frost seemed to blanket the ground, rendering it mute. He was writing after the fall of Stalingrad. Two hundred thousand Germans had been killed and ninety thousand taken prisoner to Siberia: these were young men, some of whom Huber had taught, their lives bitterly squandered. The repressed anger that had welled up inside him for a decade against Hitler began to unleash. Slowly, painstakingly he crafted his words, absorbed in the task of communicating the details of recent atrocities for a student audience. In a way he was doing what he did regularly, typing out lectures in the early hours, except that these were clandestine words designed to ignite.

Sixth and Last Leaflet

Fellow Students,
Our people are deeply shaken by the fall of our men at Stalingrad. Three hundred and thirty thousand German men were senselessly and irresponsibly driven to their deaths by the brilliant strategy of our World War I corporal. Führer, we thank you!

'Führer, wir danken Dir' was the slogan used over and over at all mass rallies and appeared elsewhere on huge banners. The text continued:

The German people are in ferment. Will we continue to entrust the fate of our armies to this dilettante? Do we want to sacrifice the remaining German youth to the base ambitions of a Party clique? No, never! The day of reckoning has come – the reckoning of our German youth with the most abominable tyrant our people have ever been forced to endure. In the name of German youth, we demand Adolf

Hitler's state restore our personal freedom, the most precious treasure that we have, out of which he swindled us in the most wretched way.

We grew up in a state where all free expression of opinion has been suppressed. The Hitler Youth, the SA and the SS have tried to drug us, to revolutionize us, and to regiment us in the most promising years of our lives, normally devoted to acquiring education. 'Philosophical training' is the name given to the despicable method by which our budding intellectual development is smothered in a fog of empty phrases. A system of selection leadership at once unimaginably devilish and narrow minded, trains up its future party bigwigs in the 'Castles of the Knightly Order' to become Godless, arrogant, and conscienceless exploiters and executioners – blind, stupid hangers-on of the Führer. We 'intellectual Workers' are the ones who should put obstacles in the path of this caste of overlords . . .. *Gauleiters*[35] insult the honor of female students with crude jokes, and the German women students at the University in Munich have given a worthy response to the besmirching of their honor, and German students have defended their female comrades and stood by them . . . This is the beginning of the struggle for our free self-determination, without which intellectual and spiritual values cannot be created. We thank the brave comrades, both men and women, who have set us such a brilliant example.

Huber went on to say that there was only one option:

There is only one slogan for us: fight against the Party! Get out of all Party organizations, which are used to keep our mouths shut and hold us in political bondage! Get out of the lecture halls run by SS corporals and sergeants and Party sycophants! We want genuine learning and real freedom of expression. No threat can intimidate us, not even the closure of universities and colleges. The struggle is for each and every one of us, for our future, our freedom, and our honor under a regime that will be more conscious of its moral responsibility.

Freedom and honour! For ten long years Hitler and his comrades have squeezed, debased and twisted those beautiful German words to the point of nausea, as only the ignorant can, casting the highest values of a nation before swine. In the ten years of destruction of all material and intellectual freedoms, of all moral fibre in the German people, they have sufficiently demonstrated what they understand by freedom and honor. The frightful blood bath has opened the eyes of even the stupidest German – it is a slaughter that they orchestrated in the name of the 'freedom and honor of the German nation' throughout Europe, and which they start anew every day. The name of Germany will be forever stained with shame if German youth do not finally arise, fight back, and atone, smash our tormentors, and set up a new Europe of the spirit.

He then reminded students that the people were looking to them for action to rescue the nation from National Socialism, as an earlier generation of Germans had saved the nation from Napoleon, and called out to them: 'the dead of Stalingrad beseech us!

"Up, up my people, let smoke and flames be our sign!" '[36]

The blanket of night began to lift and the first cracks of pale grey appeared between the curtains. Shuffling sounds of a waking city echoed those of his own family stirring. Clara entered his room, and the artificial cloak of privacy was ruptured. She gasped at what he had composed, and the reality of his mission was suddenly stark before him.

In spite of his fear, Huber delivered the leaflet and ten thousand copies of it were distributed throughout Germany, carried on trains, dropped in mail boxes, piled for students to find after lectures throughout German universities. A few remaining leaflets were sitting in the bottom of a suitcase and Hans and Sophie Scholl decided to drop them from the main building of Munich University on 18 February 1943. A caretaker standing below the window witnessed the papers fall like doves. Aroused by his own sense of importance, he raced to inform the Gestapo who tracked down Hans and Sophie and arrested them. Many other students were discovered, too, during the wave of interrogations that ensued.[37] But the Gestapo's investigations didn't end there.

When news reached Huber at the university that the Gestapo were making numerous arrests, he hoped against hope that his own name would not be revealed. His wife was away with little Wolf; she had left the country to barter possessions in exchange for food for the family. Hearing news of the interrogations he rushed home, and before his twelve-year-old daughter Birgit's astonished eyes, burned papers and documents and set fire to books.

During the course of the following week, alone in the house with Birgit, Huber stayed awake, pacing across the creaking floorboards throughout each night. At five one morning the bell rang. Birgit ran downstairs to answer. She was missing her mother and brother and hoped they had returned early. Three well-dressed men were standing at the door and asked politely whether her father was home. She felt shy and answered with a sideways glance: 'He's sleeping in bed.' They pushed past her and mounted the stairs. Now terrified, she ran to get past them to warn her father; the men blocked her way but she ducked beneath them, blistering her nails on the balustrade and screamed, 'Poppi, Poppi, the police are here.'[38] Her father, weary after his former nights' vigilance, had fallen asleep. He had given in to exhaustion and surrendered his anxieties to the overwhelming need for rest. His daughter's words penetrated his hazy mind and he clung for a second to the familiarity of the morning, his bed linen, the familiar slant of the curtains drawn across the dark sky, the oval mirror on the oak wardrobe, the comforting walls of his home enveloping him, the tinny pitch of his child's voice. A moment later he sat bolt upright. They had come for him on Friday, 26 February 1943.

It grieved him that he had to leave his daughter on her own behind him as the three men escorted him out of the house. He was heading for trial and imprisonment. Then the shock of what now awaited him sent tremors through his body. He felt the panic thumping in his chest and he had to concentrate hard just to breathe. Stadelheim Prison emerged before him, its walls towering around him, peeling paint on unplastered bricks, metal windows with metal bars, blankets that were infused with the stale odours from previous meals, other men's last days: forced, dirty intimacy.

Unbeknown to Huber, two days earlier on Wednesday, 24 February the Nationalist Socialist Party had been celebrating: it was the founding of their new title. To mark the occasion Hitler had sent a proclamation to Munich, 'the capital of the [Party's] movement'. On this day, he exclaimed, 'the Party has to break terror with tenfold terror. ... It has to extinguish traitors – whoever they are, whatever their disguise.' The announcement specifically mentioned the universities and Goebbels then demanded on 27 February that 'hostile university members be subjected to the free use of corporal punishment'.[39] It was unlucky timing for Kurt Huber and the White Rose.

Huber learned in due course that Hans and Sophie Scholl had been beheaded and that the same fate had befallen other members of the White Rose whom he'd last seen in lectures, students chatting vivaciously, clattering down university corridors.[40] He suffered painful prison visits from his wife and family, hope and for him a sense of honour interspersed with doubt, guilt, fear. Feeling utterly out of control, he had to regain control in the only way he knew how, by retreating to the mind. He asked Clara to bring his notes on Leibniz, and while the Gestapo mounted their indictment he wrote his magnum opus – in the same prison where Hitler had been briefly incarcerated over two decades earlier. He performed similar actions to Hitler, sitting in a cell writing, but there were no gifts from well-wishers and no special treatment from the guards.[41] Moreover, Huber's text couldn't have contrasted more with Hitler's. Whereas the Führer's was vulgar, fuelled by hate and a bitter drive for dominance, Huber drafted a sophisticated tract on the inherent goodness of God's creation. He also attempted an explanation for the existence of evil.

The preparation for Huber's trial took months, all through the spring and long summer of 1943. Meanwhile, his family made an appeal for clemency. This dragged its way up through the highest echelons of the military, but the reponse was: 'I reject all petitions of mercy.' It was signed by Adolf Hitler.[42] When the trial finally beckoned, Huber learned that among the five judges was the notorious Roland Freisler, a virtual psychopath who indulged his power over defendants, relishing every last drop of indignity and humiliation he could bestow upon them. He virtually drooled when he saw Huber, a disgraced intellectual, before him. 'Whom the gods love they punish', Huber whispered to himself as he went into the dock.[43] Adding to Huber's misery was the absence of his character witness who was 'out of town', and as he stood to prepare himself for the fourteen-hour ordeal, standing for most of the time without food or drink, his defence lawyer also abandoned him. He was completely alone.

The final leaflet of the White Rose was read out in court; the audience of hand-picked Nazi officials was outraged. Freisler jeered at Huber and taunted him as he was ordered to take the stand. Huber stood and governed his composure by taking the notes he had prepared for his own defence. He spoke: 'What I had in mind was the awakening of the students, not through organising, but through the power of the sheer word, not to arouse to acts of violence, but to give them insights into what heavy damage has been done to our political life.' Huber quoted one of the Führer's alleged favourites, the German philosopher Johann Gottlieb Fichte: '*And you must act, as if, on you and your actions alone the fate of Germany depends and the responsibility were yours.*'[44]

Freisler applauded in mock sincerity and followed with a tirade of sneers, insults and gestures of humiliation. 'I don't know any Professor Huber or any Dr. Huber. I know defendant Huber. He doesn't have the right to be a German, he's a bum,' he laughed.[45] The Nazis had stripped Huber of his doctorate and professorship. Next they took away his life. 'Those sentenced to death on the right side,' yelled a guard, 'those to prison on the left.' Huber was ushered to the right. The Leibniz treatise was to remain unfinished, as the Nazis wouldn't give permission to extend the stay of execution to enable its completion.

Huber would have to face death alone, but this was not what concerned him most. He felt anxious for his family. Powerless to help them, he feared for the aftermath of Nazi persecutions that were common towards 'criminal families'. His four-year-old son and young daughter, what hardships would they face without him there to protect them? As he wrestled with his anxieties he felt the love for his family well up deep within him and he wrote to them, thanking them for making his life rich and beautiful: 'In front of me in my cell are the Alpine roses you sent. . . . I go in two hours into that true mountain freedom for which I've fought all my life. May the Almighty God bless you and keep you. Your loving father.'[46]

Huber was summoned to his execution on 13 July 1943. It irritated him as he crossed the courtyard to the guillotine that he limped, his leg dragging behind him, and his hands trembled – the final humiliation that he couldn't stand as firmly as he would have liked. The chaplain smiled, Huber moved the muscles of his mouth to reflect the gesture. The courtyard stretched out to an infinity of grey stones on a hot, humid July day. Torn away from his final attachment, his work, he sought that last remaining place to go, from body and human cares to the world of the mind, the thought of his family, their enduring spirit, the deeper German spirit in which he still truly believed.

After the philosopher's death his family were denied his pension. Students and friends collected funds on their behalf, but the Nazis appropriated these and arrested anyone caught performing this subversive activity. Then the Gestapo paid a routine visit to Clara and ordered her to pay the equivalent of two months' salary for 'wear on the guillotine'.[47]

CHAPTER 10

The Nuremberg Trials and Beyond

After a decade's rule, Hitler's dream appeared to have been realized. Rosenberg, Bäumler, Krieck and the other Nazi collaborators had a tight hold over the universities, while opponents such as Benjamin, Adorno, Arendt and Huber had been ousted, silenced or killed. The programme to dominate the German mind had been well established.

The Reich, however, was not to last for a thousand years. Had Kurt Huber and Walter Benjamin survived another few years, they would have witnessed Europe descend under a thick blanket of carnage. In the early winter of 1945, when the sun would ordinarily have been low in the sky casting long shadows over the ground, the Allies bombed German cities so intensely that the light was all but obliterated. Huge dust clouds hovered, obscuring the chaos and debris below. Then the unnaturally dark winter turned into spring and a few small glimpses of the softening season emerged.

As his defeat became inevitable, and his generals started to question his leadership, Hitler began to panic. In his bunker in Berlin, this great 'philosopher-leader' who had seemed infallible raged like a madman. He turned to those still supporting him and immediately made a number of decisions that he acted upon, such as marrying Eva Braun.[1] After their wedding the news reached him that Benito Mussolini had been captured by Italian partisans, executed, and his body hung upside down for public display in the marketplace of Milan on 28 April 1945, before being beaten and pelted by the furious crowd.[2] On hearing this, Hitler now repeated the order that his and Eva Braun's bodies were to be destroyed 'so that nothing remains': 'I do not wish to fall into the hands of enemies who for the amusement of their whipped-up masses, will need a spectacle arranged by Jews.' [3] On 30 April while the Battle of Berlin raged above, Hitler resorted to his last gory act.

The death of a monster is always shrouded in speculation and myth, and so there were varying stories surrounding the fate of the Führer, alleged sightings and speculation that he had been murdered. The most authoritative version was that cyanide capsules were in his possession, and to check that they worked Hitler tried them out on his Alsatian Blondi – the pet promptly died a horrible death.[4] He then supplied his newly wed wife with the poison and went with her into his private suite in the bunker. Martin Bormann, Goebbels, Heinz Linge (the Führer's valet) and others waited outside the door. After an interval they entered: 'Hitler was lying on the sofa, which was soaked with blood. He had shot himself through the mouth. Eva Braun was also on the sofa, also dead. A revolver was by her side, but she had not used it: she had swallowed poison. The time was half-past three.'[5]

Shortly afterwards, 'two corpses were taken and placed side by side ... and petrol ... was poured over them'. A rag was dipped in petrol and set alight and flung upon the corpses. 'They were at once enveloped in a sheet of flame.'[6] Hitler's last pyromaniac fantasy had been indulged.[7]

After the Führer's demise the German forces in Berlin were finally defeated. On 7 May 1945 Germany signed an unconditional surrender and the following day became V-E, Victory in Europe, day. The sun broke through the clouds and the most terrible period in modern history had, at last, come to an end. But soon, ghostly apparitions began to appear: the numerous concentration camps with their gas chambers were revealed and, as the civilized world recoiled, the full extent of the Holocaust became apparent. Then, before the shock could be absorbed, the business of holding the perpetrators to account got underway.

The Palace of Justice in the city of Nuremberg, Bavaria, became the centre of international attention. Prominent members of the Third Reich were to be prosecuted in the 'Trial of the Major War Criminals' before the International Military Tribunal.[8]

The main courtroom in the Palace of Justice had a high ceiling from which cold-looking lights glared. The walls were wooden panelled with ornate carvings of state. The rest of the room was a fairly modest affair with a bare floor and simple wooden pews as in a church. The Soviet, British, American and French flags hung behind the judges' bench. The wooden tables were piled with sheets of paper, reflecting the harsh light from above. On the left was the dock for the defendants, in front of them the German defence counsels – all members of the former Nazi Bar Association. Behind a glass screen listening through headphones were the translators, and opposite them the presiding judges. In the centre the prosecuting attorneys stood, and before them was the witness box. Allied soldiers flanked the room in the full military attire of the various nations.[9]

At 10 o'clock in the morning on 20 November 1945 a hushed silence spread through the court as proceedings commenced. The chief prosecutor, Justice Robert H. Jackson, stood before the bench, shuffling his papers in preparation for his opening statement. He began: 'History does not record a crime ever perpetuated against so many victims or one ever carried out with such calculated cruelty.'[10] On trial were Hitler's generals. Some, like Hitler himself, escaped being brought to justice. Roland Freisler, for example, the sadistic judge who had sentenced Kurt Huber along with other members of the White Rose, had been killed on 3 February 1945 when American Flying Fortresses on a massive raid had dropped almost three thousand tons of bombs. Reports claimed that Freisler had 'bled to death on the pavement outside the People's Court at Bellevuestrasse 15 in Berlin'.[11]

Most leading Nazis were forced to stand trial, and after a catalogue of harrowing evidence were charged with crimes against humanity. Facing the law was Rudolf Hess, Hitler's deputy, who had watched the Führer type out *Mein Kampf* in Landsberg gaol. He had gone on 'to participate in aggression against Austria, Czechoslavakia, and Poland' and had 'signed multiple decrees persecuting Jews'. Referred to as 'the engineer tending to the Party machinery', he was spared the hangman's noose on account of his alleged mental problems: 'Defendant Rudolf Hess, on the counts of the Indictment on which you have been convicted, the International Military Tribunal sentences you to imprisonment for life.'[12]

The Reichminister for the Eastern Occupied Territories, Alfred Rosenberg, also stood trial. Throughout the trial it was agreed that Rosenberg's book the *Myth of the Twentieth Century* was, along with *Mein Kampf*, the ultimate Nazi bible. He had indoctrinated a generation of Germans and furthered the persecution of the Jews; it was his directives that had provided for segregation in the ghettos and facilitated mass murder. The court found him guilty of conspiracy to commit crimes against peace; planning, initiating and waging wars of aggression; war crimes; and crimes against humanity. He was sentenced: 'Defendant Alfred Rosenberg, on the counts of the Indictment on which you have been convicted, the International Military Tribunal sentences you to death by hanging.'[13]

On the morning of 16 October 1946, at Nuremberg, the following grisly description of Rosenberg's last moments was revealed:

> Three black-painted wooden scaffolds stood inside the gymnasium, a room approximately 33 feet wide by 80 feet long with plaster walls in which cracks showed. The gymnasium had been used only three days before by the American security guards for a basketball game. Two gallows were used alternately. The third was a spare for use if needed. The men were hanged one at a time, but to get the executions over with quickly, the military police would bring in the man while the prisoner who proceeded him still was dangling at the end of the rope.

The . . . once great men in Hitler's Reich that was to have lasted for a thousand years walked up thirteen wooden steps to a platform eight feet high which also was eight square feet.

Ropes were suspended from a crossbeam supported on two posts. A new one was used for each man.

When the trap was sprung, the victim dropped from sight in the interior of the scaffolding. The bottom of it was boarded up with wood on three sides and shielded by a dark canvas curtain on the fourth, so that no one saw the death struggles of the men dangling with broken necks.

. . . The scaffold was made ready for Alfred Rosenberg.

Rosenberg was dull and sunken-cheeked as he looked around the court. His complexion was pasty-brown, but he did not appear nervous and walked with a steady step to and up the gallows.

Apart from giving his name and replying 'no' to a question as to whether he had anything to say, he did not utter a word. Despite his avowed atheism he was accompanied by a Protestant chaplain who followed him to the gallows and stood beside him praying.

Rosenberg looked at the chaplain once, expressionless. Ninety seconds after he was swinging from the end of a hangman's rope. His was the swiftest execution. . . [14]

After the main trials ended on 1 October 1946, a whole succession of further cases took place. Judges, medics and other senior figures were all called to account for their atrocities. These proceedings for 'lesser war criminals' were conducted under Control Council Law No. 10 at the US Nuremberg Military Tribunals. The list of crimes continued to make traumatic reading.

What, however, happened to the myriad of other Germans who had bolstered Hitler – the schoolteachers, civil servants and academics? More especially, what happened to the philosopher-collaborators, those who together with Rosenberg had helped to develop and establish Nazi ideology? Rosenberg had been a senior Party member and his conviction was for actually implementing genocide. Other collaborating academics were regarded by the court as less culpable. Their crimes had been thought crimes only. But those survivors who had actually suffered under the Nazis were not convinced that trying to alter the mindset of a whole nation was any less heinous a crime than actually using a gun.

So while the Nuremberg trials were deployed to prosecute the leaders of the regime, from autumn 1945 until autumn 1946 the Allies formalized and developed de-Nazification committees.[15] These committees were then turned over to the Germans and developed into local civilian tribunals known as *Spruchkammer*.[16] Designed to weed out the influence of Nazis in the press, judiciary and cultural institutions, they also focused upon education – all institutions were assessed including the universities. In the beginning anyone who was a National Socialist Party member was listed. Names included a whole tranche of philosophers. In fact, there were soon too many names for the Allies to process, so they changed the system to assess complicity on an individual case-by-case basis. Categories of collaboration were produced ranging from the worst, *Hauptschuldiger* (Major Offender), to decreasing levels of involvement, *Belastet* (Activist), *Minderbelastet* (Lesser Incriminated Person), to the mildest, *Mitläufer* (Fellow Traveller).[17]

Two philosophers in particular came under scrutiny: Rosenberg's most ardent accomplices, Bäumler and Krieck. First off, Alfred Bäumler was captured by the Allies and assessed as *Hauptschuldiger*, the worst category of Nazi. He escaped Rosenberg's grisly end, however, and was given just a three-year sentence, for which he was interned in Hammelburg Prison.

Hammelburg had become well-known through Lieutenant General George Patton, the most popular general in America, for his son-in-law, Lieutenant Colonel John K. Waters, had been interned there. It was somewhat poignant that after the war Bäumler should be incarcerated in the same place.[18] Thereafter he was interned at Ludwigsburg, a city in Baden-Württemberg, about 12 kilometres north of Stuttgart near the river Neckar. Ludwigsburg was also notable for being the same city associated with the 1940 Nazi propaganda film, *Jud Süss* – infamous for its vilification of the Jews.[19]

Bäumler was released after only three years in custody and went to live in Eningen unter Achalm, near Reutlingen. There he produced an enormous body of work, 752 copies of documents, mainly manuscripts. He claimed to have denounced Nazism, but his post-war research is not available for public viewing and is only accessible after 'consultation with the heiress of the estate'.[20] He died in 1968.

Whereas Bäumler had been quickly captured, Ernst Krieck had not been. He was soon, however, tracked down and interned by the US occupying forces. He awaited trial in the camp of Moosburg, which had a dark past. In 1939, shortly after the beginning of the Second World War, a POW camp called Stalag VII A had been established there. Eighty thousand prisoners had been interned in this camp until the end of the war. In the corner of the fenced perimeter, obscuring the view, was a former watchtower and a sinister wooden platform from where the Nazi soldiers had surveilled the former prisoners of war, watching a large number be transported to the concentration camps of Dachau and Buchenwald where they had been killed.[21] After the war and until 1948 the camp served as Civilian Internment Camp No. 6 with up to twelve thousand prisoners.[22]

Krieck occupied a small cell containing wooden bunks that had been made by the prisoners, where he awaited trial. He could look out through his window beyond the barbed-wire fence, south towards the town of Moosburg with its two church steeples. He would have been spared the horrific ordeal that befell the previous inmates, but while he was waiting for proceedings to get underway he died on 19 March 1947.[23] No trial had taken place and so no verdict was reached. Very little is known about the exact circumstances of Krieck's death, but it seems that he simply died from natural causes.

While Krieck had died and Bäumler met with a fairly light sentence, how did other Nazi philosophers fare? With the exception of Dr Ernst Bergmann, professor of philosophy at the University of Leipzig, who committed suicide in 1945,[24] others seemed to wait for the de-Nazification committees to track them down and build legal cases against them. Max Hildebert Boehm, professor of philosophy, legal science and sociology at the University of Jena,[25] was instructed on 12 July 1945 by an Allied committee to be removed from the university.[26] In 1945, Hans Heyse, Rector of Königsberg University, likewise was also officially relieved of his post.[27] However, both Boehm and Heyse shortly afterwards continued with their careers. Boehm founded a state-sponsored Northeastern German Academy in Lüneburg where, bizarrely enough, up to the 1960s his main areas of work were on German policy regarding refugees and displaced people.[28] Heyse meanwhile only appeared to retire formally in 1953.[29]

Other philosophy faculty members across the nation manoeuvred to evade their convictions. They included Eugen Fehrle, who had 'tyrannized the Philosophy Faculty' in Heidelberg in the Nazi period.[30] He fled but was eventually caught, arrested and interned for two years in Karlsruhe Hospital. On 5 January 1948 the de-Nazification committee charged him with racist purging of the universities and using academic scholarship for political ends.[31] Described as 'fundamentally important for the destruction of the old scientific spirit of the university',[32] Fehrle was labelled Hauptschuldiger. However, he scrabbled around for affidavits from colleagues in German universities in the postwar period, then employed a highly trained team of lawyers to downgrade his official category to Mitläufer.[33] Having cheated the de-Nazification squads, in October 1950 he was granted Emeritus status at Heidelberg University by Baden's Ministry of Culture and then enjoyed a revival in popularity over the course of the next decade.[34]

Public records are sparse for many of the 1945 legal proceedings. However, in spite of the Nuremberg trials and efforts of the initial Allied de-Nazification committees, the past records of Nazi collaborators were subject to concealment and whitewashing when the Germans themselves took over the restorative process.[35] Treacherous philosophers hid their collaboration, covered up the scale of their involvement, and if caught, fought long, drawn-out legal cases. Having backed an evil regime, they fled, hid, lied, manipulated and rewrote their own history, doing whatever they could to save themselves when the tables turned.

Jewish intellectuals were outraged. The distinguished Yiddish scholar Max Weinreich – forced to flee from Poland to America under the Nazi jackboot[36] – declared that if the question of legal responsibility was one for a United Nations Tribunal, then the culpability of German scholarship was 'for the world's conscience to decide'.[37] So while the Nuremberg trials were in session from 1945 to 1946 a group of Jewish scholars met in the few surviving cafés, libraries and university buildings. They huddled together as if sheltering from a storm. Led by Weinreich, in hushed voices they asked: 'Are Germany's intellectual leaders guilty of complicity in the crimes against humanity?' 'Along with the political and military leaders, did they prepare, institute, and bless the program of vilification, enslavement and murder?'[38] Then the scholars combed through libraries, universities, publishing houses and former Nazi institutions across Germany. Collecting articles as evidence, they discussed and read incriminating material into the early hours under poor light in the postwar decrepit conditions. Amidst crumbling ruins they gathered material buried in archives, in the heart of the Nazi gaols, torture chambers and courthouses of the Reich, and managed to find thousands of papers, many of which had been kept secret for a decade. They then shipped their research across the Atlantic to Weinreich in America, who combined them with a systematic reading of scholarly publications. And as the Nuremberg trials entered their final weeks and the de-Nazification committees struggled to administer justice, Weinreich was ready to make these findings known to the world.[39] 'Only the names of the engineers who so ingeniously constructed the gas chambers and death furnaces remain in obscurity,' he commented.[40] The scholars would not.

Dr Otto Höfler, professor at the University of Munich, had eulogized Nazi ideology and vociferously argued for the continuity of ancient Germanic culture into latter-day folklore.[41] So now Weinreich exposed him. However, while he could uncover the truth he was powerless to prosecute justice. After the war Höfler was officially categorized merely as a 'Fellow Traveller'. He moved back to his native Austria where he continued to work, living in Vienna from 1951 to 1971. His views remained decidedly racist during his postwar tenure, although this did not prevent him publishing. In 1978, for example, the Austrian Academy of Sciences in Vienna published his continuing work on German folklore.[42]

Hans Gerhard Johann Hagemeyer, known as Hans Hagemeyer, had worked closely with Alfred Rosenberg in high positions in his commission in the Offices of Philosophical Information and was a senior official in Rosenberg's main anti-Jewish organization.[43] In spite of Weinreich's publicity, however, no records exist of any trial. After the war, Hagemeyer moved to the Soviet zone of occupation and lived in Bremen as a pensioner.[44]

Erich Rothacker, professor at the University of Bonn, had been a fervent Nazi, even discussing in earnest Hitler's contribution to German philosophy.[45] After the war ended he merely suffered a 'brief suspension from teaching' and then continued as professor in Bonn where he wrote and published freely in philosophy, associating with many well-known philosophers until his retirement in 1956. After his death in 1965, at the age of seventy-seven, his research archive was continued by Hans Georg Gadamer.[46]

Professor Max Wundt of Tübingen (son of the famous psychologist and philosopher Wilhelm Max Wundt) was a philosopher who studied the development of Fichte's thought.[47] A dedicated Nazi, he was promoted to professor at Tübingen from 1929 to 1945. Despite

Weinreich's exposé, current records indicate that Wundt continued to work and publish after the war into the late 1940s and 1950s. Archives hold materials connected with his life, including letters to his parents, war memoirs, some portrait photos, and his manuscripts on the history of philosophy and race.[48] To commemorate him, in 1964 Hildesheim publishers even reprinted one of his best-known treatises from the Nazi era.[49]

Weinreich uncovered a host of other Nazi collaborators such as Dr Walther Schulze-Sölde,[50] professor of philosophy at the University of Innsbruck; Dr Hans Alfred Grunsky,[51] professor of philosophy at the University of Munich, who had written a racist diatribe against Jews in philosophy; Professor Georg Stieler, Heidegger's colleague and associate professor of philosophy at Freiburg;[52] and Dr August Faust, who had enthusiastically supported Hitler.[53] Little is known about their post-war lives. The trail runs cold.

Everything ran cold in post-Nuremberg Germany. The wooden-panelled walls in the Palace of Justice rose darkly and obscurely on all sides. The official lights lost their glare as the dust settled and the wooden pews became damp as the heating dimmed. Gone were the flags and their brilliant colours, the echo of the bustle from journalists, camera lenses and officials. Even the sombre shadows of the prosecutors from the military tribunal faded. The main courtroom had a curious silence about it. In spite of the attempt to return it to normality with the petty business of ongoing adjudication, the atmosphere remained heavy. Much later, a Memorium to the Nuremberg Trials would be set up tucked away in the attic.

During the post-war years, Jewish scholars struggled for justice, but a pattern of overlooking Nazi records spread across Germany. Academic authorities did little to exorcise the demons of the university halls. For example, Oskar Becker had been Edmund Husserl's assistant.[54] After Husserl's suspension, Becker had collaborated with the Nazis. One of his most famous lectures, on 'The Vacuity of Art and the Daring of the

Artist', presented a 'Nordic Metaphysics' in typical Nazi style. However, despite being shunned by émigré philosophers, he suffered few consequences after the war. Indeed in the 1950s he received great acclaim for his work in the field of logic.[55]

Erik Wolf, the head of the Freiburg Faculty of Law under the Nazis, also seemed to get off lightly. He had become an extreme Nazi under the influence of Heidegger and had borrowed ideas of totalitarianism from Schmitt via the influence of a fellow Nazi, Ernst Forsthoff.[56] Whatever the proceedings against Wolf he continued to lead a productive and undisturbed life in post-war Germany, as his list of publications revealed: volumes of his work appear in Tübingen from the late 1940s and throughout the 1950s.[57]

You might be forgiven for thinking that this was the end of the matter, that Hitler's philosophers simply managed to evade justice. But something even worse was about to happen.

In the 1950s, academic faculties in both East and West Germany began to reappoint former Nazis. Johannes Kühn, who had contributed zealously to racist philosophy and who had been an outspoken proponent of war during Hitler's chancellorship, after a quiet period in the immediate aftermath of 1945, rejoined the Heidelberg philosophy faculty. He was soon joined by Helmut Meinhold in 1952. During the war Meinhold had been a key Nazi serving in the Institute of German Labour in the East, and in Cracow he had 'planned the depopulation and resettlement of Poland'. In 1957 he was not only reappointed to the faculty but actually made its chairman in Heidelberg. In fact, by 1957 the philosophy faculty was almost entirely dominated by former members of the National Socialist Party, including Eric Maschke, Reinhard Herbig and Werner Conze.[58] One prominent scholar wrote that 'by the mid 1950s, the [Heidelberg] philosophy faculty had become a stronghold of former Nazis or pro-Nazis'.[59] This scenario was repeated throughout East and West Germany. Having succeeded under one regime, former Nazis had wormed their way back into posts under another.

Hitler's philosophers were very secretive and never discussed their past. In fact, anyone attempting to raise the Nazi issue was very likely to be punished:

> If one thinks back to the events of 1933, one would think it would be unnecessary to waste a word about them, because most of today's adult generation ... must have been branded. ... My experiences of the years 1952–1954, however, have shown me that this is surely not the case: all the acts of National Socialism were either forgotten or were supposed to be ignored.[60]

A veil of silence descended across the university halls and this extended well into the 1960s. The next generation of students who were dependent for their careers upon their former Nazi teachers were also reluctant to challenge their masters, indeed they often defended them. So from 1945 until well into the 1960s, German philosophy departments were mired in cover-ups of atrocious pasts. Leading Nazis such as Ernst Krieck, Eugen Fehrle and Alfred Bäumler were scapegoated as fanatics, but others who had wholeheartedly collaborated avoided scrutiny; a taboo was firmly established.[61]

Even more disturbingly, there is ample evidence that former Nazi philosophers, despite their attempted cover-ups during the post-war years, remained unaltered in their views. Philosophy departments were enmeshed in a web of pro-Nazi sympathy and widespread anti-Semitism. Special forums, discussion groups and organizations were created to help them – as if they represented a special cause! For example, ironically, 'Academia Moralis' was the name of a support network at Heidelberg University run by Ernst Forsthoff, a disciple of Carl Schmitt.[62]

So what became of the more esteemed philosophers who had collaborated? Whereas many lesser names could hide in anonymity, surely famous thinkers had been so much in the public eye that it would be impossible for them to conceal their pasts?

On a clear day in 1945 Hitler's lawmaker Carl Schmitt awoke to the heavy thud of military fists upon the front door of his home. The Americans had been alerted to Schmitt's potential involvement with Nazi crimes and called at his house, placing him under arrest. (This was two months prior to the trials of the major Nazi leaders at Nuremberg.) Then for more than a year he was held in various internment camps, awaiting a decision as to whether he should be tried. Schmitt was savvy in answering questions and presented a difficult case. Like other collaborating Nazis he underplayed his role and the extent to which he had benefited from the regime. He claimed that as a jurist he was *forced* to work for the Third Reich, but given the scale of his Nazi publications and anti-Semitic writings this didn't convince anyone. He was therefore transferred to Nuremberg in March 1947 to be tried for war crimes. With the threat of retribution around the corner, Schmitt deployed his talents with intent.[63]

Meanwhile at this time the scale of the atrocities of the Holocaust were coming to light, including 6 million murdered Jewish men, women and children. As Max Weinreich explained, 'If the murdered be placed one behind the other in marching order, the column of skeletons would extend all the way from New York to San Francisco, and then all the way back from San Francisco to New York, and then from New York to Chicago.'[64] In the light of these findings, Schmitt summed up his view of his own culpability: 'the deed for which I am being held responsible . . . is essentially the publication of scholarly opinions which have led to many fruitful discussions'.[65]

Schmitt did not meet the fate of other senior Nazis. No public trial for him. He was simply released and returned to his home town of Plettenberg, and later to the house of his housekeeper Anni Stand in Plettenberg-Pasel. He refused every attempt at de-Nazification, the only sanction being that he was barred from positions in academia. Despite being isolated from the mainstream of the scholarly community, he continued his work and received a never-ending stream of visitors, among them well-known intellectuals such as Ernst Jünger, Jacob Taubes and Alexandre Kojève.

Schmitt resumed his studies of philosophy and international law from the 1950s in Germany. Although banned from an official post himself, his work became wholeheartedly endorsed in Germany's leading universities because of the efforts of Ernst Forsthoff, the Nazi who had returned to the Heidelberg law faculty in 1951. Forsthoff was also especially effective in transmitting Schmitt's ideas to the Western academic world.[66] In 1962, Schmitt gave lectures in Francoist Spain, which were then disseminated to great acclaim – in America one publisher considered it appropriate and sufficient to refer to him as 'one of the great legal and political thinkers of the 20th century'.[67] Schmitt's works were disseminated worldwide, both to the West and East, and translated into many foreign languages, including Japanese and Korean.

Schmitt always complained about being a victim of circumstances and named his house 'San Casciano', after the home of the exiled Niccolò Machiavelli who had lost favour with his patrons, the Medici family. Schmitt never apologized for his involvement with Nazism or his anti-Semitic publications in the light of the Holocaust. After living a long life, he died on 7 April 1985, aged ninety-seven.

In the meantime, while Schmitt had been defending himself, what had happened to Germany's most venerated philosopher of all, Hitler's 'superman', Martin Heidegger? In the early spring of 1945 as the Allies advanced on Freiburg, Heidegger had moved his faculty to a medieval fortress, Castle Wildenstein, in the valley of the upper Danube. There, as in a fairy tale, he retreated with one of his students, the beautiful Princess of Sachsen-Meiningen, and rumour had it that they embarked on a love affair. Throughout the summer of that year, while Freiburg was under the control of the French, Heidegger's faculty worked from their romantic hideaway. In June 1945, still as full professor of philosophy, Heidegger gave a lecture: 'All our thoughts are concentrated on things of the mind.

We have become poor, that we might become rich.'[68] For him, 'becoming poor' coincided with the defeat of the Nazis.

The French colonial infantry division running Freiburg produced a list of Nazi collaborators and Heidegger, who was locally known as a 'Nazi typique', was on the list. The first measure taken was the requisitioning of accommodation provided by the university. This included Heidegger's home: Rötebuck 47.[69] When the Freiburg philosophy faculty returned to their city, Heidegger, desperate to defend his turf, wrote:

> On what legal grounds I have been made the target of such an unheard-of proceeding I cannot imagine. I wish to protest in the strongest possible terms against this attack upon my person and my work. Why should I have been singled out for punishment and defamation before the eyes of the whole city – indeed before the eyes of the world – not only by having my home requisitioned in this manner, but also by being stripped of my employment? I never held office of any kind within the Party, and was never active in the Party or any of its organizations.[70]

In spite of his protests, Heidegger was subject to the formal proceedings of the de-Nazification of Freiburg.[71] Outraged, he protested his persecution before embarking on an elaborate defence. He reconstructed his life and career from 1933 until 1945 as one of minimal involvement with the Third Reich. 'Have you ever read *Mein Kampf*?' he was asked. His reply was that he 'found its content repugnant'.[72] He even mentioned Kurt Huber and the White Rose sympathetically during an interrogation when he was defending himself.[73] Astonishingly enough, the French military government bought all this. Heidegger was categorized as merely a 'Fellow Traveller', and recommended for Emeritus status at the university, retaining his right to teach.

The new democratic governors of Freiburg University protested – it would be a mockery if this intellectual Pied Piper, who had led so many young scholars astray, were to be treated so leniently.[74] Getting wind of this, Heidegger rushed to secure his Emeritus status. But the tide had turned and the philosopher Karl Jaspers, formerly a loyal friend but snubbed by Heidegger on account of his Jewish wife during the Nazi era, was asked to make a report. Jaspers had admired Heidegger but he could not in all conscience withhold the degree of Heidegger's involvement as a collaborator. Jaspers concluded that along with Carl Schmitt and Alfred Bäumler, all three 'strove for the intellectual leadership of the National Socialist movement'.[75]

Eventually, the university was forced to ban Heidegger from teaching, but it still allowed him to retain Emeritus status. At some point financial sanctions were imposed, but even these were lifted. And as far as his home was concerned, he merely had to suffer the inconvenience of sharing it with another family. Nevertheless, although Heidegger's treatment at the hands of the Allies was ludicrously tame in comparison to the sufferings of his Jewish colleagues, Heidegger was broken by it. What then ensued was a period in the Haus Baden sanatorium in Badenweiler, and a struggle with depression. The man who had not flinched at the idea of mass slaughter in the name of the German *Volk* collapsed under emotional strain when his own academic status was in jeopardy.

When he recovered, as he shortly did, both he and his wife scrabbled around for support – even turning to former Jewish students and colleagues. As it turned out, Heidegger successfully networked his way back into the academic world, acquiring allies from the unlikeliest of sources.[76]

In 1950, Hannah Arendt returned to Germany for the first time since the war had ended.[77] With conflicting emotions, she was going to visit Martin Heidegger. Although he had influenced Arendt's way of thinking, her devotion to Judaism meant that she had become hostile towards him. She never mentioned him in print until after the war in 1946, when she had written that Heidegger 'forbade Husserl, his teacher and friend, whose lecture chair he had inherited, to enter the faculty because Husserl

was a Jew'.[78] She often claimed that Heidegger should have resigned
rather than sign the letter firing Husserl, 'because I know,' she declared,
'that this letter and this signature almost killed him [Husserl], *I cannot but
regard Heidegger as a potential murderer*'.[79]

Arriving in Freiburg on 7 February, Arendt went straight to her
hotel, and from there sent a message. It was unsigned and simply said, 'I
am here.'[80] A short time later, dressed in her former European style,
Hannah waited in the foyer. She waited what seemed a long time.
Presently, a man in formal attire, his moustache and hair slightly greying,
appeared at the entrance. Hannah was startled but soon recovered her
outer poise – yet inwardly her nerves had reverted to those of an
eighteen-year-old girl as she recognized the man who had influenced her
for twenty years.

After their meeting, she wrote:

> Wiesbaden
>
> Alexanderstrasse 6–8
>
> February 9 1950.
>
> From the moment I left the house and got into the car, I have been
> writing this letter. And now, late at night, I cannot write after all. (I am
> using a typewriter because my fountain pen is broken and my hand-
> writing has become illegible.)
>
> This evening and this morning are the confirmation of an entire life. A
> confirmation that, when it comes down to it, was never expected.
> When the waiter spoke your name (I had not actually expected you,
> had not received the letter, after all), it was as if time had suddenly
> stood still . . .
>
> Hannah.

Heidegger promptly sent her a series of poems entitled 'Martin Heidegger
for Hannah Arendt: Five Poems'. One poem, 'You', read:

. . . .The stranger,

Even to yourself,

She is:

Mountain of joy, sea of sorrow,

Desert of desire,

Dawn of arrival.

Stranger: home of the one gaze

Where world begins.

Beginning is sacrifice.

Sacrifice is loyalty's hearth

still outglowing all the fires

ashes and –

igniting:

embers of charity,

shine of silence.

Stranger from abroad, you –

May you live in beginning.

For the friend's friend.[81]

After their reunion Arendt wrote with an abrupt change of tone. Gone
was the 'murderous monster'; in his place was a genius who ought not to
be disturbed by petty criticism about his past.[82] Hannah then embarked
on a project that would change the face of modern philosophy. She
helped to re-establish Heidegger on the world stage. To achieve this she
used, of all things, her connection with Jewish publishers to get him into
print across the world. The following letter is an example:

New York, 21 Febr. 1972

Dear Martin,

I am writing today about a publishing issue that might interest you. . . .
it was important to [the publisher] that a complete edition of your
works be produced. . . . He said he would do it immediately, including

everything that had not been published (whose scope, however he was not aware of), *with an advance to you of 100,000 DM...*

Of course, I have no idea whether you are interested. ... If you are interested, he will certainly be glad to come speak with you. If you want to approach him yourself, drop me a line and I will let him know. If you want to contact him directly yourself, his address: 1 Berlin 61, Lindernstrasse 76, telephone: 1911 (1) ...

All the best to both of you,

Hannah[83]

Hannah was joined by another unlikely thinker in support of Heidegger. From liberated France, Jean-Paul Sartre, in spite of having been a prisoner of war under the Nazis, had already incorporated Heidegger's philosophy into his own ideas. Sartre's enormous endorsement firmly helped to re-establish Heidegger on the post-war stage. This lining-up of Arendt and Sartre heralded a new era in Heidegger's life. He went back to the mountains, to Todtnauberg, and began to write again, this time about poetry and language. 'It is not we who speak language but language that speaks us,' he declared in cryptic tones. Language creates us and our world and all understanding of it. Heidegger, in the words of Sartre, 'rose up like a phoenix from the ashes'.[84]

Having manipulated the story of his involvement with the Nazi regime, played down his collaboration, meticulously edited and excluded his most incriminating works and speeches, Heidegger played the role of the innocent, abstract philosopher. Arendt, Sartre and many of the world's intellectuals bought his excuses and celebrated his genius. At no point, however, did Heidegger apologize for the harm he had caused or express any sympathy with the suffering of Hitler's victims. When pressed to comment on the Holocaust, he simply likened the loss of Jewish lives to the Germans killed during combat. And amidst all the pressure to repent, Heidegger complained to the Nazi writer Ernst Jünger that

Hitler had let him down. 'Is Hitler going to apologize to me?' he enquired.[85]

Years later Heidegger would invite the poet Paul Celan to Todtnauberg. Celan was Jewish. He had been confined to a ghetto, forced into labour and interned in a concentration camp under Hitler. His mother had been shot and his father had died, probably from typhus, also in a concentration camp. Celan was suffering from post-Holocaust trauma but he assumed Heidegger's invitation implied some profound reparation. So on 25 July 1967 he met the philosopher. But he was greeted with a cold silence. Recorded in the visitor's book at Todtnauberg were the poet's words: 'looking out at the star over the well, in the hope of a word to come in my heart'. The word never came. Soon after this meeting Celan took his own life by drowning himself in the Seine.[86]

None of this seemed to matter. Heidegger had been reappointed as a professor at Freiburg University back in 1951. Throughout the following decades he made appearances as an honorary professor, travelling widely and participating in conferences and colloquia, all dedicated to *his* work.[87] On 27 September 1959 he was decorated as an honorary citizen of Messkirch, and in Hausen in Germany he was awarded the Johann Peter Hebel Prize on 10 May 1960.[88] Being a former signed-up Nazi seemed to be no obstacle to enjoying a dazzling career in post-war Germany.[89]

If most Nazi philosophers avoided justice, what happened to the Jewish thinkers who survived? Were they reinstated in their jobs? Did those who had left return to Germany?

After a seemingly endless wait for the war to be over, those few Jewish–German philosophers who remained alive, whether in Germany or in Israel, America or other European sanctuaries, would have felt an inexpressible wave of relief. The force that had threatened to swallow up whole peoples, 'Hitler's Reich that was to have lasted for a thousand years', was at last vanquished.[90] These survivors celebrated but soon their celebrations were followed by a pang of homesickness. Questions arose in their minds: Could they go back? What would they find? How would they feel?

For one philosopher the possibility of returning home didn't arise, for he had never left. The psychiatrist and philosopher Karl Jaspers, a former friend of Heidegger and a close friend of Hannah Arendt, had remained in Germany throughout the era of the Third Reich. Jaspers had been said by the Nazis to have had a 'taint' due to Gertrude, his Jewish wife. He had resisted all attempts at Nazification and thus had been forced into early retirement back in 1937. His Chair in the faculty of philosophy had tellingly become the professorship for military policy and military sciences. Besides losing his job, a year later in 1938 Jaspers had been banned from publishing anything. He and his wife had endured over a decade of increasing terror, with the forever present threat of being sent to a concentration camp.[91] As the war came to an end, Jasper's terror was realized: his wife's name appeared on a Gestapo deportation list. American troops arrived just in time.[92]

In 1945, Jaspers was optimistic: Germany would be restored and former Nazis would be held to account. He became one of the professors responsible for reopening the University of Heidelberg, where he opposed the rehabilitation of professors with a Nazi past. However, having survived a threatened existence for so long under Hitler, Jaspers was devastated to find himself ignored as he witnessed the return of many Nazi philosophers. In 1948 he left his country, relinquishing his German citizenship in protest, and moved to the University of Basel, Switzerland where he remained for the rest of his life.[93]

For another individual, the question of returning to Germany also never arose, but for quite different reasons. Ernst Cassirer, the eminent philosopher of culture, had resigned from his rectorship at the University of Hamburg when Hitler came to power, and then left Germany.[94] At first he had found refuge in Oxford but after failing to secure a permanent post had been forced to leave, eventually becoming professor at Gothenburg University in Sweden. But in 1941 he had left that country, considering neutral Sweden to be too unsafe. Continuing his search for safety, he had gone on to find work in America. However, by the time the shores of his homeland beckoned it was too late. He died on 13 April 1945, less than a month before the Nazis were finally defeated.[95]

A further Jewish-German philosopher who had celebrated Hitler's demise was Herbert Marcuse, Adorno's friend, whose best-known works were *Eros and Civilization* and *One-Dimensional Man*. Like so many other Jewish intellectuals, he had found sanctuary in the United States. Marcuse became a US citizen in 1940, working from 1942 as an intelligence agent against the Nazis for the precursor to the CIA.[96] When the war ended he faced the very real option of returning. However, he declined and continued to reside in the US.[97]

The great friend of Walter Benjamin, Gerhard Scholem, had been born in Berlin. He had left Germany to become the first professor of Jewish mysticism at the Hebrew University of Jerusalem. During the era of the Third Reich, Scholem's brother had been murdered and many other of his close friends like Benjamin had suffered similar fates. Whatever his private affection for the place of his childhood, his feelings were buried under the years of savagery. Scholem never returned.[98]

On 8 May 1945, Hannah Arendt opened a bottle of champagne and toasted a new life for Germany. When her homeland became safe she was in the midst of writing an epic, analysing the origins of the Holocaust. From her flat in New York where she lived with her mother and husband, she worked tirelessly. For a decade she had been campaigning passionately for the plight of the Jews, offering herself as their intellectual voice and zealous spokesperson. Arendt, therefore, did not drop everything and return to Germany after the war ended but continued with her work in America. She was regularly in touch with her old mentor Karl Jaspers and had heard from him first-hand about the situation in Germany. If the 'air was so bad you couldn't breathe', she didn't want to risk going back, especially as she was perhaps the most vocal representative of the Jews. Arendt remained an exile in the US for a further six years until 1951, when she became a naturalized citizen.[99] Her epics, *The Origins of Totalitarianism* and *The Human Condition*, were soon published and she rocketed to stardom. However, Arendt's loyalty to the Jews would be called into question.

In 1960, Israeli security forces captured the SS lieutenant colonel Adolf Eichmann, who had been responsible for transporting Jews to the death camps. Among the Jews Eichmann had deported for extermination were the same women with whom Hannah had been interned in Gurs, and if it were not for her lucky escape she would have been among them. The following year Eichmann was tried in Israel, where Arendt covered the hearings as a correspondent for *The New Yorker*. Her articles were then revised and expanded for *Eichmann in Jerusalem*. Her report sparked outrage.

In *Eichmann in Jerusalem: A Report on the Banality of Evil*, Hannah was critical of Jewish leaders for organizing the Jewish community so efficiently that they had in fact, she alleged, unintentionally aided the process of genocide. She was also disparaging about the lack of resistance she claimed was shown by the Jews, and she berated the fact that they had not fought the Nazis. These comments were offensive enough to the many who had experienced the Holocaust first-hand, which, of course, Arendt never had, but the title of the book and its overall conclusion were what generated the most anger. Arendt had been disappointed to find that Eichmann, the monster who had ordered so many deaths, was merely an ordinary-looking man. She experienced no aura of power, no intelligence, no force of character, evil or otherwise, and was stunned at his 'banality'. He had no ideological motive that she could discern, no especial sadism, and was not even particularly Jew hating. He just seemed like a dull bureaucrat, merely fulfilling the role of his job. This led her to assert that evil was not essentially powerful or visible in its perniciousness, but simply mundane. The 'banality of evil' became a much-quoted phrase. This conclusion wounded the Holocaust survivors who, having experienced first-hand the atrocities of men like Eichmann, felt that they were anything but banal.

In her defence, it could be said that, like Adorno and Benjamin, Arendt was suspicious of the authoritarian tendencies of large-scale organizations. In their scale and efficiency, bureaucracies could exert enormous power. Coupled to this, they operated in abstract modes, detached from human engagement. They therefore held the potential to exercise evil. It was a point she had laboured in the *Origins of Totalitarianism*, and Eichmann for her was a perfect example, an unthinking bureaucrat who enacted evil through conformity with mass-administrative procedures. Eichmann himself contested this position during his trial. In his defence, controversially, he argued not that he had *not* acted unthinkingly but that he had followed Kant's moral philosophy, to be precise, Kant's categorical imperative. His version of Kant was that the moral law is not obeyed for specific reasons but solely because it is a law. The moral act is to be understood not as an expression of the good but as pure duty: 'your duty is . . . to do your duty'. This, for Eichmann, became the duty to follow the Führer's will. Precisely because this duty was imperative (categorical), he could avoid thinking. Eichmann's Kant, like that of other Nazis, is subject to gross distortion. But the fact remains that, like Hitler, here was another Nazi quoting Kant. It was becoming increasingly difficult to extricate philosophy from any involvement with Nazism. Arendt, however, was determined to do so. Was her drive in part to excuse her former lover?[100]

There was a further crushing issue. Whereas Jews the world over were desperate for a land they could call their own and were enmeshed in a gruelling attempt to gain one, Arendt was becoming vocally anti-Zionist. During her visit to Jerusalem to report on the Eichmann trial, she even went so far as to liken the new Israeli police to the Nazis. Arendt prompted the writer Saul Bellow to comment sourly on intellectuals in *Mr Sammler's Planet* (1969). Likewise, Isaiah Berlin noted her change of heart: 'when I first met her in 1942 her fanatical Jewish nationalism *which has now turned into its opposite* was, I remember, too much for me'.[101] Had her visit to Heidegger in 1950 modified her Jewish enthusiasm?

Whatever the ambiguities resulting from her feelings for Heidegger, Hannah never returned to live in Germany. She stayed in America where the controversy surrounding her is illustrated by her death in 1975. Hannah died unconsecrated by a religious ceremony (her ashes are buried at Bard College, New York State where Blücher taught), and the obituary in *The New York Times* tersely noted that she had 'no religious affiliation'. Although there are many uncertainties surrounding Arendt, one thing is certain: she never wanted to return back 'home', not even in death.

It seemed as if none of the Jewish exiles wanted to return 'home'. The horrors had been too immense and the purging of society too little. They remained scattered across America, Israel and Europe. There were, however, exceptions, a very small minority who were brave or determined enough to go back to the land that had been overridden by the Third Reich. These few, only 4 per cent of the total who had been expelled, decided to confront the past.[102] They included Karl Löwith, the German-Jewish philosopher who had been a student of Heidegger. He had fled the Nazis, spending years in Japan and America.[103] In 1952, Löwith returned to teach as professor of philosophy at the University of Heidelberg. He commented on the swathe of former pro-Nazis around him. How did he tolerate the unpleasant atmosphere, working side by side with those who had helped Hitler spin his web?

Max Horkheimer, Adorno's great friend and leader of the Frankfurt School, also returned to Germany. An émigré to the US, he went back to Frankfurt in 1949 where a year later in a blaze of optimism the Frankfurt Institute reopened. Soon Horkheimer became Rector of the University of Frankfurt, where he made great institutional as well as intellectual contributions to German philosophy. He continued to teach until dark shadows once again converged.

Of those German-Jewish philosophers returning to their native land, the most prominent was Theodor Adorno. He had journeyed home by way of France.

> 257 Paris 28.10.1949
>
> Mumma my animal,
>
> This is just to tell you . . . of my safe arrival. . . . Despite a turbulent crossing – we arrived an entire day late – no sea-sickness, thanks to the new remedy.
>
> Seeing Paris again after 12 years was deeply moving to me. It is indescribably beautiful amid all the poverty . . .
>
> Teddie.[104]

In the winter of 1949, Adorno arrived to survey the ruins of his home. Even four years after the war had ended, Frankfurt had only a quarter of its houses still standing; the rest were either bare skeletons, ruins or rubble. The Old Town was a wreck; most of the bridges over the river Main were shattered; the opera house, theatre, stock exchange and university had all been crippled by the bombings. Amidst these ruins a mass of impoverished people, evacuees and refugees had returned 'home'.[105] Adorno wrote:

> At first the city, in the area around Bockenheimer Warte, did not seem in such a bad state, but the old town centre is a desolate dream where everything is in a terrible mess. The Fahrgasse, for example, no longer exists at all. Avoided seeing our house until now. . . . In spite of everything it is still Frankfurt, and the feeling of coming home is stronger than everything else. A miracle that this city, of which three-quarters has been destroyed, nonetheless almost conveys an impression of normality. Food excellent, room overheated, as is my large one at the

University. Only the people's clothes are shabby, and there are no elegant women at all any more.[106]

Adorno's family home had been bought at a fraction of its value under the Nazis. He confronted the owner, later explaining in a letter that he had suffered a 'violent shock. It was the only time that I lost my nerve: I called him a Nazi and a murderer . . .' The house had been blasted by an incendiary bomb and the only homely part remaining was a ground-floor room with a parquet floor, on which Adorno could still make out 'the imprint left by his mother's piano'.[107] In that imprint was the shadow of his lost years.

His feelings were confided to his mother. He wrote:

> your lovely old dressing table was still there in Oberrad, as well as some other things of ours (a picture by the hall and one by Agnes Meyerhof); they seemed so very peculiar amid the . . . ruins. Was also in the garden which has a large piece of property added to it – very alien. The quarter around Schöne Aussicht is the most miserable of them all – not only houses, but entire stretches of road destroyed, so that I no longer know my way round at all, unless a single house, such as that of the Mannskopfs, suddenly accosts me in my childhood area. In place of number 9, absolute nothingness; no. 7 replaced by an entirely new building.[108]

Just like the shadow of the piano in his former home, amongst the architectural and human wreckage Adorno found glimpses of the old German culture – a richness of music, art, literature and thought. The old European-ness was still tangible in the hearts and minds of the population, and this was satisfying to him after his years in exile.

The desire to return to live in Germany was not sufficient, however. His overwhelming need was to regain employment. Having been expelled in 1933 from his post as a university lecturer, Adorno hoped that he might be reinstated. However, he could gain only a temporary post standing in for Horkheimer. By 1950 he was still without a secure job. The university seemed to make no attempt at reparation to someone who had been hounded out of their post by the Nazis. In fact, Adorno's experience mirrored a national trend: 'neither the universities nor the postwar state and national governments ever made a systematic effort to bring the victims of the [Nazi] purges in academia back to Germany'.[109]

Investing his energy elsewhere, Adorno reformed the Frankfurt Institute for Social Research with Max Horkheimer, and his *Minima Moralia* was published to great acclaim. However, still with no definite prospects of employment in Frankfurt, and in fear of losing his rights back in America, he was forced to leave once again and make the journey back across the Atlantic: 'I am traveling with an infinitely heavy heart,' he wrote.[110] Like many other émigrés Adorno had no networks of support or influence in Germany, and so whereas the universities were reappointing former Nazis, Adorno's battle to be reinstated in his post was arduous. Horkheimer, on a visit to Adorno, noted that 'forgetting and cold deceit is the intellectual climate that works best for the heirs of the Nazis'.[111] Adorno's nerves were fraught and the new battle that appeared before him was gruelling.

Finally, with much help from Horkheimer, and in light of the acclaim from Adorno's publications, the university could no longer refuse him. In 1957 he returned to Frankfurt and was made full professor at the University of Frankfurt. The former Nazi, Helmut Ritter, shortly after a faculty meeting, exclaimed that to make a career in Frankfurt you only had to be a protégé of Horkheimer and a Jew. Horkheimer was deeply upset and stood down in protest. Outraged by the continuing anti-Semitism at the university, Horkheimer retired early in 1958.[112]

Adorno was now left single-handedly carrying the flame for Jewish-German philosophy. And carry the flame he did, publishing the masterpieces *Dialectic of Enlightenment* co-authored with Max Horkheimer, *Jargon of Authenticity*, *Negative Dialectics* and *Aesthetic Theory*, many of them written during his time in exile. He also helped advise on the

reconstruction of the new democracy of the Federal Republic of Germany
and was an accomplished contributor to West German musical culture,
undertaking studies of Bach, Beethoven, Schubert, Wagner, Offenbach,
Ravel, Mahler, Strauss and Sibelius. He was also interested in the music
of direct contemporaries, Hanns Eisler, Kurt Weill and Ernst Krenek as
well as Bartók, Berg, Schönberg and Webern.[113] The courage to think,
especially to think critically and not be seduced by appearances, was the
most important way to stave off being duped by evil regimes, Adorno
argued. He was always advocating the importance of subtle things such
as critical reflection as the best weapons to fight butchery. Against a back-
drop of still-seething anti-Semitism, while the earth was still barely able
to contain its horrific secrets as many new mass graves were being uncovered, his ideas became regarded as 'melancholy' – for he was pessimistic
that society could ever rid itself of the threat of barbarism.[114]

In his *Group Experiment* (1955), Adorno revealed residual National
Socialist attitudes – widespread anti-Semitism and unthinking conformity
– among the recently democratized Germans. His study was slated by the
former Nazi social psychologist Peter R. Hofstätter, who accused Adorno
of wanting to burden the nation with guilt.[115] Adorno poignantly replied:
'it was the victims who were forced to bear the burden of the horrors
of Auschwitz, not the people who did not want to know about it'.[116]
Adorno also undertook criticism of Heidegger, describing the former
Nazi's ideas as a mere 'jargon of authenticity'. He wrote: 'weakness . . .
march[es] into Heidegger's philosophy. Authenticity is supposed to calm
the consciousness of weakness, but it also resembles it.'[117] For his critique
of Heidegger he also provoked the anger of Arendt. She attacked Adorno,
focusing upon his relationship with Benjamin – something that deeply
wounded him. Adorno for his part couldn't stomach Arendt's allegiance
to Heidegger and her perpetuation of the latter's brand of philosophy,
believing that she was inadvertently a carrier of Nazism into philosophy.
These two German-Jewish émigrés with so much in common nevertheless stood poles apart.

Adorno would sometimes play the piano in his Frankfurt apartment, which he had decorated in a simple, modest style, barring one dramatic image. The rooms revolved around Paul Klee's *Angelus Novus*, a reproduction of the original owned by his dear late-departed friend, Walter Benjamin. Many visitors came to his and Gretel's home, including Gershom Scholem, Max Horkheimer and other Frankfurt School members. After years of fear and then the stresses of returning to a Nazi-infused atmosphere, his health was sorely affected. With high blood pressure and a traumatized heart, Adorno desperately craved peace. However, this was not to be.

During the mid to late 1960s, radicalized students made Adorno the target of their demonstrations. In a letter to Samuel Beckett, he wrote: 'The feeling of suddenly being attacked as a reactionary at least has a surprising note.'[118] But things only deteriorated further. Adorno was mobbed and hounded until one day a group of female students blocked his lecture platform. They removed their tops and bras, trying to humiliate him with their bare breasts. Adorno feared that this political radicalism had the same bullying mentality as Nazism, the horror of which still affected him. What began as a thoughtless jibe had tragic consequences. In a poignant echo of Walter Benjamin, Adorno took flight to the mountains. There, as happened to Benjamin years before when fleeing from the Nazis, he suffered palpitations. On 6 August 1969, Adorno died of a heart attack, aged sixty-five.

If during their lifetime Hitler's philosophers dominated and Jewish thinkers were forced to retreat, what happened posthumously? Surely time would sift the wheat from the chaff, and where in life justice had failed them history itself at least would be just. After the dust had settled and time moved inexorably forwards, which reputations waned and which endured?

'Carl Schmitt is famous. Possibly the most-discussed German jurist', a notable scholar proclaimed at the beginning of the twenty-first century.

During the decades after the war a great many professors in Germany, the United States, France, Italy and elsewhere wrote about Schmitt at considerable length; bibliographies swelled to contain more than 1,600 entries. Then, in the latter part of the twentieth century came the 'Schmitt renaissance',[119] an even greater revival of admiration for his work, occurring throughout some of the world's most authoritative institutions.[120] Schmitt now appears on the curriculum of many university degree courses in Britain, America and across the Western world. *Harper's* magazine ran a special feature on him in August 2007, and other major scholarly journals have celebrated him and even dedicated special editions to his work.[121] The blurb on a recent translation of *The Nomos of the Earth* claims Schmitt offers 'prospects for a new world order' and 'a reasoned, yet passionate argument in defence of the European achievement', and that he is instrumental 'in creating the first truly global order of international law'.[122] There even exists a periodical, *Schmittiana,* that collects and reproduces newly discovered Schmitt memorabilia; his correspondence, memoirs, bibliography and gossip are all objects of fervent scholarly commentary.[123]

Schmitt's involvement with Nazism is excused as an unfortunate period which we must not allow to prejudice us to the importance of his academic ideas. Many high-ranking scholars even go so far as to defend Schmitt's anti-Semitism, claiming, as he did himself, that it was merely a necessary tool for him to survive Nazism: at worst, so it goes, he was guilty of opportunism. A recent critic, however, bravely countered that 'Schmitt's anti-Semitism was at the core of his work – before, during, and after the Nazi era. His influential polarities of friend and foe ... emerge from a conceptual template in which *"the Jew" is defined as adversary'.*[124] Certain key thinkers point out that 'Schmitt's post-1933 writings on Jewish [issues] ... had a central importance for both Nazi aims and his work as a whole',[125] and that 'his anti-Jewish attitudes permeated the very structure and grounds of Schmitt's thought and categories'.[126] Confronted with the vast pits of human corpses in the mid-1940s, one wonders whether the subtleties in the debate about Schmitt's motives miss the main point. As

Weinreich commented: 'Had the war lasted one year more, probably not a single Jew in Europe would have remained alive.'[127]

Before his death, Heidegger, far more so than Schmitt, had become arguably the most famous thinker of the century: 'Martin Heidegger is perhaps the twentieth century's greatest philosopher, and his work stimulated much that is original and compelling in modern thought.'[128] In Germany, Heidegger never went out of fashion. From the 1950s onwards, he has been arguably both the most influential and revered mind of the nation.[129]

Beyond Germany, devotion to the 'Master of Messkirch', largely due to Sartre's endorsement, spread throughout former occupied nations such as France.[130]

One prominent scholar explained: 'In France . . . Heidegger's thought has taken root since 1945 in a very specific way and . . . the political persona of the philosopher has faded into the background, completely overshadowed by his intellectual significance.'[131] Famous names such as Louis Althusser and Michel Foucault carried Heidegger's flame further into the later twentieth century, and then Paul de Man 'made it possible for Heidegger to expand to the United States and subsequently the entire world, to the point of making him appear the chief representative of what has been called "continental philosophy".'[132] British and American universities planted him firmly at the centre of their curriculum, and beyond these borders Heidegger became revered in areas as far-flung as Latin America, Africa and Asia – notably Japan.[133] His 'empire' even extended beyond philosophy into literature, theology, psychology and cinema – a film, *The Ister*, would celebrate his 'genius', and the BBC would make a documentary dedicated to his life.[134]

After his death in 1976, as well as during his lifetime, of course, Heidegger seduced Nazi extremists and liberals alike, conservatives as well as radicals. Apologists and revisionists excused or denied his collaboration, but Heidegger scholarship has never abated, intellectual admiration often outweighing any potential moral distaste.

If Heidegger is the current star of continental philosophy, Gottlob Frege provides the cornerstone for the Western analytic tradition. Frege never espoused political or moral ideas within his philosophy. He was strictly a logician, employing a rigid separation between critical thought and strongly held personal views. In his work he was rigorous. In his personal views, however, he held uncritically the worst conventional prejudices of his place and time: 'Adolf Hitler correctly writes ... that ... Germany has not had a clear political goal ...'[135] Nevertheless, in spite of his anti-Semitism and admiration for Hitler, Frege influenced greats such as Bertrand Russell and Ludwig Wittgenstein. An encyclopaedia entry notes: 'He is considered to be one of the founders of modern logic, and made major contributions to the foundations of mathematics. As a philosopher, he is generally considered to be the father of analytic philosophy.'[136] Given that analytic philosophy is dominant throughout Western universities, it is worrying that the founder of this tradition, Frege, held such morally repulsive views – and moreover that for the majority of students this issue will never even be raised.[137]

Meanwhile, what has become of Hitler's opponents in the practice of philosophy in the twenty-first century? The martyr Kurt Huber's philosophy and musicology are out of print. Huber was the only philosophy professor actively to resist the Nazis. He appears on no philosophy syllabus throughout the Western world, not for his posthumously published classic on Leibniz, neither for his awesome contribution to musicology and aesthetics. Indeed, although his bravery is recorded in a brief mention in certain academic departments, his intellectual prowess remains as quiet in the Western world as it was under Hitler.

Twentieth-century Jewish-German thinkers like those from the Frankfurt School, while spawning a tradition of political and philosophical criticism and scepticism in an attempt to provide a buffer to authoritarianism, have struggled to be accepted in the mainstream philosophy syllabus. Walter Benjamin, Hannah Arendt and Theodor Adorno, in spite of their enormous accomplishments, have never been admitted into the philosophy canon in the English-speaking world. Horkheimer, Marcuse and Cassirer are also marginalized into other academic fields, while Karl Jaspers, Gerhard Scholem and Karl Löwith have almost been completely forgotten.

The situation of Europe's intellectual culture, therefore, provides food for thought. The dissemination of the ideas of Schmitt, Heidegger and the dominance of Frege throughout British, American and continental universities today leaves a worrying aftertaste. So too the dark strand in Germany's intellectual heritage, which is rarely mentioned. The marginalization of many Jewish-German thinkers from mainstream philosophy is also a concern. Many students are happily oblivious of the context of the ideas taught in their discipline, the past involvements of great thinkers that might be unpalatable to many. Philosophy is descended from the 'moral sciences', and in view of this heritage its practitioners need to remain conscious of its disturbing trajectory.

Epilogue

I began this story with a memory. A memory of playing as a child in our grandmother's garden in Suffolk in the 1970s. There we unearthed part of a skeleton which had lain buried at the end of an undulating path at the rear of the garden for years. I began, too, with a memory of my grandparents' stories about the Second World War, and recalled an ethical dilemma presented before us students during a medical lecture: Should we use information gained from medical experiments conducted by Nazis upon the Jews, even if this could save lives?

In philosophy, many issues lie dormant. Underlying some of the most seductive and widespread ideas are practitioners such as Heidegger, who never condemned the Holocaust. Should we teach their ideas, blithely encourage students to read *Being and Time*, the works of Schmitt or the logician Frege, oblivious to the context of their words? Of course, the problem in philosophy is a central one – if this discipline cannot set an ethical standard then which one can? And what value are the thoughts of men who are unable to reflect critically upon the most brutal of human regimes?

These are questions for the reader to ponder. My task here has been to uncover the lives and context of German philosophers who were active under, and in some cases after, the Third Reich, just as during childhood we had dug for clues about an old skeleton.

On family walks along the Suffolk coast I had climbed into old pill-boxes, imagining soldiers hiding there for hours in the cold mud and hard stones, fearing an invasion by Hitler. The pillboxes had been designed to guard against the Nazis, but there was little to guard against the invasion of ideas. Without vigilance, might cryptic words not disguise prejudice, and the seeds of Hitler's philosophy carry forwards to new generations?

Notes

Introduction

1. See, for instance, the compelling and erudite treatments by J. Cornwell, 2000.
2. Kant lived prior to the formation of the German nation state in Prussia but is commonly regarded as a 'German' philosopher.

Chapter 1

1. E. Hanfstaengl 2005, p. 85.
2. Ernst Hanfstaengl was later to become a prominent figure on account of to his intimate friendship with Hitler and later role in the Nazi Party. He was a gifted pianist, and Hitler loved to hear him play the piano.
3. See G.D. Rosenfeld 2000, for an excellent analysis of Munich's buildings and their fate during the war.
4. This was also expressed later by Hitler in *Mein Kampf* See A. Hitler 1980, p. 597.
5. E. Hanfstaengl 2005, p. 85.
6. Ibid.
7. The description is taken from the photograph *Landsberg Prison* by Heinrich Hoffmann, 1924, black and white.
8. See M. Deiler, 'Landsberg Prison Documents 1923/1924: Adolf Hitler's Imprisonment', in *Civil Association for the Study of Contemporary Landsberg*, Issue 1, 2005. For a map of the prison during Hitler's time, see *Lageplan Festungshaftanstaltz Vom 31. März 1924*, in the same publication series.
9. Descriptions are taken from the photographs *Unterhaltguns und Tagesraum Festungshaftanstalt* by Heinrich Hoffmann, 1924, black and white.
10. In answer to the question, 'What impression does Hitler make on one?', H. Rauschning 2004, p. 13.
11. The description emanates from the photo *Adolf Hitler in der Festung Landsberg* by Heinrich Hoffmann, 1924, black and white.
12. E. Hanfstaengl 2005, p. 64.
13. This is a quote from Hitler's view of the Rembrandt painting; see E. Hanfstaengl 2005, p. 64.
14. E. Hanfstaengl 2005, pp. 121–2.
15. A. Hitler 1973, p. 110.
16. Ibid., p. 105.
17. Ibid., p. 111.
18. H. Frank 1953, pp. 46–7.

19. Hermann Fobke describes Hitler's day at Landsberg in W Jochmann 1963, quoted in I. Kershaw 1998, p. 240.

20. Recent research on *Mein Kampf* (see Othma Plöckinger's book, the relevant part of which is summarized in I. Kershaw 2009, p. 147) shows that Hitler typed vol. 1 of *Mein Kampf* himself and did not dictate it (though he did dictate parts of vol. 2, which appeared only in late 1926).

21. 'Twenty years later, his personal physician, Dr. Theo Morell, declared that his illness might be psychogenic.' A. Hitler 1973, p. 326.

22. E. Hanfstaengl 2005, p. 123.

23. Hess studied with Professor Karl Haushofer, himself a student of the English geographer Halfred Mackinder. See H. Trevor-Roper 1988, p. xxxi; and also G. Kearns 2009.

24. E. Hanfstaengl 2005, p. 123.

25. A. Hitler 1980, p. 3.

26. Ibid., p. 3.

27. Ibid., p. 4. My emphasis.

28. Ibid.

29. Ibid., p. 26.

30. H. Rauschning 1940, p. 89. Note that Rauschning's alleged observations of Hitler were thrown into serious doubt by past historians, so much so that they were 'long regarded as spurious.' Hugh Trevor-Roper comments that 'If any still doubt its genuineness they will hardly do so after reading the volume now published.' He refers to *Hitler's Table Talk* and points out that Rauschning was one of those entrusted with recording Hitler's table talk in the early years. The quotes I use from Rauschning are consistent in their representation of the Führer's character with other accounts such as those of Martin Bormann endorsed by Trevor-Roper.

31. A. Hitler 1980, p. 5.

32. From Adolf's sister's (Paula Hitler) testimony, 8 December 1938, in the National Archive, Washington, D.C., referenced in I. Kershaw 1998, p. 20.

33. See A. Hitler 1980, p. 32.

34. Ibid., p. 5.

35. Ibid., p. 584.

36. Hitler's speech of 10 April 1923 in A. Hitler, vol. 1, 1942, pp. 42–4.

37. Hitler's 'Reden' (edition of 1933), p. 122, reprinted in A. Hitler, vol. 1, 1942, pp. 86–7.

38. A. Hitler 1980, p. 21.

39. Ibid.

40. German Text, *Dokumente der deutschen Politik*, vol. 1 (1935), pp. 28–9. The translation given above is an adaptation of the official English translation published in *The New Germany Desires Work and Peace*, p. 19; cited in A. Hitler, vol. 1, 1942, p. 568.

41. See I. Kershaw 1998, p. 250.

42. A. Hitler 1980, p. 392.

43. I. Kershaw 1998, p. 252; see A. Hitler 1980, pp. 387–94.

44. I. Kershaw 1998, p. 252.

45. Ibid., p. 240.

46. Ibid., p. 84.

47. A. Hitler 1980, p. 141.

48. Hitler, Reichstag, 23 March 1933, in N. H. Baynes, vol. 1, 1942, p. 264.

49. Lagarde, 1827–1891, wrote that: 'the Jews, now numbering two million, can never be assimilated', in A. S. Lindemann 2000, p. 69, and 'I cannot wish that Jews be allowed to live with' the Germans, in T. W. Ryback 2010, p. 139.

50. T. W. Ryback 2010, p. 140.

51. Chamberlain's works would become precious literature and part of Hitler's lifelong private collection. See ibid., pp. 134 and 97. Earlier, before Hitler's incarceration in Landsberg, Dietrich Eckart, his friend and mentor, had passed on this particular influence.

52. Published in 1890. See T. W. Ryback 2010, p. 134.

53. Rembrandt was, of course, Dutch. See H. J. Hahn 1995, p. 193.

54. T. W. Ryback 2010, p. 67.
55. See ibid., p. 50. Spengler in his *The Decline of the West* had combined Nietzsche with simplistic biological ideas derived from pseudo-Darwinism into an avocation of life as a 'struggle for domination', H. J. Hahn 1995, p. 196.
56. A. Kubizek 1973, p. 188. This presumably refers to the Karl Marx Hof library in Vienna, subsequently badly damaged during the war. See I. Kershaw 1998, p. 41.
57. H. Rauschning 1940, p. 255.
58. T. W. Ryback 2010, p. 69.
59. Ibid., p. 132.
60. H. Trevor-Roper 1988 or I. Kershaw 1998.
61. A. Kubizek 1973, p. 188.
62. A. Hitler 1980, p. 392.
63. Ibid., p. 20
64. Ibid., p. 33.
65. A. Hitler 1988, p. 720.
66. Ibid., p. 89.
67. Hitler, Karlsruhe, 13 March 1936, opening electoral campaign speech, in N. H. Baynes, vol. 1, 1942, p. 633. (My emphasis).
68. H. Rauschning 1940, p. 255.
69. A. Hitler 1988, p. 291.
70. E. Hanfstaengl 2005, p. 342.
71. A. Hitler 1988, p. 316.
72. E. Hanfstaengl 2005, p. 234.
73. H. Rauschning 1940, p. 255.
74. S. P. Tansey and N. Jackson 2008, p. 75.
75. Hitler, 27 November 1937, part of a speech while laying the foundation stone at the Faculty of Military Science, see A. Hitler, vol. 1, 1942, p. 600 (my emphasis).
76. F. McDonough 2003, p. 56.
77. R. B. Downs 2004, pp. 328–9.
78. T. W. Ryback 2010, p. 130.
79. Given on 22 June 1933. T. W. Ryback 2010, p. 122.
80. A. Hitler 1988, p. 20. Kershaw also endorses this claim, see I. Kershaw 1998, p. 91.
81. A. Hitler 1988, p. 720. Hitler's amateurism is, of course, evident here. Every German philosophy student would have known that Hegel was from the German Idealist tradition, not a pragmatist.
82. R. B. Downs 2004, pp. 328–9.
83. A. Hitler 1988, p. 358.
84. E. Hanfstaengl 2005, p. 361.
85. E. Hanfstaengl 1994, p. 206.
86. A. Hitler 1988, p. 720.
87. A. Hitler, *Kulturtagung, Nuremberg*, 6 September 1938, in A. Hitler, vol. 1, 1942, p. 598.
88. Ibid.
89. A. Hitler, 'Opening of the second exhibition of German Art', Munich, 10 July 1938, in A Hitler, vol. 1, 1942, p. 605.
90. A. Hitler, *Kulturatagung, Nuremberg*, 6 September 1938, in A. Hitler, vol. 1, 1942, p. 597. The incorrect spelling is in the original.
91. H. Rauschning 1940, p. 254.
92. F. McDonough 2003, p. 56.
93. See W. Shirer 1960.
94. E. Hanfstaengl 2005, p. 223.
95. Ibid., pp. 223–4.
96. J. Giblin 2002, p. 46.
97. A. Hitler 1988–89, pp. 389–416.
98. E. Hanfstaengl 2005, p. 224.

99. Ibid., p. 290.
100. H. Rauschning 1940, pp. 254–6.
101. A. Hitler 1988, p. 720.
102. H. Rauschning 1940, p. 275.
103. For our purposes, lederhosen can be considered traditional Bavarian clothing. However, their actual history is somewhat more complex.
104. F. Wagner 1948, pp. 8–9.
105. E. Hanfstaengl 2005, p. 352.
106. A. Hitler 1980, p. 16.
107. A. Hitler 1988, p. 241.
108. Ibid., p. 240.
109. Ibid., p. 206.
110. Ibid., p. 241.
111. A. Hitler, a speech opening the House of German Art, Munich, 18 July 1937, quoted in Hitler, vol. 1, 1942, p. 584.
112. I. Kershaw 1998, p. 252.
113. A. Hitler 1980a, p. 294; 22–23 February 1942, quoted in I. Kershaw 1998, p. 47.
114. E. Hanfstaengl 2005, p. 54.
115. W. Shirer 1960, p. 102.
116. A. Hitler 1973, p. 113.
117. E. Hanfstaengl 2005, p. 124.
118. W. Schwarzwaller 1989, p. 193.
119. A. Hitler 1980, p. 416.
120. Ibid., p. 414; my emphasis.
121. H. Rauschning 1940, p. 8.
122. J. Giblin 2002, p. 48.
123. A. Hitler, vol. 1, 1942, p. 134.
124. See, J. Giblin 2002, p. 48.
125. A. Hitler, vol. 1, 1942, p. 136; my emphasis.
126. Ibid., p. 137.
127. Ibid., p. 134; my emphasis.
128. Ibid., pp. 138–39; my emphasis.

Chapter 2

1. Throughout this book the term 'German' will be used to refer to the cultural, social and linguistic communities that later became the basis of the German nation.
2. Known as the 'Province of Prussia' from 1701 to 1773, Königsberg was its capital although other cities were seen as more vibrant.
3. M. Kuehn 2001, p. 65.
4. Ibid., p. 66.
5. Ibid., pp. 115–16.
6. R. Scruton 1982, pp. 4–7.
7. M. Kuehn 2001, p. 109.
8. Kant's pupil, Reinhold Bernhard Jachmann, in R. Scruton 1982, pp. 3–4.
9. Reinhold Bernhard Jachmann, quoted in R. Scruton 1982, p. 4.
10. M. Kuehn 2001, p. 114.
11. See E. Cassirer 1981, p. 227, where he views Kant as holding 'the ever-more-exact apprehension and the ever deepening understanding of the thought of freedom'.
12. Reinhold Bernhard Jachmann, quoted in R. Scruton 1982, p. 4.
13. P. L. Rose 1990, p. 93. Defenders of Kant point out that in other works he was less hostile to the Jews. This may be so, but nowhere did he retract the deeply damaging claims outlined above. Furthermore, Kant's very definition of reason was one that excluded Judaistic modes

of thinking. Given that for Kant reason was foundational to everything of value in human life, ethics, politics, etc., this is surely telling.

14. I. Kant, 1997b *Lectures on Ethics*, p. 27. Herder reported Kant saying this in his lecture, see M. Mack 2003, p. 5.
15. I. Kant, *Anthropologie*, in *Werke*, 12:517ff. in P. L. Rose 1990, p. 94.
16. Later Jewish-German philosophers would make a profound interpretation of the German Enlightenment and its complex but inextricable link to Nazi barbarism, see M. Horkheimer and T. Adorno 1992.
17. I. Kant 1996, p. 276.
18. M. Mack 2003, pp. 39–40.
19. I. Kant, 1997a, p. 133.
20. See P. L. Rose 1990, pp. 117–32.
21. T. Ryback 2010 p. 129.
22. Ibid., pp. 129–30.
23. J. G. Fichte 1995, p. 309. See P. L. Rose 1990 p. 120, for a discussion of Fichte's anti-Semitism.
24. G. W. F. Hegel 1988, p. 90.
25. G. W. F. Hegel 1977. See also P. L. 1990 Rose p. 109, pp. 110–18.
26. Y. Yovel 1998, p. xii.
27. G. W. F. Hegel 1978, pp. 182–3.
28. G. Ritter 1965, p. 59.
29. A. Schopenhauer 1974, II, pp. 261–4; P. L. Rose 1992, p. 92.
30. See L. Feuerbach 1957, and P. L. Rose 1990, p. 254.
31. Karl Marx was, of course, himself a Jew, with allegedly 'self-hating' anti-Semitism. Hitler later associated all socialism with Judaism.
32. *On The Jewish Question* first published in *Deutsch-Französische Jahrbücher*, 1844, see K. Marx 2000. Note that some attribute anti-Semitic attitudes to the early Marx only. For a fuller account see J. Carlebach 1978.
33. R. Wagner in a letter dated 29 April 1866, in S. Spencer and B. Millington 1987; see also P. L. Rose 1992, p. 105.
34. R. Wagner in P. L. Rose 1992, p. 37.
35. This was first published under a pseudonym in 1850. See, R. Wagner, 'Judaism in Music,' in E. M. Brener 2006, pp. 301–17.
36. R. Wagner, 'Judaism in Music', in E. M. Brener 2006, p. 302.
37. A. Rosenberg 1933, p. 132, in D. J. Goldhagen 1996, p. 398.
38. Description from the photo, 'The parsonage at Röcken in Prussian Saxony where Nietzsche was born on 15 October 1844', in R. Hayman 1995, p. 200. Note this is the rear view.
39. Nietzsche in R. Safranski 2003, p. 352.
40. Ibid.
41. See R. Hayman 1995, pp. 13–25.
42. R. Safranski 2003, p. 43.
43. R. Hayman 1995, pp. 128–33.
44. Ibid., p. 316.
45. Description taken from the photo, 'Nietzsche's small, simply furnished room at Sils-Maria', in R. Hayman 1995, pp. 200–1.
46. Note also the controversial *Will to Power*, a book written not by Nietzsche himself but compiled after his death by the Nietzsche Archive, allegedly from notes scattered across several different periods of his life. There are complexities about the publication date of this work and about whether it is representative of any of Nietzsche's views.
47. See K. Ansell-Pearson 2002 for an excellent, authoritative interpretation of Nietzsche.
48. It is characteristic of his contradictory nature that he also, in other places, advocated democracy.
49. This is, of course, a very brief summary and condenses many complexities. For a superb account of the development of Nietzsche's thought see R. Safranski 2003.

50. F. Nietzsche in R. Hayman 1995, pp. 128–9.
51. R. Hayman 1995, p. 128.
52. F. Nietzsche in R. Hayman 1995, p. 79.
53. Ibid., p. 358.
54. R. Hayman 1995, p. 129.
55. F. Nietzsche in R. Hayman 1995, p. 142.
56. F. Nietzsche, in R. Safranski 2003, p. 339.
57. S. E. Ascheim 1992.
58. R. Safranski 2003, p. 329.
59. S. E. Ascheim 1992, p. 128.
60. T. Hardy in *The Daily Mail*, 27 September 1914; *Manchester Guardian*, 7 October 1914, quoted in S. E. Ascheim 1992, p. 130.
61. She was at this time the widow of the famous anti-Semite Bernhard Forster.
62. F. Nietzsche, *Der Wille zur Macht*, section 982 (note of 1884) in R. Hayman 1995, p. 359. See K. Ansell-Pearson 1997 for a very different view of Nietzsche's 'biological man' than that which was appropriated by the Nazis.
63. F. Nietzsche *Der Wille zur Macht*, section 981 (note of 1887) in R. Hayman 1995, p. 359.
64. S. E. Ascheim 1992, p. 152. Nietzsche's present to Wagner was Albrecht Dürer's 'Knight, Death and the Devil', R. Hayman 1995, p. 133.
65. F. Stern 1961, pp. 279, 284. Note that it is an assumption that Nietzsche was a profound and self-critical philosopher with integrity, whereas these other 'nationalist' thinkers were, by contrast, superficial, crude and amateur.
66. P. de Lagarde in F. Stern 1961, p. 61. n. 12.
67. Langbehn was so drawn to Nietzsche that he even offered to look after him after his mental collapse. See F. Stern 1961, pp. 107–8.
68. J. Langbehn in F. Stern 1961, p. 141. n. 5.
69. *Rembrandt*, 49th ed., pp. 348–51, in F. Stern 1961, p. 141.
70. Published in 1879. See A. Lindemann 2000, p. 128.
71. G. Ritter 1965, p. 118.
72. Ibid., p. 59.
73. Ibid., p. 118.
74. F. Stern 1961. p. 295.
75. Thus far 'Germanism' had been based upon a sense of the German people as a cultural community with a shared language, history, art and spirit. Jews were excluded in so far as they were *culturally* alien. All that was about to change.
76. E. J. Browne 1995, p. 6.
77. C. Darwin 1958, p. 24.
78. See A. J. Desmond and J. R. Moore 1994.
79. R. C. Bannister 1989.
80. E. J. Browne 1995, pp. 244–6.
81. W. Bölsche 1906, p. 28.
82. Ibid., pp. 26–7.
83. Ibid., p. 19.
84. Ibid., p. 18, my emphasis.
85. E. Haeckel 1883.
86. W. Bölsche 1906, p. 309.
87. See D. Gasman 1971, pp. 82–104.
88. Ibid., p. 95.
89. E. Haeckel 1876, p. 170.
90. G. J. Stein 1988, p. 56.
91. D. Gasman 1971, p. 161.
92. W. Bölsche 1906, p. 320.
93. Ibid., p. 320.
94. Ibid., p. 321.

95. Ibid., p. 15.
96. J. Keegan 1988, p. 8; K. J. Bade and A. Brown 2003, pp. 167–8.
97. T. W. Ryback 2010 pp. 89–90; G. Ritter 1965, p. 118.
98. D. Gasman 1971, p. 172.
99. See T. W. Ryback 2010, pp. 132–3.
100. He also studied with a student of Haeckel's.
101. D. Gasman 1971, p. 150.
102. Ibid., pp. 150–1. See also J. Cornwell 2003 for the influence of Darwinist ideas upon military science.
103. This book was 'a final summary of the resentments and aspirations of the would-be conservatives', and against warnings of the 'sentimental brutality' of the German right. It went on to become hugely influential. Joseph Goebbels was particularly influenced. See F. Stern 1961, pp. xxix–x.
104. Moeller in F. Stern 1961, p. 257, n. 23.
105. F. Stern 1961, pp. 282–3.
106. Lagarde was also influenced by Darwin.
107. H. J. Hahn 1995, p. 196, n. 85.
108. J. Glover 2001, p. 376.
109. Ibid., pp. 376–7.
110. Ibid., p. 377.
111. 'The greatest achievements in intellectual life can never be produced by those of alien race but only by those who are inspired by the Aryan or German spirit', N. H. Baynes 1942, vol. 1, p. 728. 'The influence of this intellectual Jewish class in Germany ha[s] everywhere a disintegrating effect. For this reason in order to bar the spread of the process of disintegration it [is] essential to take steps to establish a clear and clean separation between the two races', ibid., p. 733.

Chapter 3

1. Video, US government archive, 18 SFP 9231 INSK.
2. Ibid., 18 SFP 186–9231 INSK.
3. R. Cecil 1972, p. 14.
4. We focus on the philosophical mindset. For a broader view of the Nazi ideological conquest see Richard Evans's masterly work, R. J. Evans, 2006.
5. R. Cecil 1972, p. 4.
6. *Nationalsozialistische Deutsche Arbeiterpartei – NSDAP.*
7. H. Härtle ed., 1970, p. 69.
8. R. Cecil 1972, p. 52.
9. Ibid., p. 9 n. 19.
10. Not everyone believed Hitler's claim about Rosenberg's weakness See R. Cecil 1972, p. 43.
11. H. Härtle ed., 1970, p. 278.
12. Sir W. Teeling. Typescript in Archives of the Royal Institute of International Affairs, Chatham House, London.
13. R. Cecil 1972, p. 101.
14. Ibid., p. 14.
15. Ibid., p. 67.
16. A. Rosenberg 1930, p. 525.
17. H. Härtle, ed., 1970, p. 89.
18. A. Rosenberg 1930, Introduction.
19. R. Cecil 1972, p. 72.
20. Sir W. Teeling Typescript in Archives of the Royal Institute of International Affairs, Chatham House, London.
21. R. Cecil 1972, p. 93.
22. S. Krosigk 1951, p. 261.

23. A. Speer 1970, p. 110.
24. R. Cecil 1972, p. 102.
25. N. Lebovic 2006, p. 31.
26. See A. Bäumler 1923.
27. See A. Bäumler 1931, pp. 180–3. Italics in the original.
28. See A. Bäumler, H. Brunträger, H. Kurzke 1989, p. 185.
29. Supporters of Heidegger usually argue that he is critical of Bäumler. Note that Nietzsche's sister working for his Archive compiled this work, *Will to Power*, and that it is not necessarily reflective of Nietzsche himself. See C. Diethe 2003.
30. L. Poliakov and J. Wulf 1959.
31. See J. Schriewer 1982; W. Helmut 2000.
32. E. Klee 2005, p. 341.
33. Ibid.
34. Including the Reich Institute for the History of the New Germany and the Nazi Lecturers Association.
35. See M. Natanson 1973.
36. See H. Ott 1993, p. 174.
37. Ibid., p. 176.
38. Elfride was the wife of the then up-and-coming philosopher Martin Heidegger.
39. H. Ott 1993, pp. 175–6.
40. Ibid., p. 175.
41. Ibid.
42. R. Safranski 1998.
43. Ibid., p. 174.
44. M. Weinreich 1999, p. 19.
45. S. P. Remy 2002, p. 80. In 1937 after Jaspers was expelled, his Chair in the faculty of philosophy tellingly became the professorship for military policy and military sciences – occupied by the historian Paul Schmitthenner, who created the 'seminar for the history of warfare'. See S. P. Remy 2002, p. 38.
46. During the Hitler era, hundreds of compositions, manuscripts, letters, and even artworks that Felix Mendelssohn had painted were smuggled to Warsaw and Cracow, and then dispersed around the world after Germany occupied Poland.
47. M. Weinreich 1999, p. 57.
48. 'General Principles for the Compilation of Blacklists', W. Herrmann, (Berlin Librarian), undated typescript in the Bundesarchiv Koblenz, reprinted in G. Sauder 1983, pp. 100–26.
49. Ibid.
50. V. Weidermann 2008.
51. R. Cecil 1972, p. 146.
52. H. Heine 1820, *Almansor* in H. Heine and M. Windfuhr (ed.), 1994.
53. This was the first political murder of an opponent to the Nazi regime outside of Germany, and caused worldwide indignation. See R. Marwedel, 1987.
54. M. Weinreich 1999, p. 25.
55. Ibid., p. 27.
56. Ibid., p. 46.
57. C. Koonz 2003, p. 201.
58. M. Weinreich 1999, p. 49.
59. See A. E. Steinweis 2006, p. 105.
60. M. Weinreich 1999, p. 23 n. 39.
61. Ibid., pp. 270, 287.
62. R. Cecil 1972, p. 146.
63. E. Krieck in M. Weinreich 1999, p. 21.
64. Ibid., n. 35; emphasis in the original.
65. Ibid., p. 16.
66. V. Farias 1989, p. 80, n. 5.

67. Ibid., p. 76.
68. H. L. Childs 1938, p. 62.
69. Ibid.
70. Ibid., pp. 77–8.
71. Ibid., p. xxxvi.
72. R. Cecil 1972, p. 154.
73. This was stressed in the volume laid out before him that was written by German university professors, the preface to which he signed.
74. M. Weinreich 1999, pp. 124–5; my emphasis.
75. 'Breslau', in Jewish Virtual Library, A Division of the American-Israeli Cooperative, 2012.
76. The national decree banning Jews from the civil service was known locally as the 'Baden decree' in the region of Baden.
77. S. P. Remy, 2002, p. 110.
78. See A. Gallin 1986, pp. 96–99.
79. See D. J. Goldhagen 1996.
80. M. Weinreich, 1999, pp. 46–50.
81. Ibid., p. 46.
82. Ibid., p. 45.
83. Ibid., p. 25.
84. Heyse was born 8 March 1891 in Bremen.
85. See R. Wolin, 'Fascism and Hermeneutics', in W. Bialas and A. Rabinbach 2007, p. 119.
86. H. Heyse 1933, p. 12.
87. The philosophy faculty had members who would be regarded by modern faculties as inter-disciplinary, such as folklorists.
88. S. P. Remy 2002, p. 184.
89. Adolf Hitler, 30 January 1939, in N. H. Baynes, ed. and trans., 1942, vol. 1, pp. 740–1; my emphasis.
90. E. Krieck in M. Weinreich 1999, p. 74, n. 100; my emphasis. The date of the speech is 1939 not 1938 as given by Krieck.
91. M. Gilbert in M. Weinreich 1999, p. xi.
92. M. Weinreich 1999, p. 240.
93. R. Cecil 1972, pp. 147–8.
94. A. Bäumler cited in M. Weinreich 1999, p. 24; my emphasis.
95. M. Weinreich 1999, p. 49.

Chapter 4

1. J-W. Müller 2003, p. 18.
2. G. Schwab 2007, p. 4.
3. C. Schmitt 1963, p. 46.
4. J. W. Bendersky 1983, p. 15.
5. C. Koonz 2003, p. 57.
6. Ibid., p. 57.
7. Ibid.
8. Ibid., pp. 56–61.
9. J. W. Bendersky 1983, p. 45.
10. F. Blei 1936, p. 1,218.
11. J. W. Bendersky, 1983, p. 130.
12. C. Schmitt in E. Hüsmert 2005, p. 199.
13. Ibid., p. 194.
14. Ibid., p. 197.
15. Image from 'Berlin Charlottenburg, Café Kutschera', postcard, 1911. See also G. Balakrishnan 2002, p. 76.
16. See J-W. Müller 2003, p. 37.

17. C. Schmitt, personal archives, referenced in V. Farias 1989, p. 138.
18. J. W. Bendersky 1983, p. 204. Note that Koonz quotes 298,860 – surely an error. C. Koonz 2003, p. 58.
19. C. Koonz 2003, pp. 58–9.
20. For more detail see J. W. Bendersky 1983, p. 204.
21. *Westdeutscher Beobachter*, 1933, pp. 1–3, in J. W. Bendersky 1983, p. 204.
22. H. Goering in D. J. Goldhagen 1996, p. 457.
23. C. Schmitt 1933, pp. 9–10.
24. Ibid., pp. 11–12, 21.
25. C. Schmitt 1940, pp. 199–203. Originally published in 1934, pp. 945–50.
26. J. W. Bendersky 1983, p. 218.
27. M. Weinreich 1999, p. 40.
28. C. Koonz 2003, pp. 207–8.
29. Ibid., pp. 208–9.
30. J. W. Bendersky 1983, p. 224.
31. C. Schmitt 1936a, p. 185.
32. C. Schmitt 15 October, 1936b, p. 1,198.
33. M. Weinreich 1999, p. 74.
34. J. H. Kaiser, 1968 Bd. 2, 319–31.
35. Ibid.

Chapter 5

1. A. Hitler 1988, p. 720.
2. V. Farias 1989, p. 116.
3. S. Friedländer 1997, p. 57.
4. V. Farias 1989, p. 116.
5. Ibid., p. 84.
6. R. Safranski 1998, p. 241.
7. H. Sluga 1993, p. 3.
8. There is ample evidence of the elevated status that Heidegger had within the Reich. Certain of his speeches were published alongside those of Hitler and Rosenberg, see E. Faye 2009, p. 53.
9. The rectorship was granted on 21 April 1933.
10. By the same student leadership that organized the book burnings, V. Farias 1989, p. 116.
11. H-G. Gadamer, 'Thinking the Unthinkable', in *Human All Too Human*, BBC documentary, 1999; my emphasis.
12. V. Farias 1989, pp. 75–6.
13. Jaspers in V. Farias 1989, p. 118.
14. R. Safranski 1998, p. 3.
15. H. Ott 1993, p. 180.
16. See, for example, E. Faye 2009, pp. xvi, 30, 69.
17. H. Arendt and M. Heidegger 2004, p. 7.
18. For an excellent analysis of *Being and Time* see S. Mulhall 1996; and for a lucid and authoritative account of Heidegger, see M. Inwood 2000.
19. Note that this signified a rejection of Kant, who considered space of principal importance, although there are signs that Kant gave priority to time in the 'Schematism of the Concepts of Pure Understanding', in I. Kant 1999.
20. J. Fritsche, 1999, p. 341.
21. There were several other female 'companions', including the intellectual Elisabeth Blochmann, who was Jewish and who, according to Michael Inwood (15 September 2011, private correspondence), Heidegger helped get to England.
22. Written from Todtnauberg, 21 March 1925, in H. Arendt and M. Heidegger, 2004, p. 9.
23. Ibid., p. 3.

24. Ibid., p. 22.
25. Ibid., p. 26.
26. Ibid., p. 29.
27. Ibid., p. 31.
28. Ibid., p. 3.
29. Ibid., p. 4.
30. Ibid., p. 5.
31. Ibid., p. 6.
32. Ibid., p. 22.
33. Ibid., p. 6.
34. Ibid.
35. Ibid., p. 27.
36. Ibid., p. 50.
37. Only seventeen days after the books by German-Jewish philosophers were burnt in Berlin.
38. See V. Farias 1989, pp. 96–112.
39. Ibid., p. 99.
40. Ibid., p. 108, Heidegger quotes Plato's *Politeia*.
41. The 'Horst-Wessel-Lied' was the anthem of the Nazi Party from 1930 to 1945 and the co-national anthem of Germany from 1933 to 1945. See G. Boderick 1995, pp. 100–27.
42. H. Ott 1993, p. 152.
43. V. Farias 1989, p. 113.
44. H. Ott 1993, part III; J. Young 1997.
45. V. Farias 1989, pp. 119–20, on 10 February 1934.
46. After the war, Heidegger took great care to hide the incriminating letters.
47. V. Farias 1989, p. 117.
48. H. Ott 1993, p. 157.
49. Ibid., p. 156.
50. V. Farias 1989, p. 117; my emphasis.
51. H. Ott 1993, p. 164.
52. E. Faye, 2009, p. 34.
53. Ibid., p. 38.
54. H. Ott 1993, p. 254.
55. Ibid., p. 243.
56. 'The command structure of the new German reality,' he argued, 'should be based on principles of "inheritance" and "health", which are in turn dependent upon the historical and political development of *Volk*'. W. Bialas and A. Rabinbach 2007, p. 103.
57. Ibid.
58. H. Ott 1993, p. 242.
59. V. Farias 1989, p. 191.
60. E. Faye 2009, pp. 252–3.
61. M. Heidegger 2000, p. 199; my emphasis.
62. R. Safranski 1998, pp. 319–20.
63. H. Ott 1993, pp. 291–2.
64. See E. Faye 2009.
65. H. Ott 1993, p. 277.
66. Ibid., p. 281.
67. Ibid., p. 277.
68. Ibid., p. 295.
69. V. Farias 1989, p. 277.
70. Ibid., p. 260.
71. Ibid., p. 84.
72. See the magnificent study by E. Faye 2009.
73. H. Ott 1993, p. 137.

Part 2 Hitler's opponents

1. There are many interesting tales to be told of Austrian Jewish thinkers, but these are stories for another book. Here we concentrate specifically on German-Jewish thinkers. Note that Karl Popper left Vienna in 1937 fleeing Nazism. While interned as an enemy alien (sent from the UK to New Zealand), he wrote *The Open Society and its Enemies*, a book which can plausibly be read both as having been written in opposition to Nazism and addressing the fundamental question about the relationship between various mainstream political philosophical thinkers (Plato, Hegel, Marx) and totalitarianism. Popper's life as a young philosopher and the focus of his early political writing were completely shaped by the rise of Nazism. Many of the greatest philosophers of the twentieth century were Jewish (at least by Hitler's definition), for instance, Wittgenstein, Popper, Kripke, Ayer, and many more.

Chapter 6

1. Image described from 'Jews being expelled from Germany after 1933', photograph, Bildarchiv Preussischer Kulturbesitz, Berlin.
2. W. Benjamin 2006, pp. 110–11.
3. Description based upon a black-and-white photograph taken by Netty Kellner, in the remarkable biography by M. Broderson 1996, p. 117.
4. W. Benjamin and G. Scholem 1992, p. 36.
5. Entry in *Kürschners Deutscher Literaturkalender*, 1930, cited in M. Broderson 1996, p. 190.
6. J. Selz 1991, p. 355.
7. M. Broderson 1996, p. 202.
8. Ibid.
9. B. Brecht 1976, p. 218.
10. W. Benjamin and G. Scholem 1992 p. 27 (note that Scholem had emigrated to Palestine).
11. Ibid., p. 47.
12. Ibid., p. 61.
13. My emphasis.
14. W. Benjamin and G. Scholem 1992, p. 34.
15. H. Benjamin 1977, p. 210.
16. W. Benjamin and G. Scholem 1992, pp. 46–7.
17. Ibid., p. 54.
18. W. Benjamin 2006, pp. 37–42.
19. M. Broderson 1996, pp. 1–6.
20. G. Scholem 1983, p. 130.
21. W. Benjamin, vol. 3, 1972–89, pp. 194–9; M. Broderson 1996, p. 21.
22. W. Benjamin 2006, pp. 71–2.
23. Ibid., p. 59.
24. Ibid., p. 125.
25. M. Broderson 1996, pp. 93–4.
26. Letter to G. Scholem, 30 July 1917, in W. Benjamin 1994, p. 91.
27. W. Kratf 1973, p. 71.
28. C. Wolff 1980, p. 66.
29. Note that this was the relationship which Benjamin had referred to in his 30 July letter as 'dying away in Zurich'. M. Broderson 1996, p. 97.
30. M. Broderson 1996, p. 100.
31. W. Benjamin 1995–2000, vol. 1, p. 271.
32. G. Scholem 2003, p. 12.
33. W. Benjamin 1995–2000, vol 1, pp. 289, 296.
34. E. Leslie 2007, p. 51.
35. U. Marx, G. and M. Schwarz, and E. Wizisla, eds, 2006, p. 112.
36. Ibid.

37. Said by Ernst Block around 1920, in M. Broderson 1996, p. 100.
38. W. Benjamin 2006, pp. 97–8.
39. W. Benjamin and T. Adorno 1999, p. 100.
40. E. Leslie 2007, p. 104.
41. W. Benjamin 1999, p. 621.
42. W. Benjamin 2006, p. 93.
43. E. Leslie 2007, p. 104.
44. W. Benjamin 1999, p. 598.
45. W. Benjamin 1972–89, vol. 4, 1, p. 383.
46. E. Leslie 2007, p. 108.
47. Ibid., p. 105.
48. W. Benjamin 1992, pp. 61–9.
49. W. Benjamin and G. Scholem 1992, p. 65.
50. Ibid., pp. 68–70.
51. Ibid., pp. 70–3.
52. Ibid., p. 77.
53. Ibid., p. 76.
54. Ibid., p. 82.
55. Expressed in a letter to Gretel Adorno on 1 November 1938. See W. Benjamin 1994, p. 578.
56. M. Broderson 1996, p. 244.
57. Ibid.
58. W. Benjamin and G. Scholem 1992, p. 259.
59. Ibid., p. 263.
60. M. Broderson 1996, p. 250.
61. W. Benjamin and T. Adorno 1999, p. 340.
62. Ibid., p. 240.
63. Lisa Fittko, 'The Story of Old Benjamin', in W. Benjamin 1974–89, vol. 5, pp. 1,185–6.
64. M. Broderson 1996, p. 254.
65. W. Benjamin 2006, p. 100.

Chapter 7

1. T. Adorno 2006, p. 170.
2. Ibid.
3. Ibid., p. 312.
4. Ibid., p. 40.
5. Ibid., p. 74.
6. Ibid., p. 81.
7. Ibid., p. 354 (my emphasis).
8. See J. D. Riva and G. Stern 2006, p. 24; p. 162.
9. T. Adorno 2006, p. 138.
10. T. Adorno 1991–92. p. 301.
11. T. Adorno 2006, p. 298.
12. Ibid., p. 298.
13. Ibid., p. 48.
14. Ibid., p. 40.
15. Ibid., p. 5.
16. Ibid., p. 114.
17. Ibid., p. 69.
18. Ibid., p. 70.
19. Ibid., p. 36.
20. Ibid., p. 40–1.
21. Ibid., p. 41.
22. Ibid., p. 50.

23. Ibid., p. 93.
24. Ibid., p. 95.
25. E. Bahr 2007, p. 5.
26. *Los Angeles Times*, 14 May 2006, B2, in E. Bahr 2007.
27. T. Adorno 2006, pp. 117–19, original type-written letter with printed letter head and handwritten postscript.
28. Ibid., p. 50.
29. Ibid.
30. Ibid., p. 53.
31. M. Horkheimer and T. Adorno 1992.
32. T. Adorno 2006, p. 73.
33. Ibid., p. 108.
34. Ibid., p. 171.
35. Ibid., p. 47.
36. Ibid., p. 322.
37. Ibid., p. 133.
38. Ibid., p. 123.
39. Ibid., p. 167.
40. Ibid., p. 56.
41. Ibid., p. 80.
42. B. Brecht in T. Adorno 2006, p. 106.
43. Ibid.
44. Ibid., p. 131.
45. Ibid., p. 144; p. 153.
46. Ibid., p. 150.
47. Ibid., p. 151.
48. Ibid., p. 152.
49. Ibid., p. 50.
50. Ibid., p. 54.
51. Ibid.
52. Adorno, for example, completed *Hegel Three Studies* and *Kant's 'Critique of Pure Reason'*.
53. T. Adorno 2006, p. 6.
54. Ibid., p. 5.
55. Ibid., p. 85.
56. S. Müller-Doohm 2005, p. 17.
57. Ibid., pp. 18–19.
58. T. Adorno 1970, pp. 117ff.
59. S. Müller-Doohm 2005, p. 28.
60. L. Lowenthal 1987, p. 203.
61. S. Müller-Doohm 2005, p. 32.
62. E. Pfeiffer-Belli 1986, p. 51.
63. S. Müller-Doohm 2005, p. 37.
64. T. Adorno 2006, p. 137.
65. S. Müller-Doohm 2005, p. 44.
66. R. Becker-Schmidt 1991, p. 210.
67. S. Müller-Doohm 2005, p. 159.
68. Ibid., p. 129.
69. T. Adorno 1971, p. 49.
70. The Archive of the Dean's Office of the Philosophy Faculty of the Johann Wolfgang Goethe University, Frankfurt. Adorno's personal file, cited in S. Müller-Doohm 2005, p. 177.
71. S. Müller-Doohm 2005, p. 178.
72. From the Theodor W. Adorno Archive, Frankfurt am Main.
73. S. Müller-Doohm 2005, p. 188.
74. T. Adorno and A. Berg 1994–2003, p. 297; E. Wilcox 1997, pp. 365ff.

75. T. Adorno 'Letter to Horkheimer, November 2nd 1934', in M. Horkheimer 1995, vol. 15, p. 262, 1985–96. See also L. Jäger 2004.
76. I. Berlin to Bernard Williams, unpublished letter, 12 September 1982, Archive, Wolfson College, Oxford.
77. Ibid., 19 May 1989.
78. I. Berlin, unpublished letter to Robert Craft, 28 October 1965, Archive, Wolfson College, Oxford.
79. From a forthcoming essay by Anthony Quinton: kindly quoted in private correspondence with H. Hardy, Oxford, 28 February 2009.
80. L. Mitchell 2009, p. 78.
81. Ibid., p. 79.
82. Helen Opie in private correspondence with the author, Friday, 16 October 2009.
83. T. Adorno and A. Berg 1994–2003, p. 296.
84. T. Adorno 1992, p. 7.
85. M. Horkheimer 1995, vol. 16, p. 392, in S. Fischer 1985–96.
86. Adorno, 2006, p. 56.

Chapter 8

1. The Reichstag fire was an arson attack on 27 February 1933. See F. Tobias 1963.
2. Dachau was the first regular concentration camp established by the Nazis in March 1933. See H. Marcuse 2001.
3. On 10 May 1933 upwards of forty thousand people gathered in Berlin to burn 'un-German' books. See United States Holocaust Memorial Museum, Washington, DC.
4. H. Arendt 1964.
5. The details of Hannah's family background and early life are taken from chapter 1, pp. 5–42, of Elizabeth Young-Bruehl's stunning biography (2004). See also chapter 1, pp. 13–22 of Derwent May 1986.
6. E. Young-Bruehl 2004, p. 6.
7. Ibid., pp. 8–9.
8. M. Arendt 2004.
9. 'The Metro', in H. Arendt and M. Heidegger 2004, p. 296.
10. K. Löwith 1986, pp. 42–3.
11. R. Safranski 1998, p. 133.
12. H. Arendt 1996, p. 190.
13. R. Wolin 2004, p. 96.
14. E. Young-Bruehl 2004, p. 53.
15. H. Arendt, 'Shadows', in H. Arendt and M. Heidegger 2004, pp. 12–16.
16. E. Ettinger 1995, pp. 21–8.
17. See H. Arendt 1996.
18. D. May 1986, p. 29.
19. E. Young-Bruehl 2004, p. 56.
20. H. Arendt 1997.
21. Ibid., p. 3.
22. H. Arendt and M. Heidegger 2004, p. 51.
23. Ibid.
24. Ibid.
25. E. Young-Bruehl 2004, p. 116.
26. D. May 1986, p. 47.
27. H. Arendt 1972.
28. H. Arendt 'Bertolt Brecht: 1898–1956', in Arendt 1968, p. 245. Walter Benjamin also commented on this poem, in W. Benjamin 1973.
29. H. Arendt 1943, p. 70.
30. See H. Arendt 1968.

31. H. Arendt 1951.
32. E. Young-Bruehl 2004, p. 162.
33. See E. Young-Bruehl for one version of this dispute and S. Muller-Doohm for another.
34. I. Berlin letter to Bernard Crick (unpublished), 4 November 1963, Archive, Wolfson College, Oxford.
35. I. Berlin letter to Sam Behrman (unpublished), 19 July 1963, and to William Phillips (unpublished), 7 May 1963, Archive, Wolfson College, Oxford.
36. H. Arendt untitled poem, 1943, in E. Young-Bruehl 2004, p. 185.
37. For instance, H. Arendt 20 November 1942.
38. E. Young-Bruehl 2004, p. 181.

Chapter 9

1. There is little material about the final moments of Huber's life. The following is a reconstruction based on the account offered by A. Dumbach and J. Newborn 2006, pp. 176–9, and by R. Hanser 1979, pp. 300–1. The facts about the prison, dates, etc., and the SS officers, are reported by them. The details of the caretaker are my own reconstruction.
2. R. Hanser 1979, pp. 300–1, and A. Dumbach and J. Newborn 2006, pp. 176–9.
3. Alexander Schmorell, member of the White Rose.
4. A. Dumbach and J. Newborn 2006, p. 85.
5. A mention of the chaplain is made in ibid., p. 178.
6. Ibid., p. 85.
7. See ibid., p. 86.
8. Description taken from a black-and-white photo, ibid., p. 142.
9. Ibid., pp. 87–8.
10. Ibid., p. 88.
11. W. H. Rubsamen 1944, p. 229.
12. I. Jens, 1987, p. 264.
13. The visiting American student Walter Rubsamen wrote this of him in an obituary published after his execution, see W. H. Rubsamen 1944.
14. Ibid., p. 226.
15. A. Dumbach and J. Newborn 2006, p. 88.
16. W. H. Rubsamen 1944, pp. 231–2.
17. R. Hanser 1979, p. 168.
18. Ibid., pp. 168–9.
19. A. Dumbach and J. Newborn 2006, p. 89.
20. Ibid., p. 25.
21. Ibid., p. 28.
22. I. Jens 1987, p. 80.
23. A. Dumbach and J. Newborn 2006, p. 66.
24. Ibid., pp. 66–7.
25. I. Jens 1987, p. 18.
26. A. Dumbach and J. Newborn 2006, p. 90.
27. I. Jens 1987, p. 216.
28. Ibid.
29. Only the White Rose member George (Jürgen) Wittenstein survived. See G. J. Wittenstein 2004.
30. I. Jens 1987, p. 18.
31. R. Hanser 1979, p. 88.
32. A. Dumbach and J. Newborn 2006, p. 191.
33. R. Hanser 1979, p. 242.
34. Although homes were supplied with electricity, it is very likely that in the wake of Allied bombardments since 1940, coal, oil and candles were frequently used.
35. These were the regional leaders of the Nazi Party.

36. A. Dumbach and J. Newborn 2006, pp. 201–3.
37. R. Hanser 1979, pp. 254–6.
38. A. Dumbach and J. Newborn 2006, p. 166.
39. Ibid., p. 162.
40. R. Hanser 1979, pp. 283–4.
41. See Chapter 1 of this book.
42. A. Dumbach and J. Newborn 2006, p. 177.
43. Ibid., p. 170.
44. Ibid., p. 173.
45. Ibid.
46. Ibid., p. 177.
47. Ibid., pp. 182–3. On 13 October 1944, Hans Leipelt, a half-Jewish chemistry student, was tried and sentenced to death. He was turned in for collecting money to support the widow of Professor Kurt Huber. He was executed on 29 January 1945; ibid., p. 181.

Chapter 10

1. H. Trevor-Roper 1947, pp. 184, 190.
2. Ibid., pp. 213–14; I. Kershaw 2000, p. 822.
3. I. Kershaw 2005, p. 47.
4. Trevor-Roper simply states that Hitler poisoned his dog.
5. H. Trevor-Roper 1947, p. 218.
6. Ibid., pp. 220–1.
7. Although Hitler's suicide was initially only a rumour among the many others circulating at the time, soon the mysterious death leaked out and rekindled the imagination of a world worn out by barbarism. The Russians were sceptical, but the Oxford historian Hugh Trevor-Roper finally confirmed both the suicide and the method, H Trevor-Roper 1947, p. 218. Many other accounts circulated then and now; see, for example, H. Linge 2009, pp. 197–208.
8. For more details see P. Calvocoressi, 1948; R. E. Conot 1983 or G. M. Gilbert, 1947.
9. Description based on black-and-white photos, 'IMT Defendants and Defense Attorneys', 10 December 1945, and 'Prosecution Reviews Nazi Chain of Command on Third Day of IMT', 22 November 1945, in Nuremberg Trials Project, Archive of Law School Library, University of Harvard, Cambridge, MA.
10. M. Weinreich 1999, p. 240. Note that Jackson's statement was made on the second day of the trial.
11. See H. W. Koch 1989, pp. 126–74; for details of his death, *The Jewish Virtual Library*.
12. K. Smith 2003.
13. Ibid.
14. Ibid.
15. S. P. Remy 2002, pp. 146–7.
16. Ibid., p. 177.
17. Ibid., p. 178.
18. D. E. Showalter 2006, pp. 404–5.
19. See S. Tegel 2007.
20. Alfred Bäumler collection, Philosophical Archive, University of Konstanz (Constance, on the Giessberg), Universitätsstrasse 10 (G 5 tract Building, Room G 511–G 514).
21. B. Jackson 2004; T. P. Griffin 2003, pp. 168–75.
22. A. Alckens 1973.
23. J. Schriewer 1982, pp. 36–8.
24. Ernst Bergmann was a Nazi Party member from 1930. See G. Leaman and G. Simon 1993, pp. 261–92, and also M. Weinreich 1999, p. 62.
25. See M. Weinreich 1999, pp. 175–6; B. Oberkrome 2007, p. 208.
26. See U. Prehn 2005; U. Prehn 2003/2004.
27. See E. Faye 2009 for more details of Heyse's Nazism.

28. See U. Prehn 2005; U. Prehn 2003/2004. Boehm died from old age on 9 November 1968 in Lüneburg.
29. See G. Leaman and G. Simon 1994, pp. 443–69; and E. Klee 2005, p. 254.
30. See S. P. Remy 2002, p. 133, and also S. P. Remy 2007, p. 28.
31. S. P. Remy 2002, p. 181.
32. Ibid., p. 133. Fehrle's and Krieck's students in the philosophy faculty had also helped to destroy academic values, namely Wilhelm Classen, Wilhelm Ganser and Waltraud Eckhard.
33. Ibid., p. 184.
34. See E. Faye 2009, p. 42; and also S. P. Remy 2002, pp. 180–5. Fehrle's main works on folklore were published in the 1950s and even posthumously into the 1970s. He died in 1957 aged seventy-seven.
35. S. P. Remy 2002, p. 177.
36. Weinreich studied and taught in Europe's leading universities and developed Jewish cultural programmes until, with the advent of the Nazi occupation of Poland, he was forced to retreat to America.
37. M. Weinreich 1999, p. 242.
38. Ibid.
39. M. Gilbert in M. Weinreich 1999, p. x.
40. Ibid., p. xi.
41. M. Weinreich 1999, p. 56, p. 271.
42. See O. Höfler 1978.
43. See M. Weinreich 1999, p. 270.
44. E. Klee 2005, p. 218.
45. See E. Rothacker 1934; M. Weinreich 1999, p. 16.
46. W. Perpeet 2005, pp. 117–18; and E. Klee 2005.
47. M. Wundt in *Neue Deutsche Biographie*, 16, 1990, p. 421.
48. Papers, 1854–1949, inventory signature UAT 228, Archives, University of Tübigen.
49. See M. Wundt 1964.
50. M. Weinreich 1999, p. 21, p. 282.
51. Ibid., pp. 48, 56–7, 270.
52. V. Farias 1989, p. 86; R. Safranski 1998, p. 253; H. Ott 1993 pp. 151, 155.
53. Born 24 July 1895, professor of philosophy at the University of Breslau, see M. Weinreich 1999, p. 124.
54. Born in 1889.
55. See E. Faye 2009, especially pp. 18–19, 262–6. Also A. Gethmann-Siefert and J. Mittelstrass, eds, 2002.
56. E. Faye 2009, p. 176.
57. See, for example, E. Wolf 1950–1954.
58. S. P. Remy 2002, p. 221.
59. Ibid., pp. 227–8.
60. Greta von Ubisch, unpublished memoirs, *c.* 1955, in ibid., p. 218. Von Ubisch was a botanist at Heidelberg, the first woman to receive a doctorate and teach at the university. She was fired on racial grounds in 1933; ibid., pp. 18–19.
61. Ibid., pp. 218–33.
62. Ibid., p. 223.
63. He also used his legal skills to defend many former Nazis. See E. Faye 2009.
64. M. Weinreich 1999, p. 241.
65. Carl, Schmitt, Interrogations by Robert Kempner, 1947, in J. W. Bendersky 1983, p. 272.
66. S. P. Remy 2002, p. 223.
67. G. L. Ulmen, review of Carl Schmitt quoted on the jacket of C. Schmitt 2003.
68. H. Ott 1993, p. 305.
69. Ibid., p. 313.
70. ibid., p. 315.
71. This eventually got underway, and on 23 July 1945 they began to assess Heidegger's case.

72. H. Ott 1993, p. 321.
73. V. Farias 1989, p. 277.
74. See letter to the rector's office, 9 October 1945, in H. Ott 1993, p. 328.
75. H. Ott 1993, p. 342.
76. Ibid., p. 348.
77. E. Ettinger 1995, p. 68.
78. Ibid., p. 66.
79. Arendt in a letter to Jaspers. My emphasis. L. Köhler and H. Saner 1985, p. 79.
80. D. May 1986, p. 76.
81. H. Arendt and M. Heidegger 2004, p. 64.
82. L. Köhler and H. Saner 1985, p. 79.
83. H. Arendt and M. Heidegger 2004, p. 193; my emphasis.
84. H. Ott 1993, p. 348.
85. R. Wolin 2003, p. 181. See also V. Farias 1989, p. 282; pp. 281–7.
86. R. Wolin 2003, p. 3. See also H. Ott 1993, pp. 367–8.
87. See S. Mulhall 1996, p. ix, who provides a superb detailed interpretation of Heidegger's principal work.
88. M. Heidegger, (1910–1976), volume 16 GA.
89. Heidegger's early publications and transcripts of his lectures are being brought out in *Gesamtausgabe*, the complete edition of his works. The *Gesamtausgabe* is projected to fill about one hundred volumes.
90. K. Smith 2003.
91. S. Kirkbright 2004.
92. Deportation was for 14 April 1945, the troops arrived on 1 April. S. P. Remy 2002, p. 115.
93. S. Kirkbright 2004.
94. A. Gallin 1986, pp. 96–9.
95. E. Skidelsky 2008.
96. J. Durham Peters, and P. Simonson, 2004, p. 485.
97. B. Katz 1982.
98. See G. Scholem 2008.
99. D. May 1986, p. 73.
100. For more details on this, see C. Bagge Laustsen and R. Ugilt, 'Eichmann's Kant', in *The Journal of Speculative Philosophy*, New Series, vol. 21, no. 3, 2007.
101. I. Berlin, Letter to Bernard Crick, 1963.
102. S. P. Remy 2002, p. 141; my emphasis.
103. See K. Löwith 1994.
104. T. Adorno 2006, p. 374.
105. S. Müller-Doohm 2005, p. 329.
106. T. Adorno 2006, p. 375.
107. S. Müller-Doohm 2005, p. 330.
108. T. Adorno 2006, p. 377.
109. S. P. Remy 2002, p. 141.
110. S. Müller-Doohm 2005, p. 348.
111. Ibid., p. 330.
112. Ibid., pp. 368–9.
113. See *Philosophy of Modern Music; Introduction to the Sociology of Music; Mahler: A Musical*; Paddison, 1993, p. 24. *Physiognomy*; and for literary criticism, *Minima Moralia, Notes to Literature*, vols. 1 and 2.
114. T. Adorno 2006, p. 377.
115. In spite of his Nazi allegiance, Hofstätter was appointed to the University of Graz in 1945, then worked in America. See W. Bergmann 1997.
116. S. Müller-Doohm 2005, p. 384.
117. T. Adorno 1986, p. 122.

118. Adorno to Samuel Beckett, 4 February 1969, Theodor W. Adorno Archive, Frankfurt am Main (Br 76/7).
119. R. Gross 2007, p. 3.
120. For example, the *Leiden Journal of International Law* published by Cambridge University Press contains many pieces on Carl Schmitt.
121. For example, Telos Press.
122. C. Schmitt 2003.
123. See R. Gross 2007, pp. 3–16.
124. Ibid., 2007; my emphasis.
125. A. Rabinbach, review, quoted in ibid., backcover.
126. S. E. Aschheim, review, quoted in ibid.
127. M. Weinreich, 1999, p. 241.
128. R. Wolin 2003.
129. Steven Remy argues that Germany remained entrenched in a culture of silence and denial about its Nazi past, so this would not be surprising. See S. P. Remy, 2002, p. 245.
130. Heidegger influenced Merleau-Ponty, Lyotard, Derrida, Foucault, Lacoue-Labarthe and Ricoeur, among many others, and his works are expounded in many multiple-volume editions in France.
131. H. Ott 1993, p. 8.
132. E. Faye 2009, p. 320.
133. In Latin America, José Ortega y Gasset incorporated his ideas. For Heidegger's impact in Japan, see G. Mayeda 2006 and G. Parkes 1987.
134. 'Thinking the Unthinkable', in *Human All Too Human*, BBC, 1999.
135. J. Glover 2001, p. 377.
136. Wikipedia, entry for Frege, 2012.
137. Richard Evans in his compelling *Lying About Hitler* takes these issues even further, addressing not just the problem of 'forgetting' but intentionally altering the truth. See R. J. Evans 2001.

Bibliography

Adorno, T. Letter to Samuel Backett, 4 February, 1969, Theodor W. Adorno Archive, Frankfurt am Main (Br 76/7).

Adorno, T. *Erziehung zur Mündigkeit: Vortäge und Gespräche mit Hellmut Becker 1959–1969*, ed. G. Kadelbach. Frankfurt am Main: Suhrkamp, 1970.

Adorno, T. 'Die Freudische Theorie und die Struktur der Faschistischen Propaganda', in *Kritik: Kleine Schriften zur Gesellschaft*, ed. R. Tiedemann. Frankfurt am Main: Sukrkamp, 1971.

Adorno, T. *The Jargon of Authenticity*. London: Routledge and Kegan Paul, 1986.

Adorno, T. 'Aus Dem Grünen Buch', West Drayton, 27 April 1934, *Frankfurter Adorno-Blätter II*, Munich, 1992.

Adorno, T. 'A Title', *Notes to Literature*, vol. 2. Trans S. Weber Nicholsen. New York: Columbia University Press, 1991–92.

Adorno, T. *Theodor W. Adorno: Letters to his Parents*, ed. C. Gödde and H. Lonitz, trans. H. Hoban. Cambridge: Polity Press, 2006.

Adorno, T. and Berg, A. *Briefwechsel 1925–1935*, ed. H. Lonitz 1997. Theodor W. Adorno Archive, Frankfurt am Main: Suhrkamp, 1994–2003.

Akehurst, T. L. 'The Nazi Tradiation: The Analytic Critique of Continental Philosophy in Mid-Century Britain', *History of European Ideas* 34, 2008, 548–57.

Akehurst, T. L. *The Cultural Politics of Analytic Philosophy: Britishness and the Spectre of Europe*, in *Continuum Studies in British Philosophy*, 2010.

Alckens, A. *Moosburg an der Isar. Eine kurze Stadtgeschichte*. Moosburg: Stadtverwaltung, 1973.

Aly, Götz and Heim, Susanne (trans. A. G. Blunden). *Architects of Annihilation: Auschwitz and the Logic of Destruction*. Princeton, NJ: Princeton University Press, 2002.

Ansell-Pearson, K. *Viroid Life: Perspectives on Nietzsche and the Transhuman Condition*. London: Routledge, 1997.

Ansell-Pearson, K. *Nietzsche and Modern German Thought*. London: Routledge, 2002.

Arendt, H. 'Die Krise des Zionismus, 3', *Aufbau*, 20 November 1942, p. 17.

Arendt, H. 'We Refugees', *Menorah Journal* 31, January 1943, pp. 69–77.

Arendt, H. *The Origins of Totalitarianism*. New York: Harcourt, Brace and Co., 1951.

Arendt, H. Interview with Günter Grass, 'Was bleibt? Es bleibt die Muttersprache', in Günter Grass, *Zur Person*. Munich: Feder, 1964.

Arendt, H. *Men in Dark Times*. New York: Harcourt, Brace and World, 1968.

Arendt, H. 'Nachwort' for Robert Gilbert, *Mich Hat Kein Esel Im Galopp Verloren*. Munich: Piper, 1972.

Arendt, H. *Love and St. Augustine*, ed. J. Vecchiarelli Scott and J. Chelius Stark. Chicago, IL: University of Chicago Press, 1996.

Arendt, H. *Rahel Varnhagen: The Life of a Jewess*, ed. L. Weissberg, trans. C. and R. Winston. Baltimore, MD: Johns Hopkins University Press, 1997.

Arendt, M. *Unser Kind*, diary, Arendt Papers, Library of Congress, Washington, DC, trans. E. Young-Bruehl, in Young-Bruehl 2004.

Arendt, H. and Heidegger, M. *Letters, 1925–1975*, ed. U. Ludz, trans. A. Shields. Orlando, FL: Harcourt Books, Inc., 2004.

Aschheim, S. E. *Nietzsche, Anti-Semitism, and the Holocaust*, in J. Golomb, ed. *Nietzsche & Jewish Culture*. New York: Routledge, 1997.

Aschheim, S. E. *The Nietzsche Legacy in Germany 1890–1990*. Berkeley and Los Angeles, CA, and Oxford: University of California Press, 1992.

Axelrod, T. *Holocaust Biographies: Hans and Sophie Scholl, German Resisters of the White Rose*. Costa Mesa: Saddleback Publishing Inc., 2000.

Bade, K. J. and Brown, A., trans. *Migration in European History: The Making of Europe*. Oxford: Blackwell, 2003.

Bagge Laustsen, C. and R. Ugilt 'Eichmann's Kant' in *The Journal of Speculative Philosophy*, New Series, vol. 21, no. 3, 2007.

Bahr, E. *Weimar on the Pacific: German Exile Culture in Los Angeles and the Crisis of Modernism*. Berkeley, Los Angeles, CA and London: University of California Press, 2007.

Balakrishnan, G. *The Enemy: An Intellectual Portrait of Carl Schmitt*. London: Verso, 2002.

Bambach C. *Heidegger's Roots: Nietzsche, National Socialism, and the Greeks*. Ithaca, NY, and London: Cornell University Press, 2003.

Bannister, R. C. *Social Darwinism: Science and Myth in Anglo-American Social Thought*. Philadelphia, PA: Temple University Press, 1989.

Bäumler, A. *Kants Kritik der Urteilskraft, ihre Geschichte und Systematik*, 2 vols. Halle Saale: Niemeyer, 1923.

Bäumler A. *Nietzsche, der Philosoph und Politiker*. Leipzig: Reclam, 1931.

Bäumler, M. Brunträger, H. and Kurzke, H. *Thomas Mann und Alfred Baeumler*. Würzburg: Königshausen & Neumann, 1989.

Baynes, N. H., ed. and trans. *The Speeches of Adolf Hitler April 1922–August 1939*, vols. 1–2. Oxford: Oxford University Press, 1942.

Becker-Schmidt, R. 'Wenn die Frauen Erst Einmal Frauen sein Koönten', in J. Früchtel and M. Calloni, eds, *Geist Gegen die Zeitgeist: Erinner on Adorno*. Frankfurt am Main: Suhrkamp, 1991, pp. 206–24.

Beistegui, M. de. *Heidegger and the Political: Dystopias*. London: Routledge, 1998.

Bendersky, J. W. *Carl Schmitt: Theorist for the Reich*. Princeton, NJ: Princeton University Press, 1983.

Bendersky, J. W. 'Carl Schmitt's Path to Nuremberg: A Sixty-Year Reassessment', *Telos* 139, summer 2007. New York: Telos Press Publishing.

Benjamin, H. *Georg Benjamin: Eine Biographie*. Leipzig: 1977.

Benjamin, W. *Gesammelte Schriften*, eds. H. Schweppenhäuser and R. Tiedemann. Frankfurt am Main: Suhrkamp, 1972–89.

Benjamin, W. *Undertsanding Brecht*. London: New Left Books, 1973.

Benjamin W. 'Unpacking my Library: A Talk about Book Collecting', in *Literarische Welt* 1931, reprinted in *Illuminations*, introduction H. Arendt. London: Fontana Press, 1992.

Benjamin, W. *The Correspondence of Walter Benjamin, 1910–1940*, ed. G. Scholem and T. Adorno, trans. M. R. and E. M. Jacobson. Chicago IL, and London: University of Chicago Press, 1994.

Benjamin, W. *Gesammelte Briefe*, 6 vols., ed. C. Gödde and H. Lonitz. Frankfurt am Main: Suhrkamp, 1995–2000.

Benjamin, W. *Selected Writings*, 2:2, 1927–34, ed. M. W. Jennings. Cambridge, MA: The Belknap Press of Harvard University Press, 1999.

Benjamin, W. *Berlin Childhood Around 1900*. Cambridge, MA: The Belknap Press of Harvard University Press, 2006.

Benjamin, W. and Adorno, T. *The Complete Correspondence 1928–1940*. London: Polity Press, 1999.

Benjamin, W. and Scholem, G. (also ed.). *The Correspondence of Walter Benjamin and Gershom Scholem*. Cambridge, MA: Harvard University Press, 1992.

Bergmann, W. *Antisemitismus in öffentlichen Konflikten: kollektives Lernen in der politischen Kultur der Bundesrepublik 1949–1989*. Frankfurt am Main: Suhrkamp, 1997.

Berlin, I. Letter to Sam Behrman, 19 July 1963, Archive, Wolfson College, Oxford.

Berlin, I. Letter to William Phillips, 7 May 1913, Archive, Wolfson College, Oxford.

Berlin, I. Letter to Bernard Crick, 4 November 1963, Isaiah Berlin Archive, Wolfson College, Oxford.

Berlin, I. Letter to Robert Craft, 28 October 1965, Archive, Wolfson College, Oxford.

Berlin, I. Letter to Bernard Williams, 12 September 1982, Archive, Wolfson College, Oxford.

Bialas, W. and Rabinbach, A. *Nazi Germany and the Humanities*. Oxford: Oneworld Publications, 2007.

Blei, F. 'Der Fall Carl Schmitt, Von einem, der ihn kannte', *Der Christliche Ständestaat*, 25 December 1936.

Boderick, G. 'The Horst-Wessel-Lied: A Reappraisal', *International Folklore Review*, vol. 10, 1995.

Bölsche, Wilhelm. *Haeckel: His Life and Work*. London: T. Fischer Unwin, 1906.

Brecht, B. *Poems* trans. J. Willett. London: Methuen, 1976.

Bredekamp, Horst. 'From Walter Benjamin to Carl Schmitt, via Thomas Hobbes'. Trans. Melissa Thorson Hause and Jackson Bond. *Critical Inquiry* 25 (1999): 247–66.

Brener, E. M. *Richard Wagner and the Jews*. Jefferson, NC: McFarland, 2006.

Brennecke, Fritz, trans. H. Childs. *The Nazi Primer: Official Handbook for Schooling the Hitler Youth*. New York and London: Harper and Brothers Publishers, 1938.

Broderson, M., trans. Malcolm R. Green and Ingrida Ligers. *Walter Benjamin: A Biography*. London: Verso, 1996.

Browne, E. J. *Charles Darwin: Voyaging*. New York: Alfred A. Knopf, 1995.

Calvocoressi, Peter. *Nuremberg*. New York: Macmillan, 1948.

Carlebach, J. *Karl Marx and the Radical Critique of Judaism*, Littman Library of Jewish Civilization. London: Routledge, 1978.

Cassirer, E. *Kant's Life and Thought*, trans. J. Haden. New Haven, CT, and London: Yale University Press, 1981.

Cecil, R. *The Myth of the Master Race: Alfred Rosenberg and Nazi Ideology*. London: B. T. Batsford Ltd., 1972.

Childs, H. L. trans. *The Nazi Primer: Official Handbook for the Schooling of the Hitler Youth*. New York and London: Harper and Brothers Publishers, 1938.

Conot, Robert E. *Justice at Nuremberg*. New York: Harper & Row, 1983.

Cornwell, J. *Hitler's Pope: The Secret History of Pius XII*. Harmondsworth: Penguin 2000.

Cornwell, J. *Hitler's Scientists: Science, War and the Devil's Pact*. London: Viking, 2003.

Darwin, C. *The Autobiography of Charles Darwin, 1809–1882*. New York: W. W. Norton and Co., 1958.

Deiler, M. 'Landsberg Prison Documents 1923/1924: Adolf Hitler's Imprisonment', in *Civil Association for the Study of Contemporary Landsberg*, Issue 1, 2005.

Desmond, A. J. and Moore, J. R. *Darwin*. New York: W. W. Norton and Co., 1994.

Diethe, Carol. *Nietzsche's Sister and the Will to Power: A Biography of Elisabeth Forster-Nietzsche*. Chicago, IL: University of Illinois Press, 2003.

Donohoe, James. *Hitler's Conservative Opponents in Bavaria, 1930–1945*. Leiden: Brill, 1961.

Dow J. R. and Lixfeld, H., eds, *The Nazificiation of an Academic Discipline: Folklore and the Third Reich*. Bloomington, IN: Indiana University Press, 1994.

Downs, R. B. *Books that Changed the World*. London: Signet Classic, 2004.

Dumbach, A. and Newborn, J. *Sophie Scholl and the White Rose*. Oxford: Oneworld Publications, 2006.

Durham Peters, J. and Simonson, P. *Mass Communication and American Social Thought: Key Texts, 1919–1968*. Lanham, MD: Rowman and Littlefield, 2004, p. 485.

Ettinger, E. *Hannah Arendt, Martin Heidegger*. New Haven, CT, and London: Yale University Press, 1995.

Evans, R. J. *Lying About Hitler: History, Holocaust and the David Irving Trial*. New York: Basic Books, 2001.

Evans, R. J. *The Third Reich in Power, 1933–1939: How the Nazis Won Over the Hearts and Minds of a Nation*. London: Penguin, 2006.

Farias, V. *Heidegger and Nazism*. Philadelphia, PA: Temple University Press, 1989.

Faye, E. *Heidegger: The Introduction of Nazism into Philosophy*, trans. M. B. Smith. New Haven, CT, and London: Yale University Press, 2009.

Feuerbach, L. *The Essence of Christianity* (1841), trans. G. Eliot. New York: Harper and Brothers, 1957.

Fichte, J. G. 'A State Within a State' (1793), in *The Jew in the Modern World: A Documentary History*, ed. P. Mendes-Flohr and J. Reindharz. New York: Oxford University Press, 1995.

Frank, H. *Im Angesicht des Galgens*. Munich: Graefelfing, 1953.

Friedlander, H. *The Origins of Nazi Genocide: From Euthanasia to the Final Solution*. Chapel Hill, NC: UNC Press Books, 1997.

Friedländer, S. *Nazi Germany and the Jews*, vol. 1. London: HarperCollins, 1997, p. 57.

Fritsche, J. *Historical Destiny and National Socialism in Heidegger's 'Being and Time'*, Berkeley, CA: University of California Press, 1999.

Gallin, A. *Midwives to Nazism: University Professors in Weimar Germany, 1925–1933*. Macon, GA: Mercer University Press, 1986.

Gasman, D. *The Scientific Origins of National Socialism*. London and New York: Macdonald and American Elsevier Inc., 1971.

Gethmann-Siefert, A. and J. Mittelstrass, eds, *Die Philosophie und die Wissenschaften. Zum Werk Oskar Beckers*. Munich: Fink, 2002.

Giblin, J. *The Life and Death of Adolf Hitler*. New York: Clarion Books, 2002.

Gilbert, G. M. *Nuremberg Diary*. New York: Farrar, Straus, and Giroux, 1947.

Glover, J. *Humanity: A Moral History of the Twentieth Century*. London: Pimlico, 2001.

Goldhagen, D. J. *Hitler's Willing Executioners*. London: Little, Brown and Company, 1996.

Golomb, J., ed. *Nietzsche & Jewish Culture*. New York: Routledge, 1997.

Griffin, T. P. *Fast Track to Manhood*. Bloomington, IN: Trafford Publishing, 2003.

Gross, R. *Carl Schmitt and the Jews*. Madison, WI: University of Wisconsin Press, 2007.

Günther, N. and Kettering E., eds, *Martin Heidegger and National Socialism: Questions and Answers*: New York: Paragon House, 1990.

Haeckel, E. *The History of Creation: Or the Development of the Earth and Its Inhabitants By the Action of Natural Causes*. New York: Appleton, 1876.

Haeckel, E. *History of Creation, Vol. 1*. London: Kegan Paul, 1883.

Hahn, H. J. *German Thought and Culture*. Manchester: Manchester University Press, 1995.

Hanfstaengl, E. *The Missing Years*. New York: Arcade Publishing, 1994.

Hanfstaengl, E. (R. J. Evans Introduction). *The Unknown Hitler: Notes from the Young Nazi Party*. London: Gibson Square Books Ltd, 2005.

Hanser, R. *A Noble Treason: The Revolt of the Munich Students Against Hitler*. New York: G. P. Putnam's, 1979.

Härtle, H., ed. *Grossdeutschland: Traum und Tragödie*. Munich: Selbstverlag, 1970.

Hayman, R. *Nietzsche: A Critical Life*. London: Phoenix, 1995.

Hegel, G. W. F. *Phenomenology of Spirit*, trans. A. V. Miller. Oxford: Oxford University Press, 1977.

Hegel, G. W. F. *Hegel on Tragedy*, ed. A. and H. Paolucci. Westport, CT, and London: Greenwood Press, 1978.

Hegel, G. W. F. *Introduction to the Lectures on the History of Philosophy*, ed. and trans. T. M. Knox and A. V. Miller. Oxford: Oxford University Press, 1988.

Heidegger, M. *Sein und Zeit*. Tübingen: Max Niemeyer, 1927.

Heidegger, M. *Reden und andere Zeugnisse eines Lebensweges* (1910–1976), vol. 16. Frankfurt am Main: Vittorio Klostermann, 2000.

Heidegger, M. *Introduction to Metaphysics*, Yale University Press, 2000.

Heine, H. and Windfuhr, M. (eds) in vol. 5 of *Historisch-kritische Gesamtausgabe der Werke/ Heinrich Heine. Hrsg. von Manfred Windfuhr*. Hamburg: Hoffmann und Campe, 1994.

Helmut, W. *Die Politische Pädagogik von Ernst Krieck und Ihre Würdigung Durch die Westdeutsche Pädagogik*. Frankfurt am Main: Peter Lang, 2000.

Heyse, H. *Die Idee der Wissenschaft und die Deutsche Universität*. Königsberg: Königsberg: Press, 1933.

Hinton, A. L., ed. *Annihilating Difference: The Anthropology of Genocide*. Berkeley, CA: University of California Press, 2002.

Hitler, A. *The Speeches of Adolf Hitler, April 1922–August 1939*, vols 1–2 trans. and ed. Norman H. Baynes. Oxford: Oxford University Press, 1942.

Hitler, A. *Hitler's Letters and Notes*, ed. W. Maser. London: Heinemann, 1973.

Hitler, A *Mein Kampf*. London: Hutchinson and Co. Ltd., 1980.

Hitler, A. *Adolf Hitler: Monologue im Fuehrerhauptquartier 1941–1944. Die Aufzeichnungen Heinrich Heims*, ed. W. Jochmann. Hamburg: A. Knauss, 1980a.

Hitler, A. *Hitler's Table Talk, Hitler's Conversations Recorded by Martin Bormann*, introduced by Hugh Trevor-Roper. Oxford: Oxford University Press, 1988.

Hitler, A., in Weber, M. *The Journal of Historical Review*, vol. 8, no. 4 (winter 1988–89).

Höfler, O. *Siegfried, Arminius und der Nibelungenhort*. Vienna: Verlag der Österreichischen Akademie der Wissenschaften, 1978.

Horkheimer, M. *Briefwechsel 1913–1936*, 1995, vol. 15, in *Gesammelte Schriften*. Frankfurt am Main: S. Fischer, 1985–96.

Horkheimer M. and Adorno, T. *Dialectic of Enlightenment*. London: Verso, 1992.

Huber, Kurt. *Leibniz*. Munich: Verlag Von R. Oldenbourg, 1951.

Hüsmert, E., *Carl Schmitt Tagebücher Oktober 1912 his February 1915*. Akademie-Verlag, Auflage 1, 2005.

Inwood, M. *Heidegger: A Very Short Introduction*. Oxford: Oxford University Press, 2000.

Jackson, B. *A Wartime Prison Camp Log, Stalag VII-A, Germany*. Albany, New York: Xiteq Books, 2004.

Jäger, L. *Adorno: A Political Biography*, trans. Spencer S. New Haven, CT, and London: Yale University Press, 2004.

Jens, I., ed. *At the Heart of the White Rose: Letters and Diaries of Hans and Sophie Scholl*. New York: Harper and Row Publishers, 1987.

Jochmann, W. *National sozialismus Und Revolution*. Frankfurter am Main: Europäische Verlag, 1963.

Joll, J. 'The English Friedrich Nietzsche and the First World War', in *Deutschland in der Weltpolitik des 19 und 29 Jahrhunderts*, ed. I. Geiss and B. J. Wendt. Düsseldorf: Bertelsmann Universitätverlag, 1973.

Kahle, P. *Bonn University in Pre-Nazi and Nazi Times: 1923–39*. London: private printing, 1945.

Kaiser, J. H. 'Europäisches Grössraumdenken: Die Steiogerung geschichtlicher Grossen als Rechtsproblem', in Hans Barion, Ernst-Wolfgang, Böckenförde, Ernst Forsthoff and Werner Weber (hrsg), *Epirrhosis. Festgabe für Carl Schmitt*. Berlin: Dunker and Humbolt, 1968, Bd. 2, pp. 319–31.

Kant, I. *Philosophical Correspondence, 1759–1799*. Chicago: University of Chicago Press, 1986.

Kant, I. *Religion and Rational Theology*, trans. and ed. A. W. Wood and G. Di Giovanni. Cambridge: Cambridge University Press, 1996.

Kant, I. *Critique of Practical Reason*, trans. and ed. M. Gregor. Cambridge: Cambridge University Press, 1997a.

Kant, I. *Lectures on Ethics*, ed. P. Heath and J. B. Schneewind, trans. P. Heath. Cambridge: Cambridge University Press, 1997b.

Kant, I. *Critique of Pure Reason*, trans. and ed. P. Guyer and A. W. Wood. Cambridge: Cambridge University Press, 1999.

Kardoff, U. von. *Berlin: Diary of a Nightmare, 1942–1945*. London: Rupert Hart-Davis, 1960.

Katz, B. *Herbert Marcuse*. London: Verso, 1982.

Kaufmann, W. *Nietzsche*. Princeton, NJ: Princeton University Press, 1974.

Kaufmann, W. *Goethe, Kant, Hegel: Discovering the Mind*. Piscataway, NJ: Transaction Publishers, 1991.

Kearns, G. *Geopolitics and Empire*. Oxford: Oxford University Press, 2009.

Keegan, J. *The First World War*. London: Hutchinson, 1988.

Kershaw, I. *Hitler, 1889–1936: Hubris*. Harmondsworth: Allen Lane, 1998.

Kershaw, Ian. *Hitler 1936–1945 Nemesis*. Harmondsworth: Allen Lane, 2000.

Kershaw, I. *Death in the Bunker*. London: Penguin, 2005.

Kershaw, I. *Hitler, the Germans and the Final Solution*. New Haven, CT and London: Yale University Press, 2008.

Kershaw, I. *Hitler*. London: Penguin, 2009.

Kirkbright, S. *Karl Jaspers: A Biography. Navigations in Truth*. New Haven, CT, and London: Yale University Press, 2004.

Klee, E. *Das Personenlexikon zum Dritten Reich*, Frankfurt am Main: Fischer Taschenbuch Verlag, 2005.

Koch, H. W. *In the Name of the Volk: Political Justice in Hitler's Germany*. London: I. B. Tauris, 1989.

Köhler, L. and Saner, H. *Hannah Arendt/Karl Jaspers Briefwechsel, 1929–1969*. Munich: Piper, 1985.

Konieczny, A. *Tormersdorf, Grüssau, Riebnig, Obozy Przejsciowe dla Zydow Dolnego Slaska z lat 1941–1943*. Wrocław, Wydawnictwo Universyłetu Wrocłowskiergo, 1997.

Koonz, C. *The Nazi Conscience*. Cambridge, MA: Belknap Press of Harvard University Press, 2003.

Kratf, W. *Spiegelung der Jugend*. Frankfurt am Main: Suhrkamp, 1973.

Krosigk, S. *Es Geschah in Deutschland*. Tübingen: Rainer Wunderlich Verlag, 1951.

Kubizek, A. *Young Hitler*. London: Mann, 1973.

Kuehn, M. *Kant: A Biography*. Cambridge: Cambridge University Press, 2001.

Lacoue-Labarthe, P. *Heidegger, Art, and Politics: The Fiction of the Political*. London: Blackwell, 1990.

Leaman, G. and Simon, G. 'Deutsche Philosophen aus der Sicht des Sicherheitsdienstes des Reichsführers', in C. Klingemann, M. Nemann and K-S. Rehberg, *Jahrbuch für Soziologie-Geschichte*, Vs Verlag, Auflage 1, 1993, pp. 261–92.

Leaman, G. and Simon, G. 'Die Kant-Studien im Dritten Reich', in *Kant-Studien* 85, 1994, pp. 443–69.

Lebovic, N. 'The Beauty and Terror of Lebensphilosophie: Ludwig Klages, Walter Benjamin and Alfred Bäumler', in *South Central Review*, vol. 23, no. 1 (spring), pp. 23–39. Baltimore, MD: Johns Hopkins University Press, 2006.

Leslie, E. *Walter Benjamin*. London: Reaktion Books, 2007.

Librett, Jeffrey S. *The Rhetoric of Cultural Dialogue: Jews and Germans from Moses Mendelssohn to Richard Wagner and Beyond*. Stanford, CA: Stanford University Press, 2000.

Lindemann, A.S. *Anti-Semitism Before the Holocaust*. Harlow, Essex: Pearson, 2000.

Linge, H. *With Hitler to the End: The Memoir of Hitler's Valet*. London: Frontline Books, Skyhorse Publishing, Inc., 2009.

Lowenthal, L. *An Unmastered Past*, ed. M. Jay. Berkeley and Los Angeles, CA, and London: University of California Press, 1987.

Löwith, K. *My Life in Germany Before and After 1933*. Chicago, IL: University of Illinois Press, 1994.

Löwith, K. *Mein Leben in Deutschland vor und nach 1939*. Stuttgart: Metzler, 1986.

Macintyre, B. *Forgotten Fatherland: The Search for Elisabeth Nietzsche*. New York: Farrar Straus and Giroux, 1992.

Mack, M. *German Idealism and the Jew: The Inner Anti-Semitism of Philosophy and German Jewish Responses*. Chicago, IL: University of Chicago Press, 2003.

Marcuse, H. *Legacies of Dachau: The Uses and Abuses of a Concentration Camp, 1933–2001*. Cambridge: Cambridge University Press, 2001.

Marwedel, R. *Theodor Lessing*. Frankfurt am Main: Luchterhand, 1987.

Marx, K. *On the Jewish Question, Part 1*. Open University, 2000.

Marx, U., Schwarz, G. and M., and Wizisla, E., eds. *Walter Benjamin's Archive*. Frankfurt am Main: Suhrkamp, 2006.

May, D. *Hannah Arendt*. Harmondsworth: Penguin Books, 1986.

Mayeda, G. *Time, Space and Ethics in the Philosophy of Watsuji Tetsurō, Kuki Shūzō, and Martin Heidegger*. New York: Routledge, 2006.

McDonough, F. *Hitler and the Rise of the Nazi Party*. Harlow, Essex: Pearson Education, 2003.

Meier, H. *Carl Schmitt and Leo Strauss: The Hidden Dialogue.* Trans. H. J. Lomax. Chicago: University of Chicago Press, 1975.

Michalczyk, J., ed. *Confront: Resistance in Nazi Germany.* New York: Peter Lang, 2005.

Milchman, A. and Rosenberg, A. *Martin Heidegger and the Holocaust.* Atlantic Highlands, NJ: Humanities Press International, 1996.

Mitchell, L. *Maurice Bowra: A Life.* Oxford and New York: Oxford University Press, 2009.

Mueller, G. *Ernst Krieck und Die Nationalsozialistische Wissenschaftsreform: Motive U. Tendenzen E. Wissenschaftslehre U. Hochschulreform im Dritten Reich.* Weinheim: Beltz Verlag, 1978.

Müller, J.-W. *A Dangerous Mind.* New Haven, CT and London: Yale University Press, 2003.

Müller-Doohm, S. *Adorno: A Biography,* trans. R. Livingstone. Cambridge: Polity Press, 2005.

Mulhall, S. *Heidegger and Being and Time.* London: Routledge, 1996.

Natanson, M. *Edmund Husserl: Philosopher of Infinite Tasks.* Evanston, IL: Northwestern University Press, 1973.

Noack, Paul. *Carl Schmitt: Eine Biographie.* Berlin: Ullstein, 1996.

Oberkrome, B. 'German Historical Scholarship under National Socialism', in W. Bialas and A. Rabinbach, eds, *Nazi Germany and the Humanities.* Oxford: Oneworld Publications, 2007.

Ott, H. *Martin Heidegger: A Political Life,* trans. A. Blunden. London: Harper Collins, 1993.

Paddison, M. *Adorno's Aesthetics: of Music.* Cambridge: Cambridge University Press, 1993.

Parkes, G. *Heidegger and Asian Thought.* Honolulu: University of Hawaii Press, 1987.

Paulsen, F. *Immanuel Kant: His Life and Doctrine.* Whitefish; MT.: Kessinger, 2007.

Perpeet, W. 'Rothacker, Erich', in *Neue Deutsche Biographie* 22, 2005, pp. 117–18 [Online version].

Pfeiffer-Belli, E. *Junge Jahre im Alten Frankfurt.* Wiesbaden and Munich: Limes, 1986.

Poliakov, L. *The History of Anti-Semitism. Volume IV, Suicidal Europe, 1870–1933.* Oxford: Oxford University Press, 1977.

Poliakov, L. and Wulf, J. *Das Dritte Reich und seine Denker.* Berlin, 1959.

Prehn, U. 'An der schmalen Grenze zwischen Wissenschaft und Politik: Max Hildebert Boehm und die Gründungsgeschichte der (Nord-)Ostdeutschen Akademie,' in *Deutsche Studien* 39 2003/2004, H. 149, S. 27–51.

Prehn, U. 'Die wechselnden Gesichter eines Europa der Völker im 20. Jahrhundert. Ethnopolitische Vorstellungen bei Max Hildebert Boehm, Eugen Lemberg und Guy Héraud,' in Heiko Kauffmann, Helmut Kellershohn and Jobst Paul (Hrsg.), *Völkische Bande. Dekadenz und Wiedergeburt – Analysen rechter Ideologie.* Münster, 2005, S. 123–57.

Pulzer, P. *Jews and the German State.* Oxford and Cambridge, MA: Blackwell, 1992.

Quinton, A. *From Wodehouse to Wittgenstein.* Manchester: Carcanet Press, 1998.

Rauschning, H. *Hitler Speaks: A Series of Political Conversations with Adolf Hitler on his Real Aims.* London: Thornton Butterworth Ltd., 1940a.

Rauschning, H. *The Voice of Destruction: Conversations with Hitler,* 1940b. Whitefish, MT: Kessinger Publishing, 2004.

Remy S. P. *The Heidelberg Myth: The Nazification and Denazification of a German University.* Cambridge, MA: Harvard University Press, 2002.

Remy, S. 'Humanities and National Socialism at Heidelberg', in W. Bialas and A. Rabinbach, eds. *Nazi Germany and the Humanities.* Oxford: Oneworld Publications, 2007.

Ritter, G. 'German Professors in the Third Reich', *Review of Politics* 8, April 1946, pp. 242–54.

Ritter, G. *The German Problem,* Columbus, OH: Ohio State University Press, 1965.

Riva, J. D. and Stern, G. *A Woman at War: Marlene Dietrich Remembered.* Detroit, MI: Wayne State University Press, 2006.

Rose, P. L. *Revolutionary Anti-Semitism in Germany from Kant to Wagner.* Princeton, NJ: Princeton University Press, 1990.

Rose, P. L. *Wagner, Race and Revolution.* London: Faber and Faber, 1992.

Rosenberg, A. *Der Mythus des 20. Jahrhunderts.* Munich: Hoheneichen, 1930.

Rosenberg, A. *Die Protokolle der Weisen von Zion und die Judische Weltpolitik.* Munich: Deutsche Volksverlag, 1933.

Rosenfeld, G. D. *Munich and Memory: Architecture, Monuments, and the Legacy of the Third Reich.* Berkeley, CA: University of California Press, 2000.

Rothacker, E. *Geschichtphilosophie. Handbuch der Philosophie*. Munich: Oldenbourg, 1934.

Rubsamen, W. H. 'Kurt Huber of Munich', in *The Musical Quarterly*, vol. 30, no. 2, April 1944, pp. 226–33.

Russell, B. and Wyatt, W. *Bertrand Russell Speaks his Mind*, London: World Publishing Company, 1960.

Ryback, T. W. *Hitler's Private Library: The Books that Shaped His Life*. London: Vintage, 2010.

Safranski, R. *Martin Heidegger Between Good and Evil*. Cambridge, MA: Harvard University Press, 1998.

Safranski, R. *Nietzsche: A Philosophical Biography*, trans. S. Frisch. London: Granta, 2003.

Santaniello, W. *Nietzsche, God, and the Jews*. Albany, NY: State University of New York Press, 1994.

Sauder, G. *Die Bücherverbrennung. Zum 10. Mai 1933*. Munich and Vienna: Carl Hanser, 1983.

Schleunes, Karl A. *The Twisted Road to Aushwitz*. Urbana and Chicago, IL: University of Illinois Press, 1990.

Schmitt, C. *Staat, Bewegung, Volk: Die Dreigliederung der politischen Einheit*. Hamburg: Anseatische Verlagsanstalt, 1933.

Schmitt, C. 'Der Fuehrer schutz das Recht', *Positionen und Begriff im Kampf mit Weimar – Genf-Versailles, 1923–1939*, Hamburg, 1940; also in Carl Schmitt, 'Der Fuehrer schutz das Recht', *Deutsche Juristen Zeitung*, Jg. 39, Heft 15, 1 August 1934.

Schmitt, C. 'Aufgabe und Notwendigkeit des deutschen Rechtsstanden,' *Deutsches Recht*, Jg. 6, Heft 9/10, 15 May, 1936a, pp. 181–5.

Schmitt, C. 'Die deutsche Rechtswissenschaft im Kampf gegen den jüdischen Geist: Schlusswort auf der Tagung der Reichsgruppe Hochschullehrer des NSRB vom 3. und 4. Oktober 1936', *Deutsche Juristen Zeitung*, Jg 41, Heft 20, 15 October, 1936b, pp. 1,193–9.

Schmitt, C. *Der Begriff des Politischen*, 4th edn. Berlin: Duncker and Humbolt, 1963.

Schmitt, C. *The Nomos of the Earth: In the International Law of the Jus Publicum Europaeum*. New York: Telos, 2003.

Scholem, G. *Walter Benjamin und Sein Engel. Vierzehn Aufsätze und Kleine Beiträge*, ed. R. Tiedemann. Frankfurt am Main: Suhrkamp, 1983.

Scholem, G. *Walter Benjamin – The Story of a Friendship*. New York: Columbia University Press, 2003.

Scholem, G. *Lamentations of Youth: The Diaries of Gershom Scholem, 1913–1919*. Cambridge, MA: Harvard University Press, 2008.

Schopenhauer, A. 'On Jurisprudence and Politics', in *Parerga and Paralipomena II*. Trans. E. F. J. Payne. Oxford: Clarendon, 1974.

Schriewer, J. 'Krieck, Ernst', in *Neue Deutsche Biographie*, Band 13. Berlin: Duncker and Humbolt, 1982, pp. 36–8.

Schwab, G. in C. Schmitt, *The Concept of the Political*. Trans. G. Schwab. Chicago, IL: University of Chicago Press, 2007.

Schwarzwaller, W. *The Unknown Hitler: His Private Life and Fortune*. Washington DC: National Press Books, 1989.

Scruton, R. *Kant*. Oxford: Oxford University Press, 1982.

Selz, J. 'Benjamin in Ibiza', trans. M. M. Guiney, in *On Walter Benjamin: Critical Essays and Recollections*, ed. G. Smith Cambridge, MA: MIT Press, 1991.

Shirer, W. *The Rise and Fall of the Third Reich*. New York: Simon and Schuster, 1960.

Showalter, D. E. *Patton and Rommel: Men of War in the Twentieth Century*. New York: Berkeley Publishing Group, 2006.

Skidelsky, E. *Ernst Cassirer: The Last Philosopher of Culture*. Princeton, NJ: Princeton University Press, 2008.

Sluga, H. *Heidegger's Crisis: Philosophy and Politics in Nazi Germany*. Cambridge MA: Harvard University Press, 1993.

Smith, K. 'The Execution of Nazi War Criminals 16 Oct 1946', in J. Carey, ed., *Eye witness to History*. New York: Perennial, 2003, pp. 641–8.

Spencer, S. and Millington, B. *Selected Letters of Richard Wagner*. London: Dent Publishers, 1987.

Speer, A. *Inside the Third Reich*, London: Macmillan, 1970.

Stein, G. J. 'Biological Science and the Roots of Nazism', *American Scientist* 76:1 (1988), pp. 50–8.

Steinweis, A. E. *Studying the Jew: Scholarly Anti-Semitism in Nazi Germany*. Cambridge, MA, and London: Harvard University Press, 2006.

Stern, F. *The Politics of Cultural Despair*. Berkeley and Los Angeles: University of California Press, 1961.

Stuckenberg, J. H. W. *The Life of Emmanuel Kant*. Bristol: Thoemmes Antiquarian Books Ltd., 1990.

Tansey, S. P. and Jackson, N. *Politics: The Basics*. London: Routledge, 2008.

Teeling, Sir W. Unpublished typescript in Archives of the Royal Institute of International Affairs, Chatham House, London.

Tegel, S. *Nazis and the Cinema*. London: Continuum Books, 2007.

Tobias, F. *The Reichstag Fire: Legend and Truth*. London: Secker and Warburg, 1963.

Trevor-Roper, H. *The Last Days of Hitler*. London: Macmillan and Co. Ltd. 1947.

Trevor-Roper, H. 'Introduction' in A. Hitler, *Hitler's Table Talk, Hitler's Conversations Recorded by Martin Bormann*. Oxford: Oxford University Press, 1988.

Wagner, F. *The Royal Family of Bayreuth*. London: Eyre and Spottiswoode, 1948.

Wagner, R. *Selected Letters of Richard Wagner*, ed. B. Millington, trans. S. Spencer. London: Dent, 1987.

Weidermann, V. *Das Buch der verbrannten Bücher*. Cologne: Kiepenheuer und Witsch, 2008.

Weindling P. *Health, Race and German Politics Between National Unification and Nazism 1870–1945*. Cambridge: Cambridge University Press, 1993.

Weinreich, M. *Hitler's Professors*. New Haven, CT, and London: Yale University Press, 1999.

Weiss S. F. *Race Hygiene and National Efficiency: The Eugenics of Wilhelm Schallmayer*. Berkeley, CA: University of California Press, 1987.

Wilcox, E. 'Alban Berg's Appeal to Edward Dent on Behalf of Theodor Adorno, 18 November 1933', *German Life and Letters* 50, 1997, pp. 365–8.

Wittenstein, G. J. 'The White Rose, A Commitment', in J. J. Michalczyk, *Confront! Resistance in Nazi Germany*. Frankfurt am Main: Peter Lang, 2004, pp. 191–210.

Wolf, E. *Griechisches Rechtsdenken*, 3 vols. Tübingen: J. C. R. Mohr, 1950–1954.

Wolff, C. *Hindsight: An Autobiography*. London: Quartet, 1980.

Wolin, R. *Heidegger's Children: Hannah Arendt, Karl Löwith, Hans Jonas, and Herbert Marcuse*. Princeton, NJ: Princeton University Press, 2003.

Wolin, R. *The Seduction of Unreason: The Intellectual Romance with Fascism from Nietzsche to Postmodernism*. Princeton, NJ: Princeton University Press, 2004.

Wundt, M. *Die Deutsche Schulphilosophie im Zeitalter der Aufklärung*. Hildesheim: Olms, 1964.

Young, J. *Heidegger, Philosophy, Nazism*. Cambridge: Cambridge University Press, 1997.

Young-Bruehl, E. *Hannah Arendt: For Love of the World*, 2nd edn. New Haven, CT, and London: Yale University Press, 2004.

Yovel, Y. *Dark Riddle: Hegel, Nietzsche, and the Jews*. London: Polity Press, 1998.

Index